FULL POTENTIAL

GMAT

SENTENCE CORRECTION INTENSIVE

Bara Sapir, MA & Karen van Hoek, PhD

Master Content. Upgrade your Mind. Elevate your Score!

comprehensive preparation · nuanced review · extensive practice · detailed explanations

- Includes Bonus TPNY Full Potential Handbook for test-day success.
- 200+ detailed examples and valuable tips based on real GMAT questions.
- Effective approaches for non-native speakers and different learning styles.
- Fool-proof techniques for mastering each type of Sentence Correction question.
- 30+ exercises for peak performance, drawn from sports psychology, mindfulness, and holistic health.

Additional educational titles from Nova Press (available at novapress.net):

- ➢ **GMAT Prep Course** (624 pages, includes software)
  GMAT Math Prep Course (528 pages)
  GMAT Data Sufficiency Prep Course (422 pages)
- ➢ **GRE Prep Course** (624 pages, includes software)
  GRE Math Prep Course (468 pages)
- ➢ **Master The LSAT** (608 pages, includes software and 4 official LSAT exams)
- ➢ **MCAT Prep Course** (1,340 pages)
- ➢ **SAT Prep Course** (628 pages)
  SAT Math Prep Course (404 pages)
  SAT Critical Reading and Writing Prep Course (350 pages)
- ➢ **ACT Math Prep Course** (402 pages)
  ACT Verbal Prep Course (248 pages)
  ACT Science Prep Course (364 pages)
- ➢ **Scoring Strategies for the TOEFL® iBT:** (800 pages, includes audio CD)
  Speaking and Writing Strategies for the TOEFL® iBT: (394 pages, includes audio CD)
  500 Words, Phrases, Idioms for the TOEFL® iBT: (238 pages, includes audio CD)
  Practice Tests for the TOEFL® iBT: (292 pages, includes audio CD)
  Business Idioms in America: (220 pages)
  Americanize Your Language and Emotionalize Your Speech! (210 pages)
- ➢ **Postal Exam Book** (276 pages)
- ➢ **Law School Basics:** A Preview of Law School and Legal Reasoning (224 pages)
- ➢ **Vocabulary 4000:** The 4000 Words Essential for an Educated Vocabulary (160 pages)

ISBN: 978–1–889057–55–2

Published by *Nova Press*.

P. O. Box: 692023
West Hollywood, CA 90069

Phone: 1-310-275-3513
E-mail: info@novapress.net
Website: www.novapress.net

What People are Saying about *TPNY's Full Potential Sentence Correction Intensive*:

"*Full Potential GMAT Sentence Correction Intensive* is by far and away the most advanced study aid available for the sentence correction section of the GMAT. We highly recommend this guide to all test takers seeking the 700+ scores the top business schools like to see."

—David Petersam, President, AdmissionsConsultants

"The Test Prep industry is cluttered with plenty of players, but Test Prep NY is the first program to address the issue of anxiety and stress, and how they can impact a score. I was thrilled to learn of their services and have directed many satisfied clients their way. Their holistic approach has been a terrific resource for those who need it, and their new book is yet another terrific way to share their revolutionary techniques."

—Stacy Blackman, Stacy Blackman Consulting, Inc

"I'm a big supporter of Bara and her book *Full Potential GMAT Sentence Correction Intensive*. While most companies abbreviate their prep strategy for a broader audience, Bara has maintained her focus on test prep for those who are looking for the very best. This book is a definitive guide for GMAT Sentence Correction questions, and if you are looking to attain the highest score on the GMAT, this is a book you should own."

—Conrad Egusa, Founder, 2minuteGMAT.com

"Test Prep New York is revolutionary in the field of test prep. Only they are addressing the biggest hurdle for test-takers: anxiety. With their help the GMAT can become much more than a test.. It can become a gateway to understanding how your mind works and moving past common blocks of fear and nervousness. TPNY can help you reach your full potential on GMAT sentence correction. But more important, they can help you reach your full potential in life."

—Katie Malachuk, Harvard BA, Stanford MBA,
Author of Earn It: A Stress-Free and Proven Approach to Getting Into Top MBA Programs

"I have always found Bara Sapir's/TPNY's creative, comprehensive and knowledge-driven approach to the GMAT admirable. I'm thrilled that she has come out with a book that I can suggest to my clients!"

—Emily B. Wolper, founder and president, E. Wolper, Inc. Admissions Consulting

"Almost everyone at some time, or every time, has struggled when it comes to test taking. Fear no more... Celebrate... For you now have available the key to set you free. The Test Prep New York Full Potential Sentence Correction gives the most thorough blueprint available to ensure building confidence in yourself to achieve and succeed. Follow the brilliant instruction that has been laid out for you and step into a brighter future."

—Tom Nicoli, BCH, CI, www.ABetterYouHypnosis.com

"Bara Sapir's/TPNY's progressive test preparation technique is good for test-takers who want an edge when taking the test, as well as test-takers who require extra assistance. The model is effective because it teaches mediation of cognitive, academic, attentional, and emotional control. This book contains the necessary ingredients to succeed on the GMAT—it skillfully teaches the essential components of test taking through a clever blend of aggressiveness, logic, and relaxation. After practicing the techniques herein, the trepidatious test taker can expect to enter testing arenas with a greater confidence to achieve that may have alluded them in the past."

—Dr. Jason Smith, School and Clinical Psychologist

"Bara Sapir and Test Prep New York are the best at what they do—she truly understands the emotional process of what a student goes through and tailors the right program for each specific student."

—Brad Grossman, Principal, Grossman& Partners

"Test Prep New York approaches test prep in an innovative and integrative way, and goes above and beyond the traditional ideas of what constitutes success. This book delivers on all levels and raises the bar in the field. It teaches students study habits that include mind/body approaches for affect regulation, retention, and focusing strategies that take into account individual learning strategies as well as limiting core beliefs. Students will never think of tests and their abilities in the same way."

—Melissa Tiers, DCH, www.melissatiers.com,
Author of Integrative Hypnosis: A Comprehensive Course in Change

"After thirty-one years in the secondary classroom, watching the anxiety and stress levels faced by test takers, I was incredibly impressed by the fantastic program that TPNY has put together. I was utterly amazed at the talent, precision, intelligence, and brilliance of TPNY's Full Potential® program and only wished for the opportunity to bring it into my former classroom. It is an asset and a motivational tool for teachers, hypnotists, students, and anyone else. The perfect blend of all of Sapir's education and the product's professionalism make this an intriguing program that deserves a closer look from anyone wishing to improve test-taking results. I'm almost jealous of those still taking tests who have the chance to use this unique and fascinating method to relieve stress and anxiety."

—Barbara A. Blinn, MA, CH Educational Consultant

"I had never realized my full potential. I always scored lower on actual exams than on practice exams. Then, after working with Test Prep New York and the Full Potential® program, I was able to gain the confidence, focus, and skill sets to increase my score. I was able to walk into the exam relaxed, focused, and confident!"

—Andrew, TPNY student, New York Stock Exchange, Emory

"Bara Sapir's innovative, holistic approach to test prep teaches us that academic excellence can come easily and effortlessly when we choose to integrate self-care and calming messaging into our daily routine."

—Shira D. Epstein, Ed.D, Assistant Professor, Davidson School of Jewish Education, JTS

"After studying with larger test prep programs and taking the GMAT three times with continually disappointing results, I contacted TPNY. After only 4 hours of the Full Potential® program I gained confidence, learned to channel my energy and mental state into a positive zone, eliminated anxiety, and was completely relaxed and prepared on test day. Most important, my score increased by 80 points. I highly recommend Test Prep New York's Full Potential® program to anyone who really wants to reach their potential and get the score they need."

—Ken, TPNY student, New York University

"That the folks at Test Prep New York could create yet another impressive study aid is a terrific achievement. And despite their sane refusal to set the whole thing to music this time (you have to get their Full Potential Audio GMAT to get some serious tunes), I'm a huge fan of not only the content, but the approach."

—Michael Moshan, Rock the SAT

"Test Prep New York's *Full Potential Sentence Correction* is a complete and thorough resource covering all aspects of the GMAT's Sentence Correction category. The book helps test-takers form a studying strategy aimed at scoring 700+ on the GMAT and then helps them drill down with hundreds of concrete, specific practice questions and a summary of key grammar rules. This manual will help test takers approach the GMAT with concrete skills, tools, and the confidence of knowing the right technique to tackle the test."

—Leila Pirnia, Founder, MBA Podcaster

"Dr. Karen van Hoek and Bara Sapir of Test Prep New York have written *Test Prep New York Full Potential Sentence Correction* to provide a unique, holistic approach to the sentence correction section of the GMAT. If you are seeking a book that teaches you the right mindset, the real skills, and the necessary test-taking techniques, this is the book for you."

—Linda Abraham, president of Accepted.com

"For 25 years I have been watching hundreds of good candidates flunk the GMAT, coming to the conclusion that their psychological mindset plays as important a role as their knowledge about the test. My reaction when I first saw this book was: Finally someone is tackling the real problem!"

—Ricardo Betti, MBA Empresarial, Brazil

"Content mastery is necessary, but not sufficient to get a top score on the GMAT. Our research suggests that as much as 1/3 of your score is determined by your ability to manage the test stress that everyone experiences. Test Prep NY is the only program I know of which combines solid content with a truly useful approach to the mental preparation required to excel on the test."

—Miro Kazakoff, Co-Founder, Testive and The MBA Show

Bara Sapir and the Test Prep NY team are a singular resource. No other test prep service comes close to TPNY's success and client satisfaction. In over a decade of advising MBA applicants, my clients have—across the board—raved about TPNY's services, philosophy and staff. More importantly, the clients I share with TPNY have the test numbers to prove their effectiveness. No doubt, *Full Potential GMAT Sentence Correction Intensive* will be another arrow in TPNY's unique quiver of teaching resources.

—Mark Meyerrose, Meyerrose Consulting, LLC

Full Potential GMAT Sentence correction offers a great combination that will benefit any aspiring MBA student. It's an excellent technical guide coupled with innovative ideas and concepts to improve one's mental preparation for test taking.

—Yael Redelman-Sidi, Admit 1 MBA

Finally, through this book, TPNY's special methods will benefit even more students dedicated to perform their best! We send many students to TPNY specifically because the success they achieve through their unique, comprehensive hybrid approach that no other company offers. These high-scoring results have helped open many doors and create opportunities.

—Louise Kreiner, New England Education Advisors

Sentence Correction Intensive
TABLE OF CONTENTS

Section II Preparation: A Map to Success

CHAPTER ONE: Setting Your Schedule

Why all work and no play is not the way to a great GMAT score. Setting up a plan that works for you.

CHAPTER TWO: Managing Your Physical Environment

Take control of your surroundings to maximize learning.

CHAPTER THREE: What Kind of Learner are You?

Discover your best learning mode and how you can maximize the benefits of studying.

CHAPTER FOUR: Three Kinds of English Learners

Some native speakers still need to learn the rules of formal written English; non-native speakers have special challenges, but also some advantages.

CHAPTER FIVE: Ready, Set, Go!

Get ready to take the mastery of your inner and outer games to the next level.

Section III Execution: The Journey

Major Areas that are Tested

Module 1: Subjects and Verbs

How the GMAT tests subject-verb agreement, verb tenses and more.

Module 2: Pronouns

When is it OK to say "it"? When is "this" wrong? How the GMAT tests pronouns.

Module 3: Modifiers

How can you tell if a relative clause is constructed correctly? How the GMAT tests modifiers.

Module 4: Comparisons

Why "New York consumes more electricity than Los Angeles" doesn't make sense.

Module 5: Parallelism

Which parts of a sentence have to be parallel – and what counts as parallel?

Module 6: Idioms

The phrases the GMAT tests frequently – and the phrases that are never correct.

Whether You Believe You Can, Or You Can't, You Are Right

Henry Ford[1]

INTRODUCTION

TEST PREP NEW YORK:
THE FULL POTENTIAL METHOD

What are the keys to success on the Graduate Management Admissions Test (GMAT)? Conventional wisdom tells us that all we need to do is work hard, and high scores will inevitably follow. Wrong. As anyone who has taken a high-stakes test knows, the real story is not always so simple.

Hard work alone is not enough for you to score your best: You can spend hours memorizing grammar rules, but if you don't learn effective test strategies or feel confident when you go into the test, you will not achieve your full potential. In fact, if you go into the test feeling anything but calm and focused, you risk a subpar performance.

The *Test Prep New York Full Potential Sentence Correction book* you hold in your hands gives you the tools you need for test taking success. Along with the most comprehensive coverage of Sentence Correction content you can find anywhere, this Test Prep New York (TPNY) guide is the only GMAT book to give you a blueprint for peak performance on the entire test. It is carefully designed to activate your whole self and awaken your full potential—heart, mind, and body—so that you will achieve your best score. You will be able to overcome test anxiety and develop the focus necessary to perform at the top of your game. The coverage of material and methods you will find here can turn a good test taker into a great test taker and a decent score into a stellar score. *TPNY Full Potential* is a revolutionary resource to enable you to achieve your best performance on the GMAT.

Full Potential principles are well established in the health, psychological, and sports psychology fields, but they are cutting edge in the field of education. In fact, at the time of this publication, we know of no other educational company that incorporates these principles. In trial tests, we found that test takers who applied a combination of these new learning techniques performed significantly higher than those who did not. As such, we began designing our Full Potential method, a system that integrates human-potential tools such as neuro-linguistic programming, hypnosis, meditation, guided visualization, Emotional Freedom Technique, Gamma Brain Waves, common-sense wellness practices, and much more to help you create the strategy you need to succeed.

The Full Potential method starts with the recognition that all the knowledge in the world won't help you if you can't access it easily and quickly while taking a test. This simple insight creates a profound shift in priorities from narrowly focusing only on content—what the test taker needs to know—to also addressing how the test taker will be able to access and utilize this knowledge during the test. The 'how' on the GMAT (and other standardized tests) involves more than just regurgitating information. Those who succeed usually draw on different faculties, from intuitive judgment to critical thinking to psychological 'buy in.' In other words, successful test takers draw on their whole self.

Our method will help you identify behaviors that don't serve the mission at hand: feelings of resistance, avoidance, and insecurity; and provide solutions for the symptoms of test anxiety and stress. Simultaneously, the method teaches techniques to engage your full potential, such as shifting your belief and behavior patterns so that you can train your mind to reach its optimal test taking state, at your will. Whether your test anxiety symptoms manifest as acute or chronic, these practices are solutions to give you peace of mind. And they have no expiration date; you can use them again and again in other situations where you don't feel your best self. These full potential techniques are for your whole life; not just those hours studying or taking tests.

This approach to learning is solidly grounded in research. Experts at such prestigious institutions as the American Medical Association and the Mayo Clinic, as well as advocates of integrative medicine such as Dr. Andrew Weil, have noted the efficacy of anxiety reduction, memory enhancement, and peak performance techniques such as those used by Test Prep New York in its training programs and in The Full Potential audio series. Professional articles supporting the use of such modalities have appeared in the most respected journals and press, including the Review of Educational Research, Cognitive Therapy and Research, the Journal of Clinical Psychology, The American Journal of Hypnosis, and US News and World Report, to name a few. Experts concur that exercise, healthy nutrition, adequate sleep, and a host of alternative healing techniques work for and are accessible to anyone who uses them. At their core, the techniques introduced here are all designed to help you believe in yourself, and then ensure that everything else in your life co-conspires for your success.

This book, like our tutoring programs, is cutting edge because it is the first of its kind to embody integrative education. Whether you use a couple of the techniques, use all of them, or decide you only want to memorize rules and practice your skill sets, the goal of this book is to introduce you to methods that have a track record of success, and for you to try them on, see which resonate with you, and then compile your own tool box for applying your most effective test taking self on test day.

THE FULL POTENTIAL METHOD WORKS

How do we know our Full Potential approach works? The authors of this book have more than a half-century of combined experience. Drawing on research-backed academic and holistic tools, TPNY coaches use the Full Potential method every day. We witness our clients' success with our own eyes. Every technique in this book has been tested and proven to work with hundreds of clients.

Testimonials from past TPNY students:

"TPNY was fantastic, especially the relaxation techniques. I am inspired and eagerly await future sessions. I can tell this is just what I need. Thank you again. I haven't felt this positive about the exam since I started studying. I already have the confidence and conviction that I will succeed."

—Christian G., London School of Economics

"The TPNY program helped me take the test while in a relaxed and comfortable state of mind. I knew I was capable of scoring high based on past practice exams but was pleasantly surprised at how well [my TPNY tutor] prepared me for the real thing. This program is the only one in the test prep industry that not only teaches one how to master the material but also how to prepare your body and mind for the actual stress of test day. I would recommend TPNY to anyone looking to master the test. They will show you the way!"

—Brian M., Wharton, University of Pennsylvania

"Bara and her team were the best thing that could have happened to me! They were able to take me to a place of calmness, focus, and motivation. I will forever use the skills I learned and apply them to other areas of my life. Since my score was the only thing holding me back from school, the 100-point increase that I scored after only a few hours of tutoring and coaching with you made the difference between being accepted and needing to chart a new course! Thank you TPNY for supporting my dream and helping it become a reality. You truly had an inspiring approach and your program has transformed my life and opened opportunities for me!"

—Marian, George Washington University

"I was beyond satisfied with Test Prep NY. I took a Manhattan GMAT course before I found TPNY and wish I just had started with them from the beginning. The test prep resources TPNY uses were much better than the MGMAT materials I started with and [my tutor's] relaxation and anxiety techniques really work. TPNY taught me great relaxation tips that I still use today when I need to de-stress. Most important, I earned the score I was aiming for by improving 170 points with TPNY!"

—Grace, Tuck School of Business , Dartmouth

To win a highly coveted spot at a prestigious institution in higher education, achieving success in standardized test taking is square one. As a former graduate business school admissions director, I found that a test score not only levels the playing field of applicants who are coming from a wide array of schools and educational backgrounds, but it also makes a profound statement to the admissions committee regarding an applicants' ability to compete in the academic rigors of their program. The challenges, I found, when meeting with various applicants, are the intellectual, emotional and psychological barriers that come with preparing for and taking the standardized test. To mitigate these challenges, look no further than Test Prep New York. Besides authoring the most comprehensive GMAT sentence correction guide available, Bara Sapir, the firm's founder and director, teaches her students to master content while improving their test-taking potential. Her students learn to reduce test-taking anxiety and banish self-limiting beliefs while also incorporating exercises to improve retention, recall and focus. Test Prep New York employs one-of-a-kind holistic methods that prepare students for a critical step in their journey to higher education.

—Mary Pat Jacobs, Director, Apply Point Admissions Consulting

TPNY has successfully helped hundreds of people improve their GMAT scores. Now, we are sharing some of our secrets of success with you. This book holds the keys to enable you to become the ultimate problem-solver: motivated, resourceful, positive, and able to perform at your best.

WILL THIS METHOD WORK FOR ME?

Most test prep books assume certain facts about you—that you grew up in the United States, speaking, reading, and writing English for example. They also assume that everyone studies best using one technique, and that everyone learns at the same pace.

The TPNY Full Potential approach is not like those other books. We know that everyone learns differently. We know that some people who have grown up in the United States are very challenged by formal English grammar. We know that non-native speakers often know formal English because that is the English they were taught.

So our assumption is that each of you is unique. Our method is designed to help you reach your own, unique combination of techniques, to best realize your full potential.

Everyone experiences a test differently. Very few people waltz through a test or even test preparation without some resistance or an emotional snag. That's especially true when it comes to the GMAT, which is typically taken by professionals who have been out of school a few years, removed from the rhythm of study, the cycle of the academic semester, and the camaraderie of academic peers. Taking the GMAT and applying to business school are both internal and external processes, and each is difficult on each of those individual levels. Most people returning to school at this time in their lives will have a 'story' about their personal journey.

Imagine the GMAT testing center with computers arranged around the room. Imagine (although this would never happen in real life) that everyone in the room draws the same Sentence Correction question simultaneously. Each individual's experience will be unique. Which one sounds most like you?

1. One person, who has a good ear for grammar, will find that the error sounds so obvious, it almost leaps off the screen.

2. The person to his right feels that three of the five choices sound fine, even though they can't all be right; she already knows she can't solve these questions by relying on her ear, but by using the grammar rules she's mastered, she's able to identify quickly the critical grammar point being tested.

3. The person to her right gets bogged down in trying to understand all the details of the long, rambling sentence instead of scanning efficiently, so she spends too much time on this question.

4. The next person over quickly recognizes the error in the original sentence, but wastes time carefully reading the (A) version of the sentence (which is always the same as the original), along with (B) and (C), which contain the same mistake.

Each of these individuals has different strengths and weaknesses that will affect how each one responds to the question, even though all are being tested on the exact same knowledge. For some, trusting instinct will work, and for others, it never will. Others can conquer a test by alternating between trusting their gut and recalling the rules, but need to know when to use each strategy.

Now let's throw the emotional and psychological responses test takers have to the test into the mix. People have widely varying reactions to the test experience. Being in the test center, obeying time limits, knowing that "this is the real thing"—all of these can be sources of stress prior to and during the test itself.

TEST TAKER 1 – One person finds that the security procedures and rigid rules of the testing center make her a bit nervous, but on the plus side, she's relieved to find that the real GMAT looks just like what she studied. She's rattled, but begins to settle into the test experience when it begins.

TEST TAKER 2 – The person next to her finds it hard to focus on the questions because her mind keeps wandering. She feels anxious and keeps guessing at how well she's scoring so far.

TEST TAKER 3 – The next person over is distracted by the timer in the corner of his screen; he feels oppressed and unnerved by the relentless countdown.

TEST TAKER 4 – The person next to him finds that being able to keep close track of the time makes him feel empowered and in control. His difficulty is that he tends to second-guess his answer choices even on questions about which he knows he should feel confident.

TEST TAKER 5 – One guy came extremely early to the testing site because he couldn't sleep the past two nights before the test. He is so nervous and spent from not sleeping that he's at a standstill, fidgeting in his chair, trying to gain the courage to just 'do it.' He feels he's practically sealed his fate with the first question, and now he's thinking that he hasn't studied enough, that he's going to fail, and that he might as well cancel his score now, go home, go back to bed, and come back in 31 days.

Each of these individuals would benefit from a different strategy to gain control of his or her less-than-ideal experience and maximize their performance. A key part of the Full Potential approach is uncovering and addressing your personal performance patterns on prior tests— both diagnostics and real. By naming and understanding the problems you have experienced before, you can draw up an action plan to ensure that you will be ready before test day for any kind of issue that might interfere with your performance. Here are some ways applying an individualized Full Potential method might assist the test takers we just described.

TEST TAKER 1 – This person gets rattled by the testing procedures, but is relieved to find that what she has studied is really on the test. Through the Full Potential method, she has learned and applied techniques to enter a calm zone before she enters the test site.

TEST TAKER 2 – This test taker finds it difficult to focus. Using the Full Potential method, she has learned how to maintain precision focus on the questions while feeling calm and fully

present with each one. In fact, over the course of a GMAT, wasteful reading habits will amount to nearly three minutes lost—enough time that

she could have gotten the last two questions correct instead of having to take wild guesses.

TEST TAKER 3 – This is our test taker who is prone to obsess over the timer. Using the Full Potential method, however, he would have

practiced using a timer in order to trust his inner clock. In addition, he would have learned how to "be present" during the test so that elements like the timer are no longer distractions and, instead, welcome tools to help navigate the test.

TEST TAKER 4 – This test taker tends to second-guess himself. Using the Full Potential method, he has learned to feel a wave of courage and confidence moving through him with each and every question.

TEST TAKER 5 – The last person is so nervous before the test that he is in danger of being physically depleted and emotionally on edge. Using the Full Potential method, he has learned techniques to enter a calm state, a state that will allow him to both get the rest he needs the night before, and calm fears that may arise during the test itself.

Some test takers need a sense of confidence; others a feeling of calm; still others need to hone a laser-like focus on testing materials. No two test takers are exactly alike, so it's essential that the unique aspects of each situation be taken into account when an action plan is created. An approach based on the idea that "Everyone who can memorize the material will do fine" won't consistently produce the same results as an individualized approach that takes into account the different strengths and weaknesses that each person brings to the task—including an individual's attitudes and beliefs about who they are and what they deserve.

Because the Full Potential method is designed to be adapted to your unique situation, this book and the programs that TPNY offers are all customizable. You will be encouraged through the book to create an individualized action plan. First, we'll provide ample exercises and techniques to identify and fine-tune how you feel, think, and perform on tests. Second, we'll address the kind of learner you are, and create a schedule so you can customize your approach to the material to make your study more effective. This priming and preparation will then be combined with a full review and plenty of practice of the sentence correction material so you can improve your knowledge base. You will be able to pursue what resonates with you personally in order to achieve YOUR Full Potential.

WHAT IS THE GMAT, REALLY?

The GMAT is designed not only to compare you to other applicants, but also to see if you demonstrate the critical thinking and other mental skills necessary to function best in the business world. No other exam is designed like this. The GMAT tests skills that are comparable to those required of a business school student and of a successful businessperson. In essence, the GMAT is designed as a metaphor for business school practices and thought. Business schools look at your GMAT performance to determine the following:

- Does this test taker take calculated risks? Or might he or she be reckless and risky?

- Do they think quickly on their feet, or become indecisive?

- Does this person think outside of the box?

- Are they moving too fast to see nuances and details?

- Will this test taker be able to communicate clearly with peers and colleagues?

- Will they be able to engage in effective negotiations and explain complex transactions?

- Can this person juggle simultaneous demands at different levels, attending to multiple details while keeping an eye on the big picture?

- Can this individual deal with texts that are loaded with unfamiliar facts—as a manager must—and understand the key relationships between ideas without being thrown off by details that are outside his or her area of expertise?

- Does this person have the critical reading skills needed for effective business communication?

The Full Potential method is the only test preparation method that approaches these exam skills as life skills, thus integrating a more holistic approach to critical thinking with the particulars of sentence correction. We understand that the GMAT is designed to test the whole person because business schools want to evaluate your current business acumen. They are investing in you. Thus, the Full Potential method addresses the whole person, and we prepare you psychologically as well as intellectually.

The ability to uncover, then correct, your own areas of weakness is an ability that will stay with you long after your GMAT experience is a distant memory. One benefit of fully mastering test preparation the Full Potential way is that you will gain a set of skills necessary for becoming a successful business professional. Learning the material our way enables you to learn how to think outside the box, take necessary risks, cut your losses, and maximize the return on your investment. With the Full Potential method, you improve your GMAT performance and you gain the skills you need to become a more insightful and focused future leader.

YOU'VE GOT TO WIN IN YOUR MIND BEFORE YOU WIN IN YOUR LIFE

JOHN ADDISON[2]

HOW TO USE THIS BOOK

TPNY Full Potential is divided into three sections: **Lay the Groundwork, A Map to Success**, and **The Journey. Lay the Groundwork** addresses the psychological aspects of the test taking process. It offers research-backed information about different methods to train your "inner game mindset."

You will not find the mindset exercises we offer in any other test preparation book. TPNY includes these exercises because scientific research has shown that human beings learn best when the mind is calm and focused, and when a person feels in control and confident. In fact, this book even includes visual exercises and suggestions of things to listen to while you're studying to promote more effective study and performance. In the last section, where you're deeply engaged in content mastery and practice, we selectively interrupt your intense sessions of learning with optical illusions and mandalas. Why? Because the most current education and psychological research promotes 'breaks' in study and constructive interruption—exercises that shift focus and induce a different type of concentration act as a mental "reboot" or "reset" button, helping your brain integrate information more effectively and helping you achieve optimal focus. In physical terms, this is similar to doing multiple weight lifting reps, stopping for a break, then resuming. Any trainer will tell you this is the most effective way to achieve results.

Using the Full Potential exercises, you will learn how to fully engage in your own learning process. You will also discover how to increase your confidence for test day, learn how to stop limiting your beliefs, and alleviate anxiety. In short, you will learn how to enter the optimal test taking zone.

This book will offer you:

- Over 100 pages addressing the mental component of taking tests, including exercises to increase perseverance, reduce test anxiety, and promote relaxation and focus.

- Straightforward, step-by-step methods to build confidence and "fire your inner critic."

- Proven methods to implement constructive behavior patterns that decrease stress and frustration and enhance learning.

- Exercises that teach you to hone your attention and sharpen your analytic skills.

- Techniques to set your intention and focus in reasonable, believable, user-friendly ways to meet your goals.

- Methods and guidance in wellness practices including nutrition, supplements, exercise, meditation, and other holistic practices, to improve your overall physical health, which will improve your perseverance and cognition.

- Tried and true techniques that will help you enter the test taking zone with optimal focus, increased confidence, and inner calm.

- Common sense advice on wellness practices to support the mental and physical demands of intense study.

- Exercises to teach you how to control your mind—instead of letting your mind control you—when obstacles like panic attacks, blanking on test questions, and physical discomfort caused by test anxiety threaten your performance.

The second part of the book, **A Map to Success**, focuses on how we learn and how to create an optimal study environment and schedule. First, you will assess how familiar you are with formal written English language skills, then identify the type of learner you are through a short survey. This information will help you develop a customized strategy for the GMAT Sentence Correction questions. Once you know the kind of learner you are and where you are on the formal English skills spectrum, *TPNY Full Potential* provides the tools to help you customize your approach to the test.

You will be able to construct a detailed plan for individualized study, including:

- A suggested timeline to assist in planning when to take your GMAT.
- A primer in time management and prioritization to organize your weekly study.
- Self-assessment tools to identify, then employ, best-use study methods related to your personal learning style.

The third and final section, **The Journey**, brings together the psychological techniques of Section I, and the personalized strategy in Section II as you study the specific questions that will be on the GMAT Sentence Correction Exam. Our comprehensive coverage of the GMAT Sentence Correction content includes detailed explanations and practice questions covering every aspect of English grammar you are expected to know on the test:

1. Subjects and verbs
2. Pronouns
3. Modifiers
4. Comparisons
5. Parallelism
6. Idioms
7. Clauses and clausal connections.
8. Special issues of meaning
9. Diction
10. Hallmarks of formal written English

In this section you will find:

- More than 200 examples, based on real GMAT questions, illustrating key grammar rules.
- Dozens of exercises, with hundreds of practice questions, to build mastery of concepts.
- Step-by-step instructions on how to best approach the question and answer sets.
- An exposé of the tricks the GMAT test creators use to make sentences more complex and confusing—and how to see through them on the actual test.

In addition, you will learn how to implement effective and efficient strategies to answer Sentence Correction questions correctly and quickly. The time you save by moving more quickly through Sentence Correction questions will provide more time for the Reading Comprehension and

Critical Reasoning questions, and help you improve your performance on the Verbal Section as a whole.

Many of you will be tempted to start right with **The Journey** section of the book. You want to get on your way, just like a basketball player wants to learn how to sink three-pointers or read an opponent's defense. However, pro basketball players will tell you that winning is not just about Execution, but about Preparation. If you are not prepared mentally for the game, your technical skills won't always pull you through.

The same is true with performing well on a test. Mastering grammar won't be enough if you are not prepared mentally.

Trust our experience. Many test takers have come to us because, in spite of knowing the content of their test backwards and forwards, they could not maintain focus on the test itself and thus did poorly. How you take the test is sometimes as important as what you know. Being prepared mentally makes a significant difference.

Start on the first page of this book, **Lay the Groundwork**, and create your own **Map to Success** before you start on **The Journey**.

BONUS OPPORTUNITIES

When you purchase this book, you get the added benefit of receiving bonus materials and learning opportunities by visiting the Resource section of our website: www.testprepny.com.

1. Two Full Potential mp3 tracks that you can download and use during your study, one for focus and the other for confidence.

2. An opportunity to evaluate your progress. After you finish all the exercises in this book, and when you feel ready for the real GMAT, test yourself with our Sentence Correction online diagnostic. Our system will evaluate whether you've mastered the material covered in the book.

3. If you're in it to win it, we challenge and invite you to send in proof of your Sentence Correction prowess: Submit original sample Sentence Correction questions and answers that YOU write yourself.

A TPNY verbal specialist will review your sample questions and let you know if you've succeeded in your efforts. (This offer is good until December 2015.)

The book you are holding now will provide you the content and training you need to master the Sentence Correction section of the GMAT. More than that, the tips and exercises here will teach you how to cultivate mental preparedness and psychological calm, and give you confidence and courage for the entire GMAT test.

Use this book wisely, trust the process, and you will learn how to study smarter, not harder. As William James said, "It is our own attitude at the beginning of a difficult undertaking which, more than anything else, will determine its successful outcome." **Now: Get busy.**

We are what we think. All that we are arises with our thoughts. With our thoughts, we make our world.

Buddha

SECTION I

PREPARATION: LAY THE GROUNDWORK

CHAPTER ONE

INNER GAME, OUTER GMAT

Any challenge we undertake occurs in two distinct arenas: the "outside" dimension—the nitty-gritty, nuts-and-bolts of the task required, and the inner dimension—the attitudes, emotions, and beliefs that powerfully shape our performance. While many people and traditions have distinguished between these inner and outer experiences, Timothy Gallwey expressed this concept in his landmark 1974 book, *The Inner Game of Tennis*. Gallwey identified the "outer game", or our external realities, as our social network, the various 'systems' in which we live (such as our familial, professional, and social rituals and interactions), and our physical environment (the food we eat, toxins to which we are exposed, our living space, and so forth). He defined the "inner game" as our emotional, mental, biochemical, energetic, and spiritual landscape.

Broadly speaking, most of our experiences involve an interplay between our inner and outer environments. We tend to think of the GMAT as occurring in the outer arena—and to some extent it does. This 'outer game' of the GMAT experience includes commuting to the test site and experiencing the test site itself—including all the conditions of registering, getting settled, seeing your 'competition' in the other test takers, dealing with the barrage of questions, handling time constraints, and managing the use of the scratch pad and computer. It encompasses almost everything you confront or respond to until you see your 'score' on the screen and feel (we hope) elated when you leave the test center.

Section II, A Map to Success, will focus on preparing yourself for the outer game. But before you can be ready for the outer game, you must first be ready for the inner game.

The "inner game" of the GMAT takes place within the test taker's mind. The inner game of the GMAT will be that voice in your head producing either negative emotions such as fear, self-doubt, lapses in focus, limiting concepts and assumptions, or, ideally, if you have worked through this section of the book, the calm, excitement, focus, and belief in yourself which becomes effortless when you are in "the zone."

Achieving mastery of the inner game will enable you to overcome the self-imposed and subconscious obstacles and patterns that prevent individuals from accessing and manifesting their full potential. Once you master the inner game, both your body and mind will adjust to achieve best performance in the outer game. In symbolic terms, Gallwey writes:

$$\text{Performance} = \text{potential} - \text{interference}$$

or

$$P = p - i.$$

Performance equals potential minus interference. According to this formula, you can increase your GMAT performance either by increasing p, your test taking potential, or by decreasing i, the inner interference most test takers experience.[3]

Final Test Taker 1 – Knowing that this is part of the process, she could have walked through this in her mind several times instead of showing up and being ambushed by the bureaucratic reality of the test.

Final Test Taker 2 – She has already taken 3+ diagnostics, so she knows the approximate score she is going to receive. Plus, she has visualized her goal score, demystifying the process and outcome so she can be fully present.

Final Test Taker 3 – He has taken enough timed quizzes and even created a kind of inner clock for himself, so he isn't distracted by the timer. Instead, he knows exactly how many questions he will complete, and how many he'll guess on. There are no unknowns here.

Final Test Taker 4 – He learns to feel confident and secure with first answers, knowing that statistically these are usually right; and has also seen first hand that this is the case. In addition, he has learned ways to fire the inner critic and quite the mental chatter, keeping him off of the distracting Habitrail he's been on through inefficient study, disappointing diagnostics, and a former test.

Final Test Taker 5 – In addition to getting enough sleep the night prior to taking the GMAT, test taker 5 knows he will take the test two times, which gives him two opportunities to do his best. While this is a high-stakes test, he is organized and prepared and can use the first test as a kind of 'dress rehearsal' if he needs to. He also knows that if it turns out that he performs his best the first time, he is prepared to forgo the second test date. Having a schedule in place, including when he'll go to sleep (most nights) leaves him in the best head space when taking this test.

If you have ever experienced these kinds of self-limiting thoughts and stress in the testing room, you can use this section of the book to decrease that internal interference. Just by learning how to stay the course, you will increase your performance.

Think of any person who excels in a skills-based activity, such as a musician or athlete. The musician practices innumerable hours to develop her physical craft with her instrument— learning the music, practicing scales, breathing, learning from the musical luminaries who came before—by listening to and reading music scores and studying old recordings. Or think of

There is always an inner game being played in your mind no matter what outer game you are playing. How aware you are of this game can make the difference between success and failure in the outer game.

Tim Gallwey[4]

Olympic and professional athletes whose practice consists of repeating, perfecting, evaluating, and training with those who can guide them through the maneuvers their sport demands. Both musician and athlete may analyze their 'skill sets' and think of ways to mechanically 'perform better'. However, during an actual performance or sporting event, the best athletes and musicians—the athletes who win games and the musicians who win our hearts—enter into a 'zone' or a 'flow' so that all their practice, learning, and 'listening' culminates in a brilliant outpouring of talent paired with pure expression. The Full Potential method provides pathways to achieve that flow.

Outer Environmental Influences	Inner Influences That Impact the Psychological State
Relationships Family Friends Professional Judgment (that of bosses and co-workers) Work Home Engagement with World Tangible Facts of the Test	Attitude Perseverance Vision Goals Time Management Spiritual Practice

Now think about listening to the consummate musician—it is not the mechanical recitation of music that we enjoy. If it were, computers would have replaced musicians already. Instead, what makes music special is the oneness between the musician and the music, the way that they move through the music—or the way the music moves through them. An exceptional musician is one who is able to bring her inner and outer game together to create something new that we sometimes call "being in the zone" or "going with the flow."

For the GMAT test taker, being able to get in this zone, to balance the flow of inner and outer, will lead to a successful performance. As with the musician or athlete, the GMAT test taker must practice the material that will be on the test. Without the outer game, the inner game won't succeed. Yet the opposite is also true. You can prep for the test night and day, but if you show up for the test feeling nervous, stressed, or lacking in confidence, you will not achieve your full potential. The goal of test prep should be to teach you how to be "in the flow," to identify what is being tested, and then to respond with grace, unfettered by fears or performance concerns.

In this section, **Lay the Groundwork**, you will learn a number of ways to enter the "flow." First, we will discuss setting goals so you can keep your eyes on the prize. Then, you will explore your emotions and learn how to handle stress when it arises. The inner game is not just about emotions—the mind itself is much more than a memorizing tool or generator of emotion. You will learn how to harness the power of your mind to take in new information, to fire the inner critic, to modify your behavior, and to achieve the optimal state for learning. Let's begin!

As you begin this journey, it's time to take inventory of your inner and outer environments. Answer the following questions to create your current map and become aware of your influences so we can begin to address your challenges and harness your strengths.

OUTER:

What are your most significant relationships?

Professional:

Social:

Familial:

As far as you are aware, how do these individuals feel about you taking the GMAT? If they don't know you're taking the GMAT, why don't they?

Do you have a quiet space to study?

Have you created a schedule, and do you have enough time set aside to study? How do you know it is enough time?

INNER:

What prompted you to buy a test prep book?

What concerns, fears, or anxieties do you have about taking the GMAT?

Are you more concerned with taking the test itself—i.e., your mastery of content (math/verbal), meeting the commitment to preparation, or the outcome/score?

Who or what is preventing you from achieving a top score at this point?

CHAPTER TWO

THE POWER OF GOAL-SETTING

Athletes always start their season by identifying their goals. Training yourself to be sure of the outcome of the GMAT, to imagine conquering business school, and even looking ahead to your future business career will help you create a game plan for success.

Both the human body and human mind can be preconditioned for success or for failure. Because of the ways neural pathways are formed and the brain filters information, we tend to notice the aspects and stimuli of the exterior world which fit our beliefs and expectations, and process that information in ways that lead to outcomes that match those expectations. We are prone, in other words, to do what is expected of us. Every serious study of education systems, youth support programs, and public assistance policies makes note of this very fact, frequently and unfortunately in its negative manifestations. Luckily, the positive manifestations of this relationship between the inner and outer games are more powerful than the negative.

Setting goals is a process of deciding what you want to accomplish, then devising a plan to achieve the results you desire. For a goal to be effective, you need to clearly articulate for yourself what you want to do, believe you can do it, and then set in motion the steps necessary to make it happen. The good news is that just being able to see that end-goal helps you to get there!

Here are a few real life examples of the power of setting clear goals and intentions:

1. Before Jim Carrey was famous, he walked up to the Hollywood Hills and wrote himself a check for several million dollars. He wrote "For Services Rendered" on the memo line. He carried this check in his wallet for years, taking it out occasionally to remind himself of his dream. To date, he's one of the highest paid actors in the world. He still carries this check with him.

2. Sean White, an Olympic gold medalist who holds many of the highest awards in snowboarding and skateboarding, won gold in the half-pipe snowboarding competition for the second time in 2010. His first run earned him a high enough score to secure the gold medal without a second run. He performed his second run anyway, as a victory lap, ending his run with the Double McTwist 1260 which he created and mastered—a move never before tried at the Olympics. White told reporters that the secret to his success in the air is visualization. He pictures himself doing a certain trick, and because of that he is able to nail it when it counts most.

3. Mark McCormack, in his book, *What They Don't Teach You at Harvard Business School*, reveals that in a study conducted in 1979 students were asked, "Have you set clear, written goals for your future and made plans to accomplish them?" Three percent of the graduates had written goals and plans; 13 percent had goals, but they were not in writing; and 84 percent had no specific goals. Ten years later, the

same people were interviewed again, and the findings were astonishing. The 13 percent of the class who had goals were earning, on average, twice as much as the 84 percent who had no goals at all. The three percent who had clear, written goals were earning, on average, ten times as much as the other 97 percent put together.

If you believe something is going to happen, as Carey and White did, you begin to direct your energy toward making it happen; conversely, if you are convinced that you cannot do something (like get a great score on the GMAT), or if you are preoccupied with anxious thoughts, more of your energy will be directed toward those negative intentions and less will be invested in achieving your goal. To get a top score, you need to be in the optimal state of mind: positive, calm, and focused.

Take a moment to think about an event coming up in your life, say, a reunion or family function. Life is a mixed bag. You may have positive and negative emotions attached to this event. You might be thrilled to see your old friends at the reunion, but nervous and scared to see an old flame. Or you might be excited about the event itself, but dread taking off work or the travel involved. For many people, the mind tends to dwell on the negative. Is this or has this been the case for you?

Turning the 'frown' into a 'smile' is easier said than done. For that reason, you need a set of written goals to focus on when time gets tough.

The following are additional exercises to help you identify your goals. You bought this book because you want a great GMAT score. That's one goal. But no one takes the GMAT solely in order to experience the pleasure of taking the GMAT! Who do you want to be and how is the GMAT going to get you there? That's your real goal. Once you identify that goal—*your goal*—you will be able to place the GMAT in perspective.

Act as if the universe is a prodigious miracle created for your amusement and illumination. Assume that secret helpers are working behind the scenes to assist you in turning into the gorgeous masterpiece you were born to be. Join the conspiracy to shower all of creation with blessings.
Rob Brezsny[5]

Exercise 1.2.1. Setting Goals

I was very taken with the Infiniti car commercial with some of the words listed below. As a self-branding process, pick 5 of the words below that you identify with and write why you identify with them and how these traits help you to be a great test taker and/or business professional. Indicate why you'd like to be identified with them. You can also add our own words, as well as ask family and friends the top 5 words they would use to describe you.

renegade, fearless, unexpected, bold, true, spontaneous, curious, intriguing, unwavering, rare, brash, provocative, intuitive, genuine, daring, uncommon, irreverent, brazen, absolute, unusual, visionary, idyllic, proud, maverick, wild, undaunted, resolute, poetic, dynamic, unconventional, strong, romantic, authentic, brave, unorthodox, radical, dreamer, soulful, leader, focused, accountable, unreasonable, connected, integrity, trend-setter, deft, triumphant, curious, devoted, happy, achiever, complete

1.

2.

3.

4.

5.

Exercise I.2.2. Vision Board

Vision boards serve the role of programming our mind to tune into the messages and intentions we want for ourselves. It's an easy and fun tool to help us attract that which we want to manifest. By creating a collage of your passions, you clarify for yourself what you want, send those messages to command central (your mind), and begin to set into motion the steps to make this a reality.

Supplies needed:

- poster board or a piece of paper

- magazines. Any will do, but include magazines which will have pictures of things you love or want in your life.

- rubber cement, *Modge Podge,* or glue stick

- scissors

INSTRUCTIONS

Step 1. Prior to creating your board, take a moment to reflect and set your intent. Check in with yourself and ask yourself what it is that you really want. Allow words, sounds, songs, and images to pop into your head. Take a moment to be with these unfiltered thoughts, which will help give a clearer direction to your vision.

Step 2. Go through your magazines and tear or cut out pictures and words that are in harmony with the intention you set for yourself. The images might be literal—for example, you might choose a picture of a successful business person, a car or private jet you like—or they might be metaphoric—for example, a mountain, standing strong and bold. Likewise you might find words that express yourself or your vision for yourself.

Step 3. Once you have the images and words together, lay them out in an arrangement that speaks to you. Maybe you are reevaluating how to perform your best on the test, or perhaps you're thinking about what this test, and business school, will offer you through the relationships and schooling you receive. Whether you understand it or not, put the images together, and trust that you are sending yourself a message.

Step 4. Glue everything onto the board. Write on the back what everything represents and where you are right now. Later, you'll have the opportunity to evaluate your life-scape through a life wheel exercise, after which you may want to revise and revisit this exercise. (See page 113 for the life wheel exercise.)

Step 5. Hang your vision board in a place where you will see it often. Now, use it as an interactive tool. Imagine you've already achieved the goals and intentions you set forth for yourself, represented through the pictures and words. Take note what comes up for you: are you invigorated? Inspired? Something else? Share it with friends and family—and encourage them to make one too. This is not only a GMAT-specific activity! It's a process that everyone can get benefit from and you repeat creating one whenever you'd like.

Exercise I.2.3. Your GMAT and Business School Goals

Now you are ready to write down some definite goals. Here are some guidelines:

1. Put your goals in writing and keep them where you can see them every day. Write them on a piece of paper that you attach to your refrigerator or bathroom mirror. Put some goals on Post-It Notes and put them up around your home.

2. Write your goals in clear and specific language and use the present tense. For example, instead of writing "I want to do well on the GMAT," write, "I will earn a 750 on the GMAT." Instead of writing, "I will try to concentrate fully," write, "I will remain focused and engaged with each and every question."

3. Create goals that are believable and reasonable to *you* (not to other people). The better you are able to articulate your own vision, the more likely it will come to pass. So don't hold back. Do you see yourself as a CEO of a multinational company? The head of a cultural revolution? The next president? No one needs to see your goals but you, so give yourself permission to think big, while believing that what you want really is possible.

Business school is really 'leadership school.' Have you begun to see yourself like a leader yet? If not, start now.

Write answers to the following:

1. GMAT Goal: I want to score _____ on the GMAT. A _____ on Verbal and _____ on Math.

2. Business School Goals: I am going to go to business school to (think about your intellectual, professional, social, skills-based and other goals):

3. An MBA will provide the following to me:

4. My lifetime goal is to be/do/have:

Exercise I.2.4. Write a Letter to Yourself

Write a letter to yourself from some point in the future. Imagine you're 60, 80 or 100 years old, writing to yourself as you are right now. Or, if writing to yourself feels too odd, imagine writing a letter from the future to a grandchild you will have.

In the letter, include what you'll accomplish as a result of getting a stellar GMAT score, and the treasures and accomplishments that await you beyond the test itself. Keep the letter and reread it to yourself when you feel anxious about your future.

For example: My darling grandchild, how could I have known that business school would unlock my potential to become the first person to create affordable medicine for everyone. Taking the classes I did gave me the resources to reconfigure priorities in the United States at a federal level and harness the corporate marketplace to create a win-win situation for everyone: a healthier nation, economy, and people. Because of whom I met, and when I met them, I had the opportunity to contribute to the world, and this resulted in my meeting my partner and creating a comfortable and exciting life for myself and our children. What I hope to pass on to you is my legacy of making a difference.

Exercise I.2.5. Visualization

Up to this point, we have identified goals in words and images. The next step is to spend time in our imagination. Daydreaming, if you will. Visualization is taking the time to imagine possibilities, either as a picture or a 'movie', of an outcome. You can use visualization for any of your goals. You can visualize acing the GMAT, getting into a top business school, entering the career you want to achieve, or creating a legacy or empire for yourself. No holds barred!

Visualization has been proven to work again and again. Researchers at Stanford and University of Chicago compared two sets of basketball players. The first group practiced playing whereas the second group only imagined practicing. The players who didn't physically practice, but visualized peak performance, improved 23-30% in their actual basket-shooting ability, whereas the test takers who only physically practiced saw little improvement. And you thought daydreaming was idle time! On the contrary!

Visualization should be a key part of realizing your goal to achieve your full potential on the GMAT (then later for subsequent goals). Do this exercise whenever you want to feel more empowered. Be sure to go through the entire 'narrative' even if you're short on time. Some people find they prefer to tape themselves and then listen to the tape.

Imagine it's test day. You feel amazing: alert, prepared, confident, and relaxed. You're well rested and have the deep belief that you've done your part in becoming prepared for this exam. You've gained knowledge of the material, practiced, taken diagnostics, and learned from your mistakes. You know there will be no surprises, even though you don't know the details of each question. You've become familiar with every type of question and you're completely ready. Notice that you answer each question with clarity and preciseness. And how great it feels.

In fact, you feel filled with extreme focus and calm. With each and every question, you notice you feel a sense of accomplishment and it feels good. As you answer each and every question, you notice you have a kind of knowing, a feeling that you've done this before and that there will be no surprises. You are on your game, in your flow. You feel this as you go through each section: AWA, Math and Verbal.

Now, imagine it's the end of the test, and you see your score on the screen. You feel the excitement and energy course through your body. You feel amazing. You want to jump up and hi-five someone. You did it! You imagine calling your friends or family outside of the test center. They are excited by your success. They love you and believe in your dreams, and they tell you this often. You knew you could accomplish this, and you did it, and you feel amazing! You know you can do anything you set your mind to, and this is just the beginning.

Your visualization does not need to be the same each time, but you need to tap into a sense of accomplishment, calm, and confidence. If you can't access this by thinking of an accomplishment in the future, think of a time in the past when you felt confident and a sense of accomplishment. Replay it in your mind and identify how you feel with that memory of accomplishment. Do this every morning and before bedtime, or whenever you want to feel more empowered.

CHAPTER THREE

THE BODY: WE ARE OUR EMOTIONS

The GMAT can feel like a "life or death" situation if you have your heart set on going to business school. You also may have reasonable concerns about taking the GMAT now, particularly if you have been away from school, tests, and academics for a while, like most GMAT test takers. So, what level of stress is appropriate?

We know that anxiety isn't all bad. Anxiety is a bit like excitement, and in just the right doses it can potentially compel a student to persevere, stay alert, perform their best, and be on their game. The problem is that many test takers cannot control that precise level of 'excitement,' nor help unconsciously thinking that the anxiety/excitement is a positive thing leading to better scores. This simply isn't always the case.

This misperception has its roots in the most basic, animal part of our selves. In a famous experiment, behavioral psychologist B.F. Skinner placed several hungry pigeons in a cage that had an automatic mechanism that delivered food at regular intervals. He discovered that the pigeons came to associate the delivery of the food with whatever actions they happened to have been performing when the food was administered. For example, the bird's wing may have been up and flapping, or the bird may have been leaning or hopping on one leg. The pigeons, once they received food, continued to perform the same actions—and even elaborated upon them. From this behavior, Skinner suggested that the pigeons believed they were influencing the automatic feed with their physical "rituals."[6]

Just as the bird behaves as if there is a causal relation between its behavior and the appearance of food (even though, in truth, such a relation is lacking), many test takers mistake their anxiety from earlier test taking experiences as the cause of their great scores just because both occurred at the same time. Skip ahead a few years. Now the same test taker hasn't taken a high stakes test or been in school for quite a while. He may feel confident about his ability to take the GMAT because he has prepped the test questions and doesn't immediately feel anxiety—until he goes into take the test, and then anxiety about test taking, about grammar, math, or about his new potential career materialize. This anxiety may even overwhelm him in a way it never did when he was in school.

Why? Because on past tests he did well in spite of—or even because of—the little bit of anxiety that was present. At first, the anxiety was likely at a low-enough level that it helped, rather than hurt, his score. It helped keep him focused and engaged. With these earliest tests, his unconscious mind mistook his anxiety, not his knowledge of the test material, as the cause of his success. This is the same dynamic exhibited when the pigeon mistook his 'dance' for the reason he was receiving food. If he is like most of us, the test taker has experienced an increase of anxiety as he passed though school and college and into the adult world to shoulder adult responsibilities. That anxiety/excitement that was once a spark of energy has snowballed into something that is a barrier to achievement.

If you spend weeks or months stressed out by the idea of the GMAT, or if you experience too much anxiety on the test day, you will likely not give your peak performance. That's why, as part of your test preparation, you need to make sure that you are not suffering from too much test anxiety. Here is a list of warning symptoms. If you have any of these symptoms, you need to read this chapter carefully and do all of the exercises.

1. You have trouble getting started on your homework/study.

2. You are easily distracted, even once you have started the test.

3. You feel, believe, and voice concerns that you won't do well on the test, despite your best efforts.

4. You have physical symptoms during or before the test, such as sweaty palms, upset stomach, headaches, tension, and difficulty falling asleep.

5. You find it hard to concentrate, follow instructions, or understand questions during the test.

6. You have a history of poor performance on tests.

7. You often remember material after the test that you forget while taking the test.

If you experience any of these symptoms, you are not going to test well—or at least not at your best. The brain and body function and feel best when you enter an exam feeling confident and focused. These positive emotions have both biochemical and psychological benefits. Emotional health, like intellectual and physical health, is a lifestyle choice. You can't neglect your emotional health for weeks or months, and then expect to feel positive and stress-free on the day you take your test.

To achieve your optimal emotional health for the exam, you will have to start changing your beliefs and habits. Changing your emotional outlook may seem difficult, even impossible. It may go against your sense of who you are: "I'm just an anxious person." "I am a pessimist." "Stress makes me work harder."

Spiritual teachers, therapists, and neuropsychologists all agree that we can change this aspect of ourselves. Let's explore what happens to the body, biochemically, when we experience a negative emotional state. Our bodies respond to every thought or feeling we have with a biochemical flow. In 2001, research by doctors at the University of Colorado showed that stress causes the nervous system to begin secreting the same chemicals our immune system produces when it detects an infection in our body. The brain responds as if a 'real' infection has occurred. We get low-level fevers and our white blood cells increase in number as our body conserves energy to be used in a fight against foreign invaders. We also suffer the same behavioral changes, including a decreased desire for food and water, more negative thoughts, and a reduction in cognitive ability. The same doctors discovered that this stress reaction could occur as much as ten days after the initial stressor. Stress, anxiety, and worry, it turns out, make us physically sick.[7] And sometimes these reactions are immediate, getting in the way of our test taking prowess.

And that is just what we can perceive as the 'symptoms' of stress, et al. But let's dig a little deeper into how this works. When we experience any kind of physical or psychological stressor, the hypothalamus, pituitary, and adrenal glands, or, as they are collectively called, the HPA axis, are stimulated, and there is a temporary increase in cortisol levels.[8] Experiencing chronic exposure to stressors/distress contributes to increased cortisol levels, which can diminish a variety of immune functions (reduce the number of lymphocytes, slow wound healing, etc.) and enhance certain undesirable immune functions (reduce the number of lymphocytes, slow wound healing, etc.) and enhance certain undesirable immune functions (e.g., inflammation)[9]. And to continue with this smarty-pants explanation, stress also increases the amount of inter-leukin-1, a pro-inflammatory cytokine (a macrophage, which is one of the first cells to respond to an infection) in the hippocampus.[10] The interleukin-1 binds to pockets of neurotransmitters, signaling to the brain that you're sick. In short: the more your body pumps out these chemicals, the more you actually feel sick, at a cellular, and then later an actual physical level. Good times these are not.

Now let's translate this science into some guideposts for your own experiences. Consider the following scenarios in which you might feel anxiety and sheer panic:

1. You avert a car accident.

2. You suddenly realize you forgot to do something very important.

3. It is late at night, and as you are walking down a dark, unfamiliar street you hear a strange noise behind you.

4. Your company is downsizing and your boss has been let go. The next round of in-house pruning takes place after the weekend.

In each case, you probably will feel what is commonly called the 'fight or flight' syndrome. You might feel your stomach drop, grow dizzy, experience sweaty palms, or have any other of a host of physical responses. This biology is one of the most primitive parts of who we are—we see it overtly in the animal kingdom. If you were truly fighting for your life, or trying to escape from some critical situation, this chemical cocktail of adrenaline and cortisol would be essential to provide the strength and wherewithal to respond quickly and intuitively for your survival.[11]

The problem with this fight or flight syndrome, particularly when it is chronic, is that the chemicals it produces wear away at our bodies. People living in situations where they actually need to fight for their lives frequently live shorter lives. For example, Ewa Ruminska-Zimny, a noted social affairs officer for the U.N., charted in her work the rising mortality of people living in Eastern Europe after the fall of the Soviet Union and significantly blamed the intense stress those populations suffered after the collapse of the Soviet system. It is well-known that people living in war-torn countries have a shorter life expectancy, even when discounting violent deaths resulting from the war as well as other factors, such as food rationing and the spread of illness and disease.

The bottom line? High stress is the way the body protects us from a danger now, even though the long term cost is potentially shorter, less productive life in the future.

Is there an alternative? Yes! There are no negative consequences from having too much calmness or happiness. In fact, when we feel positive, our bodies produce a different set of hormones and chemicals that have positive effect on our physical and mental health. In 1974, Herbert Benson, a doctor at Harvard, proved through extensive research and experimentation that a variety of calming exercises (which we'll get into in more detail later in the book) that he grouped under the heading The Relaxation Response, produced in patients almost mirror images of the negative reactions their bodies produced while under stress. Blood pressure dropped, muscle tension decreased, heart rates returned to normal, and a host of other beneficial actions in the body occurred when the mind was calmed with focused, positive thoughts. We do not yet know the full extent of the power of the individual brain, and probably never will. The fact that so many patients in so many pharmaceutical tests demonstrate signs of improved health even when only receiving placebo drugs, however, implies the level of control we all have over our own wellbeing. The mind, it seems, is one of the most powerful healers of all.

So how does Positive Reappraisal work? As stress and negative emotions are detrimental to physical health, positive reappraisal is a "cognitive process through which people focus on the good in what is happening or what has happened."[12] It may reduce distress and/or enhance positive emotion. The Positive Emotion Broaden-and-Build theory states that positive emotions broaden people's day-to-day thought-action repertoires and widens the variety of thoughts and actions that come to mind[13], for example, joy, interest, contentment, etc. As one gains a wider scope of attention, cognition and action, it leads to building of physical, intellectual and social resources.[14] And an increase in positive emotions, increases personal resources.

A study was conducted in which participants were shown film clips to induce specific emotions (joy, contentment, fear, anger).[15] With a control group that was shown a neutral clip, the subjects were shown the clip and afterwards asked to list the different activities they'd like to do right then. The responses were recorded on a sheet with up to 20 blank lines. The positive emotion subjects identified more activities relative to the negative emotion subjects and the neutral control group.

Experiments like this and those utilizing electromyography (EMG, a technique for recording the electrical activity produced by skeletal muscles) show that positive thinking increases the range of thoughts and emotions one experiences.[16]

How can we change our emotions so that we flush ourselves with calm rather than stress? First, we can encourage our body to produce beneficial chemicals through exercise and good nutrition. We have to take care of our bodies if we want our bodies to provide us with peak performance. We also can flood our bodies with calming chemicals by using body-based practices like meditation and yoga. The next chapter teaches you basic meditation techniques you can use to calm your mind.

Finally, if we really want to reach our full potential, we have to learn how to change negative feelings into positive ones, which means we have to do the hard work of reframing what we believe about ourselves and our abilities. We'll work on four different ways to reframe our behaviors—hypnosis, EFT, NLP and Gamma Brain Wave Learning—in the rest of this section.

Exercise I.3.I. The Urgency Index[17]

Circle the number that best represents your normal behavior or attitude using this scale:

		Never	Sometimes			Always
1	I seem to do my best work when I'm under pressure.	0	1	2	3	4
2	I often blame the rush and push of external things for my failure to spend deep introspective time with myself.	0	1	2	3	4
3	I'm often frustrated by the slowness of people and things around me. I hate to wait or stand in line.	0	1	2	3	4
4	I feel guilty when I take time off from work.	0	1	2	3	4
5	I always seem to be rushing between places and events.	0	1	2	3	4
6	I frequently find myself pushing people away so I can finish what I'm doing.	0	1	2	3	4
7	I feel anxious when I'm out of touch with the office.	0	1	2	3	4
8	I'm often preoccupied with one thing when I'm doing something else.	0	1	2	3	4
9	I'm at my best when I'm handling a crisis situation.	0	1	2	3	4
10	I often eat lunch or other meals while I work.	0	1	2	3	4
11	I keep thinking that someday I'll be able to do what I really want.	0	1	2	3	4
12	It's difficult for me to really complete things without the pressure of a deadline.	0	1	2	3	4
13	I often give up quality time with important people in my life to handle situations at work.	0	1	2	3	4
14	I feel like I've really been productive if I've checked off a lot of items on my "to do" list.	0	1	2	3	4

		Never	Sometimes			Always
15	I get irritated when I, or others, make mistakes, or when things don't go right or get delayed.	0	1	2	3	4
16	I start thinking about what I have to do at work within a few minutes of waking up.	0	1	2	3	4
17	I have a hard time slowing down and relaxing when I reach the end of the workday.	0	1	2	3	4
18	When something cancels or I get unexpected free time, my first thought is what work I can fill the empty space with.	0	1	2	3	4
19	I have a hard time creating sacrosanct space in my life into which work doesn't intrude.	0	1	2	3	4
20	While I'm working, I feel the pressure of all the other things I have to do that are hanging over me.	0	1	2	3	4

Add together your scores and place the total here:

0 – 30   Low Urgency Mind-Set

30 – 50   High Urgency Mind-Set

51+   Urgency Addiction

Being the good business school students that you are, you'll compute that the only way you'd fit into the Low Urgency Mindset is if your average answer was < 1.5. In our experience this has been rare.

Exercise 1.3.2. Stress Behavior Inventory

There are many evaluative tools available to help you ascertain whether you're stressed or anxious, but you probably already know the answer yourself. Associate and identify what kinds of stress you feel now and how you would like to feel.

1. I experience these symptoms when I need to take a test:

   a. I have trouble sleeping before a test.

   b. During a test, I get an unpleasant physical response. Circle your response: sweaty palms, twitches, rapid breathing, stomach ache, other:_____.

   c. I have trouble focusing during a test.

   d. I feel very self-conscious while taking a test.

   e. I get bored or distracted in the middle of a test.

2. Go back over the symptoms in question 1b. Do you experience any of these symptoms when you are not taking a test but are doing homework or other test prep work?

3. Describe how you would want to feel before and during a test:

4. Describe an optimal testing situation (i.e., lighting, temperature, sound, time, how you feel, etc.).

Exercise 1.3.3. How Do You Move?

Physical exercise should be an important part of your test preparation process. Why? Because the benefits of exercise, beyond feeling great and looking good, include increased ability to cope better with stress as well as improving the brain's functions.[18] In numerous studies, physical activity has been shown to help the brain work better. Exercise causes an actual physical and chemical response inside the brain that helps people perform better than without it. For many GMAT test takers, a life sitting at a desk is the norm. For the youngest of the test takers, 1-3 years out of college, this more sedentary posture might be a departure from a more active life prior. With habits engrained, and the time-demands of the job, implementing a more active lifestyle may be optimistic and unrealistic—but inserting even the littlest bit of physical activity can have profound affects on your test performance. Just look at some of the data:

Several studies done by the California Department of Education found that there was a positive relationship between physical activity and academic performance. Their studies suggested that when a substantial amount of school time is dedicated to physical activity, academic performance meets and may even exceed that of students not receiving additional physical activity.[19] Another study measured the cognitive abilities of the participants in four areas: memory, executive functioning, attention/concentration, and psychomotor speed, both before enrolling in an exercise study, and four months after. The results proved that those who exercised demonstrated significant improvements in the higher mental processes of memory and in "executive functions" that involve planning, organization, and the ability to mentally juggle different intellectual tasks at the same time.[20] So while training for the New York, Boston (or insert your city here) Marathon may not be in your near future, you can incorporate small steps to incorporate physical activity to improve your brain health. Now, for those of us pressed for time, let's figure out what kind of physical exercise works best for us.

First, circle your answers to this question: Right now, I exercise this much every week:

1 day/wk   2 day/wk   3 day/wk   5 day/wk   every day

For: 0-30 min 30-60 min   60-120 min   >120 min

If you already exercise 3x or more per week, or more than 120 minutes a week, you can skip this exercise!

If you now exercise only 1 day/wk or for less than 30 minutes, please see a doctor before starting any new exercise plan. And make sure to start your exercise plan gradually!

Circle which statement best applies:

1. I am the kind of person who (choose the one that best fits you):

    a. Likes to challenge myself

    b. Likes to work with others

    c. Likes to compete against others

2. I have excellent (choose the one that best fits you):

    a. hand-eye coordination

    b. leg strength

    c. arm strength

    d. endurance

If you put down:

   1a and 2a, then you may enjoy golf

   1a and 2b, then you may enjoy walking, running, rock-climbing, or skateboarding

   1a and 2c, then you may enjoy weight lifting, swimming, or kayaking

   1a and 2d, then you may enjoy running, swimming, or vinyasa yoga

   1b and 2a, then you may enjoy golf or pick-up basketball, soccer, or flag football

   1b and 2b, then you may enjoy running with others

   1b and 2c, then you may enjoy weight lifting with a friend

   1b and 2d, then you may enjoy running with a partner or playing soccer

   1c and 2a, then you may enjoy tennis, badminton, or golf

   1c and 2b, then you may enjoy soccer or basketball

   1c and 2c, then you might enjoy racquet ball, hand ball, and tennis

   1c and 2d, then you might enjoy soccer, ultimate Frisbee, or martial arts

CHAPTER FOUR

MEDITATION

Meditation is an ancient practice of quieting the mind and the body in order to move into a deeper state of relaxation or awareness. When someone engages in a meditation practice, the benefits extend beyond the calming act of meditation itself, helping the practitioner achieve greater focus, deliberation, and clarity. Meditation has even been shown to improve brain function. Researchers at the Dalian University of Technology and the University of Oregon ran studies in 2010 that proved that regular meditation actually spurs new growth of the fibers that connect neurons within the brain. Meditation can actually grow your brain![21]

Meditation is used by many different world religions and cultures to help practitioners observe and understand their minds, and to give the unconscious mind time to process and integrate information. The person meditating learns to "let go" of whatever the mind gravitates to and the emotions that follow. By learning to release yourself from your thoughts and emotions, you become better able to control the mind's direction when you are not meditating.

For some of us, the mind is like a leaf blowing in the wind—forced here and there by the direction of the gale. If things are going well, you might feel happy, but if they are going badly, you will not. For example, if you take a diagnostic after studying a long time, you might first feel invigorated, excited, and 'up' for the challenge. If, however, you discover when scoring your test that you missed questions you thought you should have answered correctly, you feel discouraged, overwhelmed and confused. That discouragement and confusion may then be carried over to other activities and areas of life. The mind has now interfered with your abilities. It is not serving your best interests, which is, of course, one of its primary functions.

With regular practice, meditation will help you to observe and understand your own mind so that you can learn to let go of your negative feelings instead of letting them control you. Meditation also gives your unconscious mind time to process and integrate information. Like sleep, meditation is a gift you give to your mind, a chance for it to rest and recharge.

The incorporation of meditation, the 'sister' to exercise, provides you with a sense of time in which nothing, literally no-thing, is supreme. A counterbalance to exercise, meditation provides you with the opportunity to slow the body and quiet the mind, which in turn activates focus, perception, and mental equilibrium. Like physical activity, however, you need to carve out the time to do your meditation practice, and you will receive more benefits as your practice becomes more consistent.

For the GMAT test taker, meditation helps to cultivate a consistent feeling of calm and ease, even in the most difficult circumstances. In general terms, someone who meditates experiences the world as one where its component parts fall naturally into place and thus make logical and emotional sense. Shifts of perception take place and productivity increases.

Now you may be thinking that in theory, meditation sounds great, but you're not spiritual or into yoga. You may even thrive under pressure (though we've shown how constant anxiety is not good for anyone over the long run). Or you might come up with many excuses as to why you can't meditate (no time, not my 'thing,' it's too 'new age', I can't relax or can't turn my brain 'off,' etc.). To this, all we can say is: just give it a try.

The last thing a test taker needs is an inner dialogue appraising their every move, or expressing some self-negating thought. That just doesn't promote optimal test taking.

Meditation helps silence that inner critic. Once you engage in a regular meditation practice, you will find that you have created a calm oasis within yourself that you can return to again and again, even without meditation. It's a real benefit during a test like the GMAT to be able to take a deep breath and return to a place of calm.

My friend and colleague Jay Michaelson is a big advocate for, and teacher of, meditation. He has written about harnessing the 'real potency' of attending one's religious institution (in this case, it was synagogue but it applies just as aptly to church, mosque, etc.) in both sporadic and consistent terms. My take away–and extension of his idea– is that as GMAT test takers, if we only seek the immediate 'spiritual' benefits derived sporadically, in only what is deemed designated times and places, of hypnosis, meditation or even massage, we aren't really benefiting fully from our practice. In other words, consistently engaging in meditation or some of the practices we have introduced in this chapter as a lifestyle choice allows you to reap the real benefits. We may get a kind of immediate or momentary 'high,' but the consistent sense of feeling present can flow into our everyday life, seeing the ordinary as extraordinary, and allows the brain to simply work better because it's 'on'. For the GMAT test taker, the benefit translates to feeling present, focused, and able to engage fully with the question sets, during study and through taking the test itself.

Meditation is also much easier to begin than most people believe. You don't need any equipment to meditate. Even though many people enjoy meditation classes because they believe working with teachers deepens their practice, you can meditate right now, sitting in your chair, with this book in front of you.

The exercises that follow provide a brief introduction to meditation. Remember, it doesn't need to be a long process: five to fifteen minutes of meditation performed regularly can have profound effects. If you find you like it, there are many resources available for you to continue and deepen your practice—check out the appendix of this book for some of them. In addition, look up meditation online, and see if local options or online courses are appealing and convenient. Chances are, finding a method and/or teacher is the best way to go, and like any new practice or hobby, experimenting with what works best for you is the way to go.

Exercise 1.4.1. Beginning a Meditation Practice

Find a quiet room with few distractions. Feel free to personalize the space where you do your meditation: you may want to light a candle, or put up photos or affirmations.

While you can do meditation at any time, we recommend morning because the mind is calmer then than it is later in the day. In any case, set aside a regular daily time.

Allow yourself enough time for your meditation. Though your first meditation practice may be only 3-10 minutes, set aside 20 minutes or more so you don't feel rushed. After you do your meditation practice, if you have extra time, you can take a brief nap, stretch, or do something else to take care of yourself.

Sit in a comfortable position. Many people prefer to sit cross-legged on the floor. If that's not comfortable, find some other position. Chairs can be distracting, but if you cannot sit comfortably on the floor, use a chair. Likewise, if you need back support, feel free to sit against a wall. The aim is to be in a position where you can allow your body to rest and soften while your mind remains alert. The first time you meditate, you may want to simply focus on how the different parts of your body feel when you sit for 10 minutes in one position.

It is helpful to set an intention before you start. Identify why you are doing the meditation: are you hoping to increase your focus and confidence, or do you just want to expand upon your inner peace?

A BREATHING MEDITATION

One easy way to start a meditation practice is to focus on an easily observable rhythm in our own bodies: our breathing.

Sit with your eyes partially closed or fully closed, and turn your attention to your breathing.

Breathe naturally, preferably through the nostrils, without attempting to control your breath, and become aware of the sensation and sound of your inhale and exhale.

Allow, with each breath, a deepened opening: loosen your face, neck, hands, stomach, and other areas of your body that are 'holding on.' Start by recognizing the tension in your head, and releasing it, then move slowly down your body towards your feet. While you do this, continue to focus on your breath and once you are relaxed, continue to be aware of your breathing.

At first, your mind will likely be busy with inner chatter. You might even feel that your mind has become busier now that you're trying to clear it in order to focus on your breath. In actuality, your mind is always noisy like this, but in this state, you're just more aware of it. While you might be tempted to follow the thoughts as they arise, resist that. Remain singularly focused on your breath. If you discover your mind has wandered, gently lead your attention back to your breath.

Notice how your body changes during breathing. Notice the rise and fall of your chest. Notice how your body feels against the floor or chair, the sounds as they arise from within the body, or those outside of it.

After some time, maybe 5 minutes, or 10 minutes, or longer once you become used to this practice, begin modulating your breath, taking a deeper breath in, and then a deeper breath out, once, twice, three times.

Open your eyes. Stretch, and allow yourself to rise slowly.

Repeat this as many times as necessary until the mind settles on the breath.

One of our clients kept this on her refrigerator while working with us and is still using it 5 years later. She told us that it was one of the most powerful exercises we offered her, so we chose to include it in our manual.

A mantra is a saying that is repeated in such a way that your mind sinks into the music of your words and thoughts, and ideas spark up on their own from your subconscious. They help us sit in the great knowledge that we are all spiritual beings having a human experience and that we are all capable of excellence, always.

To fully absorb the possibility of being in a truly mindful state, sit in a comfortable place, preferably on the ground with crossed legs, and place these words in front of you. With half-closed eyes, read out loud. Listen to your words. Let their shape linger on your tongue, their vibrations and meanings swim in the silence you've made for yourself.

Say at least one mantra once a day, and the entire thing at once, once a week, during each month you are studying. If one or more of the categories feels right, say it more often. If there are things you want to add, add them. If there are things you want to take away, then take them away. This is merely meant to be a reflection of you at your core essence, a reminder of how fantastic, dedicated, and courageous you have been to come this far on your journey to enrich your life by going back to school. You know yourself the best, so adapt as needed.

Release and Move Through Mantra – The past is behind me. I shed it, and let it go… I embrace life… I let go of the past and whatever has happened before me… I welcome the positive…I embrace life… I am open to new things… I accept the love and creative possibility in all things… I understand that the unknown might be surrounding me, but that from that place of mystery comes fruitful possibility… In that darkness comes the spark of ingenuity, shift and change… From this place, I remain free, liberated… I can allow that flow to be… And I can forgive, and see opportunity for change at each step… My future is choice, and is secure. Change is good and I welcome it… I trust myself… Newness is exciting and freeing… I celebrate the past that brought me here to this moment in time… I can move on knowing my foundations are firm in shifting to a new direction. Transition is like the butterfly, trusting the cocoon will bring it the ability to fly… And I can fly… I lounge in this moment… There is beauty in this cycle, and I'm drawn to its freedom… To embrace this very point in time where I can choose, have faith in my decision, and be in peace… I make this happen…

Relax and Open Mantra – Release tensions… Feel good… Feel relaxed… Let go… Open… My life is full of possibility… Of love… Of breathing deeply and freely… To land and… Go to sleep easily… Relaxed… My body is strong… Is supple… My mind keeps still… As again and again… I let go… I am still… I am calm… Relaxed… Tranquil… Rest comes easily… Harmony is within me… Peace comes like the tide… Again and again…Like the sun rising… Setting the world alight… I move with the wind… I feel at ease… With myself… With others… With the peace around me… Flowing through my fingers like the wind… I move with it… I enjoy this stillness, this flow, this ripple, this strength… I have all the time I could ever need… Beauty is everywhere… I am in flow… I am… I am… **I make this happen…**

Accept and Love Self Mantra – I roar... Feeling the spiral of strength within me...Belting out the courageous... The strength within... I am confident... I embrace change, connection moments, abundance, shifts.... I am healthy... Strength lives within me... I am clear, focused, and see my future as an extension of this very moment... I walk placidly amid the haste... Softness with strength by my side... Within me... Delighted by the moment... I lift my heart towards the sun, my head tilted back... I feel the warmth... I am powerful... My path is clear before me, it extends out from me... The future is safe... I am determined... The time is now... I choose to make things happen... I am bold with boundless energy... The details reveal what the bigger picture relays... That I walk with courage... Live in high spirits... I am self-reliant, bold, free, passionate, engaged with life and living... I seek adventure, enjoy charm... Joy springs from within me... I believe in myself... I have faith in my vision... I attract strong people... I live in the moment, enthusiastic... My inner strength grows... Flows like the river... **I make this happen...**

Nourishment and Living Healthy Mantra – I feel great... Amazing... I am free...Clear... Movement is easy and my mind is free... I love my body... Strength comes from within... I take care of myself... Great food, air, sunshine, friends, thoughts, ideas, possibilities... I feel nurtured and nourished... There is a bounty in living in the now and in embracing free-dom... I am always drawn to healthy foods... I embrace life... One good... I am in excellent shape... I nurture my body... I step back from the canvas of my life... And assess that I feel fresh and alive... Breathing freely and deeply... I embrace nature... I exercise daily... Feeling relaxed... I drink an abundance of water... I soar through life... I am happy... I choose wholesome foods... Foods full of nutrients and strength-giving properties... To help me maximize my potential... There is beauty in my strength and softness... I feel nourished in the now... Each cell taking in the energy, the light, so I can feel radiant and vibrant... I am cheerful and spirited... Lusty... The core of my being is light... happiness dwells within and is shared by me... I love my life... Living foods always... I respect this earth that is my home... **I make this happen...**

Magnified Happiness Mantra – In that kernel deep within me, I feel the growth, like a seed that grows and reaches towards the sun... Happiness dwells in me, my heart is open and free... I feel passion, am passionate and live with a zest for life... My life is enriching... And I feel boundless love... I feel open and share my feelings... I trust in myself... I welcome a colorful life... I nurture my emotions, my body, my mind... I feel both softness and strength... I welcome earthly pleasures... Love... I celebrate my body... I celebrate sensual pleasures... I express and experience my sexuality with confidence... I know that love lives in everybody... I am sensitive to my needs... My life is stimulating... Exciting... I feel happiness well up and raise me up... I embrace the romance and mystery in life... Welcome the surprises... One good... I respect the earth and nature around me... I trust in my feelings for others... I share love with the world... I am open to new friendships... I nurture my body, my spirit, my soul... I feel and experience beauty everywhere... Love is healing... Strength lies within... I feel integrated with all that is around me... I revel in this moment... I celebrate the now... **I make this happen...**

Expand Gratitude Mantra – I have much to be thankful for... My life is full of happiness... And I choose to be happy... In this mindset I feel cheerful... I am cheerful... I am liberated... I feel liberated... My choices make me feel alive, and I feel refreshed as I move through my day... I make both thoughtful and spontaneous decisions to satiate my curiosity and drive...

I explore who I am in each decision I make and experience that I have... I feel gratitude for who I am, celebrate each opportunity and choice that has come to me... I celebrate me... My world is comprised of simple pleasures... I embrace my inner child... I welcome color and passion... I feel energy... I live a charmed life... I feel free... Feel love... I feel connected to the people around me and send love out to the world... I enjoy playing and being playful... I nourish myself... I always have what I need... I respect the elements outside of me and the elements within me... I live in the moment... I welcome joy... I see the love in all things... I have a joyful life... The spirit of creativity dwells with in me... I invite new friendships... New connections... Happiness abounds... I am free in spirit... I rejoice in life...
I make this happen...

Spark Creativity Mantra – My mind is free and germinates ideas from thoughts, colors, sounds, shapes... Scents entice me to feel old and new things at once... Collages in front of me... I linger in the moments... I love life... Creativity flows from within and sparks... My recall is excellent... I see the world in both usual and unusual ways and act on my ideas... I ponder in a sea of possibility... All things are possible... I have befriended my mind... I am flexible, I see outcomes, I am excited by the options... My memory is excellent... I hear and listen to my intuition... I am delighted by my strong vision... I focus and understand easily... Intuitively... I have a way of knowing... I am resourceful, inventive, and in the now... My life germinates new ideas... My mind feeds my appetite... I am resourceful... My mind is quick... Sharp... Imagination weaves and flows through me... Life inspires me... I respect the sparks of flame... I create opportunities... My path is clear before me...
I make this happen...

Abundant Bliss Mantra – Knowledge and bright ideas come to me easily... I am free... My vision is strong and sharp... I am poised, and sit on a throne of abundance... My court is of equals... And we all live in this abundant, beautiful place... It is radiant and beautiful, and holds all we need and hold dear... I feel comfortable with all aspects of being: intellectual, physical, spiritual, emotional... I choose abundance... My life is affluent in every realm... Knowledge and being able to perform to my capabilities come easily... I invest in myself with confidence and ease... Feeling good, I feel my sustenance... Depth... Being... I attract the wealth of living and being alive... Joyful... I feel comfortable with using my knowledge for good... I act now for the good of all... Drawing from the deep well of joy... Transformations and evolutions are abundant... I am joyful... Blissful... Seizing the moment... The day... I am powerful... I accept wealth... Freedom... I quickly seize opportunity... I know how to maximize my potential... My life is plentiful... I am fruitful... I am free from my possessions and live in comfort... I am generous... Prosperity surrounds me... I create opportunities...
I make this happen...

I choose: Yes.

CHAPTER FIVE

THE INCREDIBLE MIND: HYPNOSIS

A variety of techniques can help diffuse and eliminate stress. Wouldn't it be better, though, if you could prevent stress in the first place? The key to controlling emotions like stress is changing your beliefs. When you set goals and teach yourself to truly believe you will achieve these goals, you will create the kind of positive attitude you need to achieve your full potential.

Beliefs arise in your mind, so the first step to changing your beliefs is to understand how the mind works. When you understand how the mind works, you will know more about why we are the way we are, how our minds process new ideas and information, and how we can take control of our ability to create new habits, beliefs, and behaviors.

You can think of the mind as 'command central,' the place where all your functions and intentions are manifest. The major parts of the mind are the conscious—the part of you that is aware of what you are doing and thinking, and the unconscious, the part of the mind that is usually hidden even to ourselves but emerges in dreams, drug-induced states, and hypnotic trances. The threshold between the conscious and the unconscious mind is known as the "critical faculty."

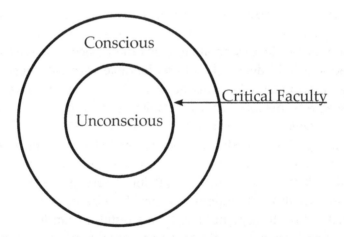

The conscious mind is the part of you that you are aware of as you engage with your environment. For example, you are aware that you are reading these words right now. Short-term memory, the place where you store things when you're 'cramming' for an exam, resides here as well. Generally speaking, the conscious mind focuses on one thing at a time and can only really juggle between a few things with relative effectiveness.

The conscious mind is logical and analytical, providing reasons for why you do what you do. Its domain is willpower and temporary memory—both critical elements tied to your short-term goals. The conscious mind is also the part of the mind that deals with judgment and decision-making. Should you continue reading this book, or should you put it down to complete a work task, participate in some social opportunity, or fulfill an obligation like cleaning up your apartment? As you weigh these decisions, actively thinking things through, you are using your conscious mind to sort through the options.

The unconscious mind, on the other hand, is engaged in a multitude of things of which you're completely unaware, even while you're reading this. The unconscious is in charge of keeping a lot of your bodily functions on track. For example, as you read this, your eyes blink, your heart beats, and you are breathing in a rhythmic pattern. These bodily functions occur just below your current awareness, but if they weren't happening, you wouldn't be around reading this.

In addition to keeping your body functioning properly, your unconscious mind is responsible for a vast range of mental operations, including dreams, intuition, creativity, imagination, and insight. It also holds onto its own set of beliefs, thoughts, and feelings, which may be pleasant or unpleasant, including feelings of pain, anxiety, or conflict. It holds the memory of everything that we have ever experienced, even though we aren't always able to access the memories easily all the time.

The critical faculty acts as the boundary or membrane between the conscious and unconscious minds. Any idea that the conscious mind wants to incorporate has to be checked out by the critical faculty, which will determine whether the new concept matches the unconscious mind's model of reality. If it doesn't match, there will be resistance: the new idea won't be fully integrated into the individual's knowledge base or the individual will have difficulty accessing and applying it later.

For example, suppose the conscious mind wants to learn the rule for when you need to use the subjunctive form of a verb (if you don't know what that is, don't worry; by the end of this book, you will). The critical faculty examines the rule to see whether the new information matches the beliefs held by the unconscious mind. Let's say that the unconscious mind doesn't have any strong opinions on this particular rule of English grammar, so the rule itself isn't a problem, and with practice it is incorporated into your body of knowledge. But suppose the unconscious mind holds negative beliefs formed through years of schooling about your level of grammar knowledge, beliefs such as "I've never been good in English classes" or "Grammar bores me to tears, and the best way to deal with it is to ignore it". While the conscious mind is trying to learn the rule, the unconscious mind may be determined to shut it out. Which one do you think will win?

With cursory study only, the individual will load the rules into short-term memory (conscious mind), but not fully absorb them. When the time comes to apply the rules on the test, he or she may feel nervous and uncertain and quite possibly blank out, which will support the unconscious (and critical) mind's belief of not being great at grammar. Too often, the beliefs of our unconscious mind become a self-fulfilling prophecy.

The key to changing unwanted, unhelpful, or unuseful behaviors is to bypass the Critical Faculty and implant into the unconscious mind what the conscious mind wants. There are a couple of ways we can achieve this. One is by making the knowledge second nature. If you have ever studied for a test by using rote memorization over a 3–6 month period, you have used this method. This method is great for studying for a test, but you may not have 3–6 months to study, and even if you did, you need to make sure your studying overrides the unconscious mind's resistance. You have to want to do great on your test as much as master the content and critical thinking necessary to succeed on the test. If at one time getting nervous served you for some reason, you need to short circuit that desire and replace it with a new desire.

The other way to bypass the Critical Faculty is to use the exercises that follow in this and the next three chapters (self-hypnosis, neuro-linguistic programming, and EFT) to reprogram the unconscious mind. These techniques allow you to enter the zone so you can access the knowledge base you've amassed for yourself.

The most successful way to use these techniques and achieve your full potential is to learn how to enter an emotional state of relaxation and acceptance. The ultimate state of relaxation is the trance state. In this highly focused state, we are more susceptible to suggestions and what is called change-work. The word "trance" sometimes has negative connotations attached to it, but trance is actually a very natural state. Anytime you find yourself drifting off into your own thoughts, or are in the 'state' just prior to falling asleep, you are in a state of trance. Have you ever zoned out while driving on the highway and wondered how you got to your destination safely, without any memory of driving there? Have you ever been so engrossed in watching a movie or reading a book that you didn't even notice when someone else entered the room? Have you ever watched a fire's flames dancing in a fireplace, or watched a candle burn, and been lost in your own thoughts? These are all naturally occurring examples of trance.

Your attention in a trance state, also known as a hypnotic state, is narrowly focused and heightened. This is useful because other stimuli in the environment are ignored or blocked out of your conscious awareness. Your unconscious, however, is taking in everything, including the direct suggestions you feed it. Don't believe it? The prestigious British Medical Journal describes hypnosis as "the induction of a deeply relaxed state, with increased suggestibility and suspension of critical faculties. Once in this state…patients are given therapeutic suggestions to encourage changes in behavior or relief of symptoms…Some practitioners use hypnosis as an aid to psychotherapy…leading to an increased likelihood of psychological insight."[22]

Recent brain studies of people who are susceptible to suggestion indicate that when they act on the suggestions, the way they process information changes.[23] The experiments show that hypnotized people lost the ability to make simple decisions while others saw colors where there were none. This isn't how we'll be using this powerful tool, however. We want to implant into your mind how successful you're going to be on the test, because you believe in yourself and have taken the steps to do your best.

Hypnosis and trance is nothing new. Many cultures throughout the ages have deliberately created trance states as part of religious or cultural ceremonies. Some cultures use rhythmic drumming and dancing; others use chanting or focus their attention on a candle; still others use rhythmic prayer or even stillness to promote a trance state.

In Europe, hypnosis and trance were used and developed as therapeutic tools by a variety of people, including Franz Mesmer (1734–1815), from whose name the word 'mesmerized' is derived. Mesmer would stand his subjects quite still while he swept his arms across their body, sometimes for hours on end, likely boring them into trance. James Braid (1795–1860), a Scottish eye doctor, developed an interest in mesmerism when he found a patient in his waiting room staring into a light, with glazed eyes. Fascinated, Braid gave the patient some commands, telling him to close his eyes and go to sleep. The patient complied and Braid's interest grew.

He discovered that getting a patient to fixate upon something was one of the most important components of putting them into a trance. Then, a British surgeon James Esdaile (1808–1859), recognized the benefits of hypnotism for pain relief and performed hundreds of major operations using hypnotism as his only anesthetic. Sigmund Freud and Karl Jung were also interested in hypnosis, but didn't fully utilize it in their practices.[24]

Beginning in the 20th century, the recognized authority on really developing hypnosis was Milton H. Erickson, MD (1901–1980). As a teenager he was stricken with polio and paralyzed, but he remobilized himself. It was while paralyzed that he had an unusual opportunity to observe people, and he noticed that what people said and what they did were often very different. He became fascinated by human psychology and devised countless innovative and creative ways to heal people. He healed through metaphor, surprise, confusion, and humor, as well as hypnosis. A master of 'indirect hypnosis,' he developed his ability to the point that he became legendary, in part because he was able to put a person into a trance without even mentioning the word hypnosis.[25]

Mid-20th century, hypnosis experienced new popularity as researchers found new potent uses for it in therapy. The trance state became recognized as a highly effective scientific tool for behavior modification and healing. Even the famous Mayo clinic in New York City treated thousands of patients with hypnosis in the 1950s.

In the years since, therapists have come to recognize that trance can be the key to unlocking our Critical Faculty and embedding our personal desires for behaviors and beliefs into our unconscious mind. Hypnosis is now used to help people give up addictive substances like alcohol or cigarettes, and to overcome deep-seated fears, like the fear of flying. And for our purposes, hypnosis can be used to help you study better, feel like you're on your game, improve retention and recall, and maintain a relaxed state even when in what would arguably be a stressful situation.

Best of all, hypnotic trance is a state you can induce by yourself. That is because all hypnosis is self-hypnosis. While almost everyone can be hypnotized, the state is voluntary—you choose to allow yourself to be hypnotized. By opening yourself up to trance states, you can learn to relinquish beliefs and behaviors that no longer serve you and take on beliefs and behaviors that will make you more successful.

Imagine if you no longer experienced stress or anxiety as you approached a major test. Imagine actually believing that you can accomplish all your goals—that you will score high on the GMAT, get into business school, attain the career you have always dreamed about. Using hypnosis to subvert the critical faculty and implant those beliefs in your unconscious mind makes the unconscious mind work for the actualization of those goals, rather than resist them.

Exercise 1.5.1. Self-Trance and Direct Suggestion

The Full Potential® 3-Step Method

Do these exercises each night before you go to bed. Follow the suggested schedule.

Ideally, you'll have at least 3 weeks before your test to do this exercise, with one week for each step. However, if you have less time than that (at least two weeks), divide your time in thirds. Do step one (1) for the first block of time, then continue with step two (2) in the second block of time, then step three(3) until the day before the test day. If you only have 1 week before your test, do all three steps below. If you have less than a week before your test, do Step 1 only.

Read through the directions of each step BEFORE you actually do it, so you don't get distracted by reading and doing simultaneously.

The Full Potential® 3-Step Method
Step 1: Pre-Sleep

When you go to bed, just before you are ready to fall asleep, give yourself the following suggestion ten (10) times—adapt the exact wording to your individual needs. Use one or two of the suggestions below or make your own. Keep the intention simple:

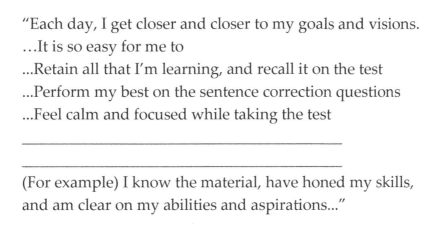

"Each day, I get closer and closer to my goals and visions.
…It is so easy for me to
…Retain all that I'm learning, and recall it on the test
…Perform my best on the sentence correction questions
…Feel calm and focused while taking the test

_____

_____

(For example) I know the material, have honed my skills,
and am clear on my abilities and aspirations…"

While you say this, imagine yourself in the testing center, in your optimal test taking state: calm, collected, and on your game.

1. To prevent falling asleep or losing count, press each finger to your thumb as you say each suggestion. Continue until you've completed saying your intention ten (10) times.

2. This may be your first attempt at this kind of hypnosis. Consistency is important, so do the exercise every night without falling asleep until you've completed the ten (10) repetitions.

3. This kind of practice is the beginning of establishing a habit of properly programming yourself with positive suggestions prior to sleep. The next day, you'll find yourself reacting very positively to the suggestions. This will be strengthened each day you do this.

OPTIONAL: Each morning when you wake up, take your "emotional pulse" and write down how you feel. You can also write down your intentions for the day, as discussed in the section on time management.

The Full Potential® 3-Step Method
Step 2: Induction

Continue with Step 1's pre-sleep technique every night.

In addition, sit twice a day (once in the morning or at noon and once in the early evening) in a comfortable position and enter a relaxed state. You'll stay in this state two to three minutes, and then allow yourself to wake up. This is how you'll do it:

Sit in a comfortable chair with your back supported.
Focus your attention on a spot opposite you, slightly above eye-level.
Soften your eyes and lower your eyelids half way, as if your eyelids are too heavy to keep open. *
Take 3 slow, deep breaths. As you inhale your third breath, hold it for 3 seconds and count backwards in your mind: 3...2...1.
Once you get to one, close your eyes fully and exhale. Pass inward focus over all parts of the body, scanning your body. Allow yourself to fully enter a deep, relaxed, restful state.
Remain in this state for approximately two - three minutes by counting down slowly from twenty-five (25) to one (1). It might help if you visualize the numbers being written on a blackboard/dry erase board, or going backward on a computer screen.
While in this state, imagine a time you felt confident, in the flow, and on your game. Enjoy the space you're in and feel the expansiveness.
When you are ready to re-energize yourself and awaken out of this state, count forward from one (1) to five (5).

Another effective technique, rather than looking at something far away, is to place your hand close to your face (1/2 – 1 inch away). The image of your hand will be fuzzy. Try to focus on your hand, with your eyes half closed. As you become more relaxed, let your hand drop to your lap, and as it does, imagine a deep wave of relaxation.

The Full Potential® 3-Step Method
Step 3: Programmed Suggestion

1. Learning to enter a relaxed state (Steps 1 and 2) can take anywhere from 2-3 days to 2-3 weeks. Once you feel you have mastered this trance technique, you will be ready to give yourself beneficial suggestions. You can stop doing the first two exercises once you start this one.

2. Use a 3x5 index card or business card which you can carry with you at all times. On the card, write one of the suggestions you've been saying to yourself, or a new one that is simple, positive, believable, and perhaps measurable. For example, you might write your dream GMAT score. Make sure to state this suggestion in the present tense.

> I will get a 720 on the GMAT

> I will enter the GMAT focused and calm

3. As in Step 2, sit down and choose a spot opposite you, slightly above eye-level. Hold the card in front of the spot and read the suggestion to yourself three (3) times. Make sure the words on the card are believable to you and allow yourself to imagine accomplishing what is written on them.

4. Once you've read the suggestion to yourself three (3) times, drop the card and take your first deep breath. Exhale. Take your second deep breath. Exhale. Take your third deep breath – hold it and close your eyes, and count backwards from five (5) to one (1): 5...4...3...2...1... Exhale and go deep into a relaxed state. Look down at the card or the image.

5. At this point, instead of counting backward from twenty-five (25) to one (1), allow the suggestion on the card to repeat in your mind. You may find that you begin to have a shift in focus: the words start to break up and become fragmented. This is perfectly fine. The important words or phrases you need to see and hear will get to your unconscious mind.

6. In approximately 2-3 minutes, when you feel it's time to rejoin your day in the world at-large, gently move yourself out of this relaxed state. You can count forward: 1...2...3... then open your eyes and start your day feeling refreshed and relaxed in every way.

Note: give yourself time for the suggestions to take hold. You will get the benefits related to your suggestion over time.

CHAPTER SIX

FIRE THE INNER CRITIC: EMOTIONAL FREEDOM TECHNIQUE (EFT)

Although you might not feel it right now, you have all the energy, focus and smarts to get a great score on the GMAT! What you might NOT have are all the skills and know-how to allow yourself to achieve your full potential. Often, it is an inner critic holding us back.

In the last chapter, we spoke about how our unconscious mind sometimes holds beliefs that stand in our way. For example, we might unconsciously believe that we are not good at taking tests, or that we don't understand grammar. The technique we learned in the last chapter, hypnosis, is a great approach for replacing those negative thoughts with positive ones.

Sometimes, however, we have to attack those negative thoughts more directly. That's because some of our negative beliefs are not unconscious. In fact, we create them consciously. They are fueled by self-talk. We are often our own worst critics.

Self-talk is something normal that we, as humans, do. Sometimes, self-talk is positive and gets us through some hurdle or experience—as when we give ourselves a pep talk. Other times, self-talk is self-effacing and negative. This is especially true if we have suffered traumatic experiences in life. Maybe you grew up in a household in which people told you were stupid or lazy. It is difficult for the young person's brain to hear such things and not appropriate them into the person's self-image. In a particularly unfair way, repeating these epithets to yourself might even be a comfort, since it reaffirms a sense of self that was created when your brain was particularly young and receptive. 'Reminding' yourself that you are lazy or stupid is a way of reminding yourself of 'who you are,' and thus of your very existence as a human being. Maybe repeating these negative self-images to yourself even served as self-defense, since it muted the hurt of hearing them from other people. Such a response is very human and sadly common. It served you at one time, but it does no longer. As an adult living your own life and pursuing your own dreams, you can reclaim the part of your mind that is holding tight to those obsolete feelings. Just as you learned them a long time ago, you can unlearn them now.

Think of yourself as having a direct line to Command Central: your brain. Your brain takes in all the messages from all the systems in your body, and delegates tasks to other parts of your body that aren't thinking so much: they're doing. When you replace that negative self-talk with affirmations of your intelligence, perseverance, and ability to excel at the GMAT, your mind says, 'That's right! We're going to make sure you have all the ingredients for success: health, alertness, and strength!' On the other hand, if you say to yourself, "I don't understand this math, I don't have time for this, I just can't improve my score," then Command Central, a non-thinking entity, responds the same way, 'Alright then, we're going to make sure you have all the ingredients to succeed at your own failure!'

There is nothing wrong with your brain. It's wired for the kind of success you ask of it. Since we're our own full-time coaches, we have to learn how to fire our inner critic and embrace our inner coach! A highly effective method of achieving this is Emotional Freedom Technique, or EFT. Place this powerful technique in your toolbox right away.

EFT was developed in the 1990s by Stanford University engineering graduate and ordained minister Gary Craig, who based his ideas on Roger Callahan's Thought Field Therapy. The EFT technique was based on the theory that negative emotions contribute to chronic distress. Traditional therapy may be very successful in exploring the origins of unhelpful feelings like negative self-image, distrust of your abilities, and fear of failure. EFT responds directly to those obstacles by helping you reframe your attitudes and modify your behavior.

EFT works by combining self-talk and positive language in a body-based process. In other words, affirmations combined with a tapping protocol which we'll describe in greater detail below. Let's unpack this.

An affirmation is a positive statement declared as true which can help you focus on goals, get rid of negative, self-defeating beliefs, and reprogram your subconscious mind. It is best to create them yourself (and don't worry, you'll have the opportunity to do so, soon!). Some examples might be anything from "I am a good person and true to myself", to "I eat well, exercise regularly and get plenty of rest to enjoy good health", to "I know I can accomplish anything I set my mind to".

In getting to the 'tapping mechanism', it can be best understood as one of the eastern medicinal philosophies. In comparison, the West thinks of 'health' as grounded in biology and curing symptoms. It is rooted in the physical realm. On the other hand, Eastern medicines such as Acupuncture and Reiki root the body's health in maintaining an even flow of energy (or chi) through points in the body, known as meridian points. Indian spiritualists and Chinese acupuncturists understand meridian points as hubs with the most energy. By touching or tapping on those hub spots (called meridian points) while addressing and correcting negative thoughts and feelings, you can actually change those thoughts and feelings.

Scientific and anecdotal studies have shown that EFT can rapidly reduce the emotional impact of incidents that trigger undesired reactions. Once the distress is reduced or removed, the mind and body will often recalibrate itself, and move towards balance and more desirable responses. To find out more of the science and research about these methods, take a look at Dawson Church's book, *The Genie In Your Genes: Epigenetic Medicine and the New Biology of Intention* (Energy Psychology Press, 2007). His book covers how western research now supports the effectiveness of things like acupuncture, reiki, and other mind-body practices.

The EFT technique can be used in conjunction with many modalities, including Hypnotherapy and Neuro-linguistic programming.

Exercise 1.6.1. Face your Inner Critic. Then Fire Him or Her

What are you really saying to yourself? Before you can fire your inner critic, you have to:

Actually listen to yourself. Is what is being said serving your intention? If it's not, turn your negative language into positive.

Make a list of all the reasons you use to justify why you can't manifest your best score. Then, change this into a solution-driven version. Write your new statements as if you've manifested the desired response already as "when" statements and continue the idea.

For example:

Change the statement "I have never been a good test taker," to "When I'm a good test taker, I can take the GMAT, or any test, and consistently perform my best."

Sometimes our inner critic appears in statements that begin with 'if.' So the previous example would look like, 'If I were a good test taker, I would be acing the GMAT.' Changing this into a 'when' statement makes your becoming a good test taker, closer to being a 'done deal.' SO: take your list and create language that will help to usher in the change you will soon manifest.

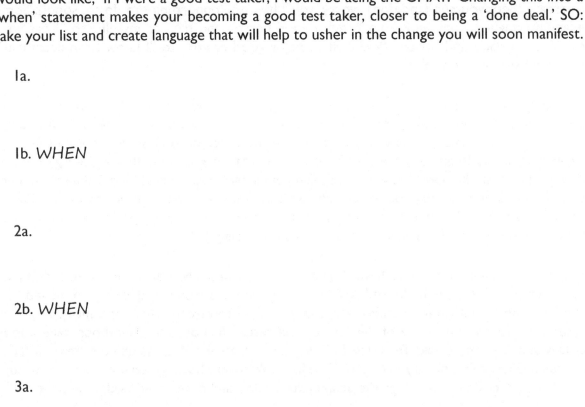

1a.

1b. *WHEN*

2a.

2b. *WHEN*

3a.

3b. *WHEN*

Exercise I.6.2. Reframe Those Negative Thoughts!

In the left hand column, list your negative self-talk. In the middle column, reverse what you've said, then on the right column, think of another way to look at the situation that is positive and empowered, and write it down. There are three examples below. It may help to work with a friend to find positive options!

Negative Self-Talk	Positive Spin	Positive and Empowered Option
When I am stressed, I feel overwhelmed and out of control.	When stress hits, I take a moment to regain composure and calm.	If I feel stress, it's an opportunity that reminds me that I have a choice to feel composed and calm, and having that choice feels great.
The GMAT is too difficult and complicated for me.	The GMAT is challenging, and I love a good challenge.	As a businessperson, I thrive on challenges. How great is it that the GMAT, a challenging test, is the beginning of this new MBA journey?!

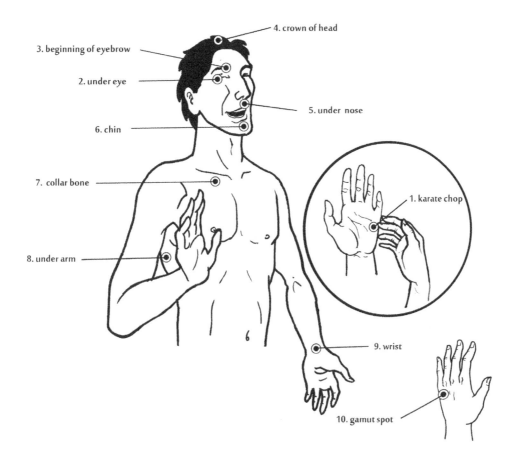

4. crown of head
3. beginning of eyebrow
2. under eye
6. chin
7. collar bone
8. under arm
5. under nose
1. karate chop
9. wrist
10. gamut spot

I don't have enough time to take the test and fulfill all the application requirements.	Mastering time management has been on my to-do list—now I can make it my top priority.	I am doing the best I can and am fully present and accountable for my actions. I'm ready to go!
1)		
2)		
3)		
4)		

Exercise 1.6.3. EFT: What Am I Feeling?

Take inventory of how you're feeling about the various aspects of your life listed below.

<u>Self Image</u>

    1. I want to be more buff

    2.

    3.

    4.

    5.

<u>Anger</u>

    1. My cubby mate is loud at work

    2.

    3.

    4.

    5.

<u>Resentment</u>

    1.

    2.

    3.

    4.

    5.

<u>Sadness</u>

    1. I am sad about my real GMAT score

    2.

    3.

    4.

    5.

Regret

1.

2.

3.

4.

5.

Guilt

1.

2.

3.

4.

5.

Shame

1.

2.

3.

4.

5.

Other Issue(s)

1.

2.

3.

4.

5.

Exercise I.6.4. How To Do EFT

Look at the diagram on the facing page. This diagram illustrates the meridian points. You may want to copy this page so you can fill it out every time you do the exercise.

1. Identify any negative emotions you are feeling right now. They can be negative emotions about the test, the test preparation process, or anything else going on in your life. Use the prior chart to help act as a template of all the things you want to shift.

2. The first time you tap around your body, create a statement that acknowledges your negative emotions and how you would rather feel. For example:

   I hate feeling _____ and I prefer to feel _____. Or

   I don't like feeling _____ because _____.

3. Now, you are going to start tapping with your left hand against the meridian points on your body. Start with tapping the fleshiest part of your hand, the bottom/side portion that extends between your pinky finger and your wrist. It is the side you'd use to break wood with a karate chop. You tap using all four fingers. See illustration.

   Then move to the points on your head, face, collarbone, rib cage, wrist, and finally to the triangle between your pinky and ring finger. You are basically moving down your upper body, from your head to your hand. You are going to go around your body several times.

   To see this in action, look up EFT videos on YouTube.

4. Assess how strongly you are feeling these emotions on a scale of 1 to 10 (where 10 is the most intense).

   Right now I am feeling:

   _____   1 2 3 4 5 6 7 8 9 10

   _____   1 2 3 4 5 6 7 8 9 10

   _____   1 2 3 4 5 6 7 8 9 10

5. Once you feel your negative emotion has shifted (which may take more than one round), proceed with more tapping rounds to identify positive feelings or perspective shift that can be drawn from the situation. Start with the statement:

   Even though I still feel _____ , I totally and completely accept myself.

6. As you begin to feel more positive, move to statements that are more completely positive, such as:

   I am able to accept happiness.

   I look forward to each day.

7. Carry out these exercises at least twice per day. For more phrases to say, see next page.

EFT MERIDIAN POINTS DIAGRAM

PHRASES TO USE WHILE DOING EFT

These phrases are adapted from *Tapping your Amazing Potential with EFT* by Betty Moore-Hafter (www.CreativeEFT.com, www.InnerTheater.net and www.EFTfree.net). They were designed to help you with any negative emotions in your life, but you can easily make them specific to the GMAT experience.

For example:

Even though I do terribly on tests, I deeply and completely accept myself and…

Would read…

Even though **I feel really nervous about my upcoming GMAT**, I deeply and completely accept myself and… I'm willing to see it differently. I know **I can ace this test!**

It may feel unnatural saying these things out loud, but try it anyway. The scientific proof speaks for itself. As well, an adaptation to this exercise can be found in the groundbreaking work by Sian Beilock, *Choke*. Dr. Beilock conducted numerous studies which proved beyond an iota of doubt that when we acknowledge our fears and anxieties, we consistently feel better, particularly in testing situations. In the next chapter, we cover the major tenets of Sian Beilock's findings and inspired by her work, we invite you to practice what we call intentional journaling.

For help in finding positive phrases, see Exercise 1.5.2.

I'm willing for _____ to change. I am willing to see myself _____. (say the positive opposite)

I'm willing to see _____ differently. I'm willing to see _____ in a positive light.

I honor myself for confronting this [difficult issue] _____.

I want to bring healing to _____ and learn from the process.

I'm choosing to make my peace with _____ and let it go. I'm choosing to take a different path.

I'm ready to let go of _____. I'm ready to welcome _____.

I choose to know and believe_____. I'm able to do whatever I set my mind to.

The truth is, _____. I am my own best ally and deserving of_____.

I'm open to the possibility that ___ can be different. I am able to perceive it differently.

I'm ok with _____.

I open myself to_____ and the possibility that things can be different than they seem to be.

I'm freeing myself from_____ and open myself to the opportunity to experience things they way I want them to be. I honor myself for how hard this has been.

I honor all my feelings, such as _____.

I honor myself for_____.

I honor this part of me that has been trying to protect me and help me. I know that I want what is really best for me.

That was then and this is now and I create my own reality.

I'm willing to forgive myself for _____. I was doing the best I could, and now I'll do better.

I'm willing to forgive _____ . She (or he) was just coming from her/his own human limitations and pain.

Even though this _____ served me in the past, it no longer serves me. I choose _____.

I'm sending a message to my mind that I want _____ and that I am able to achieve it easily.

I'm getting through to [this part of myself] _____.

I surrender what I thought I knew for a deeper truth.

I'm taking back my power. I can do well on this test. I control it; it doesn't control me.

I'm letting go of my need to control_____. All I need to do is believe that I can do it, then learn the skills necessary to make it a done deal.

I'm willing to let _____ be what it is.

I choose_____.

 I choose to feel_____.

I choose to respond with feelings of _____ and conviction.

I choose to be free of_____.

CHAPTER SEVEN

WRITING THINGS DOWN: INTENTIONAL JOURNALING

In *CHOKE: What Secrets of the Brain Reveal about Getting it Right When You Have To*, Sian Beilock, an associate professor in Psychology at the University of Chicago, dedicates herself to the study of anxiety in high stakes sports, academic, and business situations. Beilock is consumed with understanding why certain high achievers fail at high-stakes performances and tests, whereas others seem to float through the process with very little resistance or challenge. Her book provides an in-depth understanding of why this occurs, along with practical solutions that have been scientifically tested. Among them is the process of writing down your worries prior to your big test.

Writing out your worries can be an emotional 'brain dump,' and have similar effects as the process of EFT, reframing and shifting 'self talk.' In part, activating this part of the self is similar to creativity. It mirrors the exercises earlier in this book that involve the collage activity, but could also include sketching, painting, making improvisational music, dancing, etc. These mediums and activities provide the means to experience and express your feelings and get them 'out' before you engage in what you might perceive as a daunting task. Freeing yourself from these unwanted emotions means you have more time and mental focus for the task itself: the GMAT.

In a larger sense, Beilock's model works within the model of the mind that is presented in Chapter 5 (Hypnosis, model of the mind). She assesses working memory as a kind of "mental scratch pad" where everyday activities benefit from the retrieval and use of stored information. Because this part of the mind has a limited bandwidth—holding onto 4–7 things at once—when limiting thoughts and fears creep up they tax the energy needed to perform.[26]

Beilock's recipe for success—comparable to Julia Cameron's morning exercises in *The Artists Way*—is to take 10 minutes to express your feelings about your upcoming test. Her research indicates that students not given this option 'choked' under pressure, and suffered a 12% drop in the accuracy of their test answers. The group who took time to write had a 5% improvement in their score. For GMAT test takers, this could be the difference of 30 or 40 points. Or, in other words, the difference between your top choice and your safety school. Note, however, that Beilock's research also reveals that the simple act of writing itself isn't the panacea that prevents choking, but specifically writing about the feelings that test taking brings up.

Exercise 1.7.1. Journaling with Intention

Because the GMAT is designed for you to have time to write prior to the exam, we suggest that you discover whether this procedure works for you. Take at least a week—if not a month—prior to the exam for designated time to intentionally journal. You officially have permission to just 'type' out things you're thinking and feeling. Does this help quell your self-doubt or anxiety? You can also spend time when you're in the testing center jotting down your feelings on the scratch pad. Get it out and allow yourself to be a blank slate.

NOTE: This is also a great time, if you have any reservations about being able to remember equations or measurements, to "dump" them onto the page so that you don't have to scan your mind when the timer is going. If you need another scratch pad, simply raise your hand and they'll bring you one.

CHAPTER EIGHT

BEHAVIOR MODIFICATION: NEURO-LINGUISTIC PROGRAMMING

The exercises we have been exploring all fundamentally address the need to shift personal perspective in order to change undesirable habits into productive practices. You want to change procrastination into productivity, test anxiety into collected calmness, or scattered thoughts into controlled actions. Positive Self-Talk focuses on the language we use with ourselves. Neuro-Linguistic Programming (NLP) addresses the data from the outside world that we allow to affect our own inner processes.

Richard Bandler and John Grinder developed NLP in the 1970s. They based the practice on the work of three therapists: Milton Erickson (hypnotherapy), Virginia Satir (family therapy), and Fritz Perls (gestalt therapy). The combination of these three fields resulted in an eclectic therapy driven by the way the individual seeking change used language. Most recently, more mainstreamed coaches such as Tony Robbins have popularized NLP. Like the methodologies explored earlier in this book, NLP proposes that most of our fears and habits (both good and bad) are learned behavior. Its unique contribution to your personal growth as a test taker and human being is to treat the psyche as a machine that downloads or blocks the data available in the world around us. If we set our filters and spam blockers at the optimum levels, we can optimize our test taking functionality.

People are meaning-making machines. We naturally create meaning for ourselves, to explain the sense data we obtain from the world around us. We create, delete, generalize, hyper-focus and distort the world around us in predictable and systematic ways based on a myriad of our formative influences. No one escapes this process; we all live in a world that produces far more data than we can possibly process. We must make choices. NLP proposes that although we may not always behave in ways that are helpful to us, we make the best choices available to us given our unique processing of the world around us. By changing the sense data our mind accepts or rejects, we can change the way we respond to the challenges the world presents to us.

Let's take an example to more fully explain. I email a report to my boss, but do not hear back after a day. I become concerned, and come up with reasons why my boss did not email me back. I am making meaning out of an observed fact, the fact that my boss did not contact me. I may become very nervous, not eat, or I could lose sleep. I may make mistakes in some important task at work, or begin to have negative thoughts about my boss.

It makes sense to be concerned about not hearing back from my boss. I am working perfectly in that respect. In my situation and in my model of the world, I may well feel that it is dangerous or difficult to approach my boss directly. It may seem safer to make meaning myself about her lack of response. Given the way I was trained to be a corporate citizen, this may be the best choice I know how to make.

NLP teaches us, however, to focus on our experience itself, and not the meaning we may make. Making up reasons why my boss hasn't called produces behaviors (anxiety, lack of eating, lack of sleep, inability to concentrate) that are not productive and can hurt job performance. The fact is that I will never know why she did not contact me unless I ask her directly. NLP trains us to override the model of the world or our situation that we may have, and to create a new model that better fits our direct experience. In this case, once we perceive "I am anxious because my boss hasn't contacted me about the report", the response that best reduces that anxiety is "I must ask her why."

NLP empowers us to look at the 'factual' world a little more clearly. It helps me to understand the difference between the sense data I observe and the meaning I make. I can say to myself, "My boss did not return my email," and, instead of reacting with panic, ask myself, "Does it matter why?" If I think it does matter, I can follow up—not by trying to answer that question myself, but by getting more data—I can call my boss back and ask if she got the report. The point is to focus on the sense data itself and leave out the loaded 'whys.'

Test takers often let meaning-making impulses affect their performances. When a GMAT test taker thinks about taking the test, he may think back to a prior test when he became anxious or nervous. He may recall that sense data and that feeling of nervousness. Instead of taking this as a call to action, however, the student often becomes consumed with the nervousness. He may start telling himself stories about why he is nervous, like "I don't take tests well," or, "I am always anxious about tests." This attempt to make meaning only reinforces the initial feeling of nervousness. With NLP, we learn to stop at the first feeling—"I feel nervous"— and then take steps to DO something about the nervousness.

The basic tenets of NLP are these:

1. *We take in information from the outside world via our 5 senses.*

2. *There is a lot of information that we could potentially access, so our mind needs methods of prioritizing or knowing what to pay attention to; so*

3. *We set up filters that allow certain information in and reject other information. These filters may arise as a result of our current focus. For example if we are thinking of going to business school, we may notice that all our friends, colleagues, and characters on TV and news stories, seem to have connections to business school.*

4. *These filters act to delete, distort, and generalize information about reality.*

5. *This distortion, deletion, and generalization causes us to make internal representations of the external world, which we mistake for reality.*

6. *These internal representations then shape our feelings and our own external behaviors.*

The aim of NLP is to stop the process at Item 2. We need to set up filters to allow certain information in and reject other information, otherwise we would be overwhelmed by all the sights and sounds and smells and textures that surround us. You are probably touching this book, and feeling the texture of its pages. There are sure to be distinctive smells in the air— maybe from a cup of coffee you are drinking. There are also sounds in your room. Listen carefully and you may hear people talking, traffic outside, leaves brushing against walls, pages being turned. You are looking at this book, and seeing the words on the page, but also the page itself, and a bit of what lies beyond it—the table or desk or room in which you are sitting.

What if you had to pay attention to all those senses at once, all the time? You would go crazy! Therefore filters are important. All too often, however, we use filters that are unproductive. Choosing the correct filter is especially important when you are preparing for a test like the GMAT, which requires you to learn so much concrete material. You have to open your mind to rules of grammar and sentence correction, while keeping your filter closed to distractions. You have to open your mind to feelings of purposefulness and success, while keeping your filter closed to feelings of anxiety and failure.

NLP teaches you how to change your filter so that what comes through is what you need.

Exercise 1.8.1. What Are Your GMAT Filters?

What are your expectations about the GMAT?

What is realistic about this or these expectations?

How are you experiencing these expectations? What specific sensory mode do they appear in? Do you imagine seeing what is going to happen as if it were a movie (visual)? Do you imagine it as a soundtrack (aural)? Do you have a physical response (a kinesthetic feeling) based on what you imagine is going to happen?

Exercise I.8.2. Reframing The GMAT

1. Remember a time when you felt really confident—perhaps when you accomplished something or were proud of a choice you made.

Write it down here:

2. Now, unpack what that feels like. Do you experience that success as something you see (visual), feel (kinesthetic), hear, smell…or even taste? Answer the question set below that matches how you experience the world.

VISUAL: What does confidence look like? Is it a color? What is its size? Is it 3-dimensional or 2-dimensional? Is it something you see outside of you, like a location? What does the world look when you're confident?

KINESTHETIC: What does confidence feel like? Is it soft or hard? What shape does it have? Can you throw it, catch it, move around in it? How does the world feel when you are confident?

AURAL: What does confidence sound like? Is it loud or quiet? Does it have a tone or cadence? Does the sound come from outside you or inside? What does the world sound like when you are confident?

SMELL/TASTE: What does confidence smell or taste like? Is it subtle or obvious, complex or pure and simple? Does the smell or taste of confidence remind you of another kind of taste or smell? What does the world smell like when you are confident?

3. Apply these feelings of confidence to the GMAT.

If you are visual, elaborate on how the GMAT room will look as you enter it, full of confidence. Imagine the room with bright light, wide spaces, a place where you can do your best work, and the test itself appearing familiar, easy, ready for you to succeed…

If you are kinesthetic, elaborate on how sitting down for the GMAT will feel as you begin working on it, full of confidence. Imagine the feeling permeating your body, getting more intense…

If you are aural, elaborate on the sounds you will hear as you begin working on the GMAT, full of confidence. Imagine how amazing things are going to sound when you're working on the test. Imagine cheering, expressions of congratulations…

If you experience the world mainly through smell or taste, elaborate on the smells and tastes you will experience as you begin working on the GMAT, full of confidence. Imagine being bathed in your favorite smells or tastes as you begin working on the test, the sensations getting more intense as you know you are doing your best…

4. Imagine a time in the future when your concern about the GMAT is so far in the past that you have forgotten it was ever an issue. Play out the entire scene. Imagine taking the test, completing the test, seeing your great score. Imagine you've gotten the AWA mailed to you, mailed all your applications in, and are now holding your acceptance letters in your hands… Feel the sense of calm knowing you did everything to the best of your ability…

5. How do you feel upon completing this exercise?

ADVANCED EXERCISE: MENTOR MEDITATION

We can take this exercise a bit deeper and further by imagining the way someone we admire experiences his or her world and imposing that onto our own experiences. For instance:

Think of a person you know or are familiar with (such as an actor, historical character, fictional character, favorite athlete, etc.) who exudes confidence that you admire, respect, and wish to emulate. Now, imagine how it would feel if you could step into their experience, as if you are them, and see what they see, hear what they hear, feel what they feel...

Exercise I.8.3. Backwards Spin

This exercise is based on some of the most recent work being done by Dr. Richard Bandler.   In fact, I recently learned it is also being used by Landmark Education, a global educational enterprise committed to the fundamental principle that people have the possibility of success, fulfillment, and greatness. It is called the backwards spin.

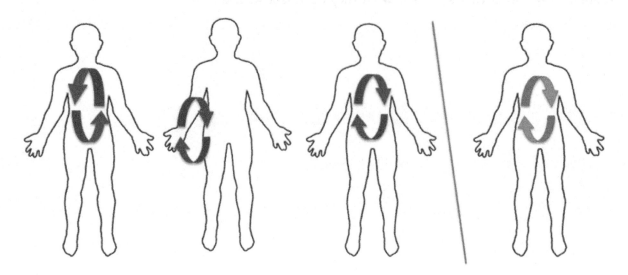

Fear, panic and strong emotions often have an internal movement that you can feel. Tap into your feelings now, close your eyes and trace the path of the energetic pull. Most fear goes up the front of the body and down the back, but some people have it go in the opposite direction, and others follow a different path. However it moves, it's likely in a circular motion. If you can't feel it, imagine a mini roller coaster inside of you moving in a loop in your torso. Close your eyes and breathe deeply. You feel that circuit of energy.

1. Notice which way the energy is spinning. Once you're able to identify it, reverse it.

2. While you keep your emotions spinning, imagine you can take them out of your body and hold them in front of you. Now, think of a time you felt inappropriate laughter, the kind of giggling that is unstoppable. Throw that laughter into the reversed spin.

3. Next, think of someone you love. It could be a friend, a partner, a family member, or a pet. Feel the love grow bigger and brighter, and throw it into the spin.

4. Think of a place you've been where you've felt completely at ease and peaceful. - Throw it in.

You can throw anything positive into the mix, including:

A memory of a time you felt confident.

The feeling you had when a friend or loved one was really present for you.

The moment you received an award or accolades for your work, etc.

Once you've thrown in 3–4 things, check in to see if you feel the fear/anxiety.

Likely you won't.

This exercise takes 2–3 minutes to do initially, but you can do it in 10 seconds after the first time. Repeat it whenever you feel unwanted anxiety.

CHAPTER NINE

OPTIMAL LEARNING: THE GAMMA BRAIN WAVE STATE

In previous chapters, we concentrated on the brain's ability to process emotion. Our focus was on reducing stress and laying the groundwork for test preparation. In this chapter, we turn to actually increasing your ability to take in and process new information. Here, we will look at the brain.

Though scientists are always trying to gain a fuller understanding of how the human brain functions, we do know that one of the processes involves neurons firing electrical impulses at each other. These impulses take the forms of waves, which we can measure.

The spectrums between feeling alert, tense, and afraid are marked by Beta waves. If you are in a state of physical and mental relaxation, while aware of what is happening around you, you're in Alpha state. Theta state is a state of sleep or deep relaxation. Theta extends into Delta, which is marked by unconsciousness, deep sleep, or catalepsy.

Gamma Brain Waves are the fastest and most potent of the brain waves, and are considered the optimal level of brain functioning as they regulate information and sensory-binding systems. Researchers believe that these Gamma Brain Waves link together all the bits of information from different parts of the brain. Research indicates that increasing the Gamma Brain Wave state improves memory, learning, and high-level mental and information processing.

People with higher amounts of Gamma Brain Waves seem to have a stronger ability to absorb and understand new information and changes in their environments. They are "peak performers." For this reason, it's an effective state to cultivate when studying.

We're just describing Gamma Brain State here. You'll get to actually experience it directly as you work through the Execution part of the book. One of the ways you will enter into Gamma Brain Wave state is by briefly interrupting your study and practice by looking at images that make you think: optical illusions and mandalas. For that reason, we've punctuated the second section of the book with these experiences. They promote a kind of intellectual 'rest' and a natural break from the rigors of intense study, while stimulating the brain in such a way that focus and information processing are rejuvenated.

Optical illusions are visual images that differ from reality. Whether our eye perceives movement, color or form when it's not there, or the object created is impossible, our eye takes it in and the mind is activated to make sense of it. Mandalas are designs that illustrate intricate geometric patterns. They are often used in meditation because they help bring a person to greater awareness and are believed to produce powerful visual and psychological effects.

Later, we will talk about the growing body of evidence that suggests even short-term meditation on optical illusions and mandalas can increase the Gamma Brain Wave state, thus improving your attention span and enhancing your cognitive abilities.

Exercise 1.9.1. Mandala Gazing

When looking at mandalas or optical illusions, allow your gaze to focus in on the image. You can also allow your eyelids to close slightly as well.

CHAPTER TEN

ADDITIONAL PRACTICES AND RESOURCES TO HELP YOU SUCCEED ON THE GMAT

In addition to the many techniques we described in some depth already, there are many other practices and resources that can support your path to success on the GMAT. We don't describe these in as much detail in part because many of these techniques require that you attend a class, purchase a product, or see a practitioner. However, these techniques are readily available and effective and any or all could be incorporated into a balanced lifestyle in preparation for the GMAT and beyond.

We've included the following topics, in alphabetical order: Acupuncture, Aromatherapy, Herbal Medicine, Homeopathy, Massage and Bodywork, Nutrition, Sound Therapy, Writing Therapy, and Yoga/Pilates.

<u>Acupuncture</u>

Acupuncture is an ancient healing modality that acts by stimulating the movement of energy (called *qi* or *chi* in Chinese). In practice, needles no thicker than a strand of hair are inserted into various traditionally determined points on the body and stimulated to cause energy movement. Our capacity to heal, live well, and maximize our potential physically, mentally, and even spiritually is governed by our access to energy flow. When that energy is blocked, our potential is diminished. When that energy is unlocked, we are capable of tremendous clarity, focus, intelligence, creativity, passion, power, love, joy, and ease.

When our energetic pathways are open, qi and blood move freely through us. This can improve general wellness as well as specific needs of the body. Certain pathways may be used that help to nourish the brain by increasing the flow of *qi* and blood to that area. Points along the spine and head may be used for these purposes. Additionally, specific points may be used that stimulate our capacity for mental concentration, focus, and memory. Acupuncture does not add anything into your system. It supports the functions already working inside you by unblocking energy, helping you to "get out of your own way."

The benefits of acupuncture include calming and quieting the mind. This helps not only at test taking time, but also indirectly by improving our sleep. This can be achieved by helping us fall asleep easier or by improving the quality and restfulness of our sleep throughout the night. A person's quality of sleep is often one of the first things reported to improve when receiving acupuncture. Many Western health insurance plans now include acupuncture in their list of subsidized health services, so check yours for opportunities.

The experience of relaxing on the treatment table and connecting with your body can also act as a practice ground for accessing that awareness in your regular day-to-day life. The more a person can remember what it feels like to be calm, centered, grounded, and at ease, as well as the closer your connection with body awareness and your breath, the easier it is to tap into and re-create that experience in your life off the table.

Acupuncture...

- Works holistically to help people access their full energy potential

- Can be used to calm and focus the mind

- Is known to improve the quality of sleep

- Clears energetic pathways to nourish the brain

- Stimulates mental clarity and alertness

- Experientially teaches people to relax

Aromatherapy

Aromatherapy is the ancient art and new evolutionary science of using plant oils as a holistic therapy for the mind, body and spirit. These essential oils are "pure essences" extracted and distilled from plants. Flowers, leaves, roots, resins, seeds, and fruits each have their own unique healing properties: Antiseptic, anti-microbial, anti-bacterial, anti-depressants, immuno-stimulants, analgesics, and others.

The application and absorption of these essential oils occurs via one of two methods: The Skin (The Integumentary System) and The Sense of Smell (Olfactory System).

Essential oils are applied to the skin via massage, compresses, topical applications via creams, and oil solutions (combined with carrier oils). They enter into the bloodstream through the skin and are circulated throughout the entire body. Aromatherapy massage is designed to maximize the benefits of essential oils by using a combination of different movements and techniques. Two of the most common are Lymphatic Drainage Massage, which facilitates and assists the elimination of toxins, and Swedish massage, which improves circulation, increases mobility, reduces pain, and eases stress and tension, promoting a healthy feeling of well being.

It is important to read all directions before applying essential oils to your skin. Some essential oils in their pure form can be too powerful to apply to the skin directly and can only be applied when diluted with carrier oils or lotions.

Oils can be applied to the olfactory system through direct inhalation via dispensers and evaporators, and are also effective because our sense of smell is linked directly to the part of the brain which regulates mood and triggers the release of chemicals. This can help regulate and balance hormones, stimulate or relax, and assist memory and creativity.

Aromatherapy can be a very helpful study aid. Certain essential oils, such as rosemary, cypress, basil, and peppermint work as stimulants to the brain. They will help you stay alert and focused. If you have a tendency to get anxious, add a few drops of lavender to promote a calm feeling. These oils can be used as single notes or in blends and inhaled through a small room nebulizer. You can also rub some in your palm and inhale at regular intervals. In fact, if you find a blend or single scent that gets you into the state you seek, then use it while studying and wear it on test day to the site!

There is another way that essential oils, either a single note or blends of several oils, can be a great support. Studies have shown that memory recall is twice as accurate when you associate the important information with a particular smell. This is an NLP technique known as anchoring. If for example you have an AHA! moment while solving a certain question, you can anchor your new insight by concentrating on it, or better yet, acting upon it, while inhaling a particular fragrance. Inhaling that fragrance again will then trigger your memory of the insight when you need it most.

A company called Scentient Beings is currently creating a special blend to serve both as an aid to concentration and as an anchor for better recall. The goal is to incorporate the oil blend into discrete scented jewelry that you wear when taking your test. (See www.scentientbeings.com.)

Listed below are essential oils for remedies to especially help the GMAT test taker. In addition we provide directions on how to administer and experience the scents:

Fatigue/Exhaustion

Stimulating oils are: Rosemary**, Basil, Orange, Eucalyptus, Ginger, Black Pepper, Peppermint, Thyme.
Rosemary is great for memory and Basil can be used to overcome stressful situations.

Relaxation

Sedative and anti-depressant oils are: Rose, Jasmine, Lavender, Sweet Orange, Bergamot, Neroli, Vetivert, Rosewood, Marjoram, Chamomile, Thyme, and Melissa.

Anti-stress and Focus

Body tonics oils: Melissa, Lemongrass, Eucalyptus, Lavender, Myrhh, Ginger, Angelica, Rosemary**, Thyme, Basil, Black Pepper, Sandalwood, Frankincense.

For Bathing

Basil, Geranium, Thyme, Rosemary**, Angelica.
**People with epilepsy should not use Rosemary.

Ratios and Directions:

Essential oils are highly concentrated materials, so use these proportions:

Topical

Add 1 drop and place on your wrists, or add to your body cream, a diffuser, burner, or spray.

Diffusers

5% of oils to water.

Oil blends for bathing and massage

3 drops essential oil to each 100 drops of carrier oil (approx. 5mls).

Bathing

6–10 drops of essential oils.

Essential Oil Distributors:

www.newdirectionsaromatics.com.

Herbal Medicine

Herbal medicine and homeopathy are used to positively influence emotional and physical health. Whether you employ them to allay your anxiety, or bring about a feeling of wellbeing and health, both are options to explore.

Herbal medicine is the use of any plant that has useful medicinal qualities. These range from super foods like ginseng, to plants that strengthen and stimulate organs of the systems like milk thistle or Echinacea, to plants that detoxify or treat infections.

Chinese herbal medicine and acupuncture represent the two major systems of Chinese medicine. Both are thousands of years old, originating long before their respective scholarly texts were written 2000 years ago. At the same time, Western herbs are just as potent and effective as Chinese plants grown in Asia, and both systems are supported by modern scientific knowledge. Herbalists with a background in Chinese medicine and acupuncture will often combine Western herbs with Chinese herbs, using principles of formula-modification to best serve the patient. Students of Chinese herbal medicine generally do, however, spend more in-class time working with herbs.

Herbal medicine is very safe when administered by a trained professional with extensive clinical experience. Herbs do not have the kind of side effects that are caused by pharmaceuticals. For example, though a well-constructed herbal formula might cause digestion problems, a simple adjustment will typically resolve the issue. A trained professional is mindful that being natural does not automatically guarantee safety, so be sure to work with a trained professional.

There are a variety of herbal medicines that address anxiety. Anxiety has varied expressions and origins that are unique to each individual. It may be genetic, biological/organic (i.e. discernible or even measurable brain chemistry imbalance), and/or related to traumatic life experiences. Any and all of these may be issues when it comes to your anxiety for the test. An herbalist will often treat anxiety with individualized herbal formulas (formulae), or constitutional homeopathic remedies. One remedy is Kava kava, a Polynesian herb which has been effectively used, though long term use may be problematic as there may be an issue with liver toxicity.

Symptomatic quick-acting or acute herbs such as passionflower, valerian, or hops can be used for nervousness. We recommend our clients get tinctures, which can be found at local health food stores. (Get certified organic tinctures if possible.)

Herbs to enhance focus and concentration include skullcap and oats, which have quick-acting symptomatic benefits. Ginko increases blood circulation to the brain, and the ayurvedic herb gotu kola is used to strengthen blood vessels and mental function. Lemon balm can also be used.

Dr. Trahan of the Olympus Healing Center in New York works with hundreds of patients, developing treatments in herbal medicine and homeopathy for these symptoms. He has seen effective clinical results in his practice using both general and more individualized and complex treatments. In fact, he reports that he has observed benefits for people who are challenged, for example, with ADD, as well as enhancements to the performance of very high functioning people.

Homeopathy

Homeopathy is an alternative medicinal system that treats patients with heavily diluted preparations which would, in larger doses, cause effects similar to the symptoms presented. (One can think of it like a vaccination, although it's a very different process.) In an unhealthy person, these diluted doses eliminate the symptoms and root causes of the disease. Homeopathy stands as arguably the most profound healing system in the world. Homeopathic medicines, also known as remedies, have a documented history of effectively treating diseases and conditions ranging from musculoskeletal, to metabolic, to psychological. They can also help with emotional issues afflicting the nervous and anxious test taker.

Discovered and developed over 200 years ago by Dr. Samuel Hahnemann in Europe, homeopathy has been used worldwide to treat simple maladies such as cold, flu, and basic injuries, as well as serious, long-term, physical pathologies and deeply rooted mental and emotional issues. Homeopathic treatments generally do not pose the risk of toxic side effects posed by many current pharmaceuticals, and are frequently comparably powerful. For instance, homeopathic remedies proved to be successful in many cases of cholera and flu epidemics in the late 1800s, as well as in the 1918 Spanish Flu outbreak, in situations where pharmaceuticals failed.

To successfully practice homeopathy requires years of study, so we recommend working with a health care practitioner who has been trained and certified.

Massage and Body Work

Massage and Body Work are effective for increasing energy and blood flow through the body. Whether you perceive it to be pampering, rejuvenating, or therapeutic, it's a great physical treat with manifold benefits. At its core, body work increases energy, decreases stress, improves quality of sleep, and heightens brain function, all incredibly valuable tools to maintain clarity and focus while taking your test. Massage is also useful to alleviate pain, improve flexibility, and increase immunity, all while making you feel good and relaxed "in the moment." All of these benefits, of course, add up to improved mental health and performance. If you've never had a professional massage before, you are in for a treat.

Frank Hughes, of Brooklyn-based Spiral Flow Massage, recommends Trigger Point Massage. This type of massage is a valuable asset in combating stress and anxiety. It focuses on holding sustained pressure for seven seconds, then releasing for two seconds to allow the muscle to receive more blood, and for metabolic waste to disperse from the muscle. This cycle is continued up to one or two minutes, or as soon as the muscle softens. He writes:

> *"The most common trigger point is located at the top of your shoulder just about an inch lateral to the side of the neck in the belly of the trapezius muscle. If you are sitting or studying for prolonged lengths of time it will surely become tight and can even cause headaches. In order to prevent this scenario from happening I suggest periodically every one to three hours to spend one minute releasing this trigger point yourself. Take your left hand with your four fingers pressed together like a raccoon's hand, place the tips of the four*

fingers on the trapezius trigger point, and with your right hand on top of your left gently press into the trigger point for five to seven seconds. Pause for two seconds and continue.

Coordinate your breath so that you are breathing in as you press and you are exhaling while you release the pressure. With each new round of pressure try to feel whether the muscle is relaxing. If the muscle is not softening, check to see if your left hand, which is contacting the trigger point, is relaxed; if it is not, it will be difficult to release the trigger point. Slow coordinated breathing combined with sustained/intermittent pressure on a trigger point is very good for the nervous system and can bring you a renewed sense of focus."

Nutrition and Sleep

There is no substitute for eating well. Nutrition provides the fuel for your body to run, and with increased pressure and a need to balance your life, it's important to eat healthy, well-balanced meals.

It is important to understand that the nourishment you need to be your best self and manifest your dreams may be very different from what your best friend or brother or sister needs in his or her body. You are "you-nique." The best way to assess if you are getting the nutrients and sustenance you need is to listen to your body. This means you must take responsibility for what you eat, when you eat and how you eat (standing up, sitting down, on the run, etc.), and assess how you feel before, during and after meals. In addition, when thinking about your future and designing the goals that are going to lead to a successful career and fulfilled life, you also need to consider sleep—how much, and the quality. Here again, your needs may differ from those of your friends and family members; your best friend may have abundant energy after six hours of sleep, though you may require a minimum of seven. The key is to embrace selfcare and the journey to discover your best self as you remove judgment from your inner guide, not only as you prepare for the GMAT, but for life. Properly nourishing yourself helps you control your mind, body, and spirit.

When preparing for an exam, particularly a high stakes exam, you already have a lot on your mind. Preparing your physical body for exam day takes time and should be a part of your overall "study" guide. Begin integrating food into that plan to boost your energy, as soon as possible. Having your mind clear and focused throughout the process will help you to retain information and remain free from anxiety. Additionally, it is in your best interest to eliminate energy-zapping foods as soon, and as quickly, as possible. Waiting until the last minute can actually hurt more than help, as suddenly removing addictive substances such as sugar and caffeine can result in headaches, sleepiness and other physical discomforts.

Energy-boosting foods include:

- Fruits and vegetables including dark leafy green vegetables, cruciferous vegetables and root vegetables

- Omega-3-rich fats such as walnuts, pumpkin seeds, flax seeds and chia seeds

- Complex carbohydrates and whole grains like brown rice, quinoa, 100% whole wheat bread and legumes

- Lean, organic, grass-fed meat

The dietary fiber, protein, and complex carbohydrates in these foods will break down slowly to provide sustained energy. An assortment of these foods in your daily diet will provide you with the vitamins, minerals, and other nutrients your body needs to function at its optimal level.

The problem, and challenge, is that many foods that are inexpensive and readily available lack high-quality, vital nutrients and actually zap, rather than increase, your energy. Eating too much will result in fatigue, sleepiness, brain fog, and an inability to concentrate. Be conscious of, and limit or completely eliminate, the following:

- Alcoholic beverages and drinks with caffeine

- Sweets including sugar, high fructose corn syrup, and artificial sweeteners

- Refined foods such as white bread, white rice, and packaged food products

- Hydrogenated oils and trans-fats like margarine

- Dairy products and foods containing gluten (a protein found in wheat, barley, and rye)—these foods can bring on bloating and other physical discomfort as many individuals are sensitive to dairy and gluten but haven't been diagnosed with an "official" disorder, such as lactose intolerance or celiac disease, that would keep them away from these foods.

You might explore ways to include in your diet the following 'brain power' nutrients, as included in Barbara Friedlander Meyer and Arnold Meyer's book *Feed My Brain, Eating to Excel*. You'll notice many of these are included above in 'high energy' foods.

Vitamins

Vitamin A: Found in liver, sweet potatoes, carrots, mangoes, spinach, cantaloupe, dried apricots, milk, egg yolks, and mozzarella cheese.

Vitamin B1: Wholegrain cereals, especially bread, fortified breakfast cereals, porridge oats, brown rice, spinach, green peas, tomato juice, watermelon, soy milk, dairy products, yeast extract, pulses, nuts, seeds, red meat, and pork.

Vitamin B2: Milk, cheese, yogurt, eggs, meats, liver, oysters, clams, fortified breakfast cereals, almonds, yeast extract, green leafy vegetables, spinach, broccoli, and mushrooms.

Vitamin B3: Red meat, poultry, fish, lean ground beef, chicken breast, tuna (canned in water), liver, shrimp, spinach, potatoes, tomato juice, nuts, pasta, and yeast extract.

Vitamin B6: Fish, pork, chicken breast, eggs, yeast extract, brown rice, soya beans, oats, whole grains, peanuts, walnuts, avocado, bananas, watermelon, tomato juice, broccoli, spinach, acorn squash, potatoes, and white rice.

Folic Acid: Dark green leafy vegetables (especially sprouts and spinach), green beans, peas, oranges, fortified breakfast cereals and bread, yeast extract, and nuts.

Vitamin C: Blackcurrants, berries, green leafy vegetables like Brussels sprouts, cabbage, spinach, broccoli, tomatoes, peppers, snow peas, mango, strawberries, kiwi fruit, citrus fruits and their juices.

Minerals

Iron: Artichoke, parsley, spinach, broccoli, green beans, tomato juice, tofu, clams, shrimp, and beef liver.

Magnesium: Spinach, broccoli, artichokes, green beans, tomato juice, navy beans, pinto beans, black-eyed peas, sunflower seeds, tofu, cashews, and halibut.

Potassium: Potatoes, acorn squash, artichoke, spinach, broccoli, carrots, green beans, tomato juice, avocado, grapefruit juice, watermelon, banana, strawberries, cod, and milk.

Zinc: Spinach, broccoli, green peas, green beans, tomato juice, lentils, oysters, shrimp, crab, turkey (dark meat), lean ham, lean ground beef, lean sirloin steak, plain yogurt, Swiss cheese, tofu, and ricotta cheese.

Chromium: Vegetable oils, liver, brewer's yeast, whole grains, cheese, and nuts.

One of the easiest and most effective habits to develop consistent energy is drinking water. The human body is approximately 70% water, and water is necessary for optimal cellular function. A good rule of thumb is to drink ½ your body weight in fluid ounces of water every day. Great food, sleep, and a dose of sunlight every day, and you're on your way to nourishing your body and mind for success.

No time to cook? No problem! Many cities offer a wide number of choices in take-out options, and consider setting aside an afternoon to cook high-quality meals that you can freeze and then eat throughout the workweek.

Sound and Music as Enhancement Tools for Relaxation and Focus

Music and sound can provide sustainable support to the test taker through enabling motivation, focus, relaxation, and creative visualization. The act of listening to music can help transport the test taker to altered states of consciousness thereby enabling a new perspective on the art of taking a test.

Music that has particular emotional meaning to the test taker can help to ease anxiety, lessen stress, be used as a mnemonic device, and aid in inspiring the test taker to challenge themselves and push through mental obstacles.

Particular qualities in music can serve different purposes for sustained focus and memory retention, such as a driving beat to inspire and awaken, lyrical instrumental melodies to quiet the mind and soothe the nervous system, or sustained drone music found in different world cultures that can facilitate spiritual feelings and a sense of connection.

In respect to quantitative results, several educational and psychological sources have suggested that certain pieces in the classical music repertoire have been linked to increased learning speed and memory. Below is a list of suggested pieces by classical composers such as Mozart, Bach, Vivaldi, Beethoven, and Pachelbel.

Suggested Listening:

Beethoven:

> Concerto No. 5 in E-flat Major for Piano and Orchestra; op. 73 ("Emperor")

Brahms:

> Concerto for Violin and Orchestra in D Major, op. 77

Haydn:

> Concerto No. 1 in C Major for Violin and Orchestra
> Concerto for Violin and String Orchestra, No. 1 in C Major and No. 2 in G Major
> Symhony No. 67 in F Major and No. 69 in B Major

Mozart:

> Concerto for Violin and Orchestra
> Concerto No. 7 in D Major, Concerto for Piano and Orchestra, No. 18 in B flat Major

Tchaikovsky:
> Concerto No. 1 in B-flat Minor for Piano and Orchestra

The Music Template

While listening to this music will have a positive effect on your learning, you can also record yourself with the material, as detailed by hypnotist Kevin Hogan on his website. Hogan details information about Dr. Georgi Lozanov, a Bulgarian psychiatrist who was the first to fuse hypnosis and music to create accelerated achievement in learning. He has provided a great step-by-step guide on how to make your own hypnotic concerts, as well as using Lozanov's suggestions on how to use the music itself.

Classical Music has been proven to help enhance learning. In fact, baroque music in particular is thought to enhance focus! Here are some works that you might want to use to enhance your process:

Suggested Listening:

Bach:

> Choral Prelude in A Minor and Prelude and Fugue in G Minor
> Fantasy in G Major
> 5 Fantasy in C Minor, and Trio in D Minor, Canonic Variations and toccata
> Symphony No. 2 for String Orchestra
> Symphony in C Major
> Symphony in D Major

Corelli:

> Concerti Grossi, op. 6, no. 2, 5, 8, 9
>
> Concerti Grossi, op. 4, 10, 11, 12
> Concerto for Organ and Orchestra

Vivaldi:

> The Four Seasons, Five Concertos for Flute and Chamber Orchestra

Step-by-Step Process:

(1) Acquire the pieces of music which are proven to enhance learning and memory. (2) Verbalize what you need to learn into some kind of recording device. (3) Close your eyes and relax before you play your concert. (4) Allow yourself to be alert and focus your mind on the concert, allowing the concert to fill your mind. (5) When the concert is over test your recall to ensure that learning has taken place!

While it falls beyond the purview of this book, please note that accelerated learning can occur by blending the articulation of material with hypnosis, relaxation and music. Katie Down is TPNY's go-to music therapist, and together with the collaboration of master improvising musicians has co-created our Full Potential Audio series. This is a a product for our clients who need to improve their test taking game. The following is a description of ways in which the music offered by TPNY's CD series can help you at this juncture: Sound and music can be used therapeutically to bring body and mind into deep states of relaxation, heighten awareness when needed, and provide inspiration to move through obstacles while taking the test. In TPNY's Full Potential Audio course, we use original music played by world class musicians who use a broad range of instruments from around the globe, including flute, Japanese shakuhachi, Indian bansuri, Australian didjeridoo, Brazilian berimbau, West African slit drums, Middle Eastern frame drum, West African djembe, Irish bodhran, Turkish riq, North Indian tabla, Middle Eastern cymbals, Tibetan bells and gongs, crystal bowls, and cello. The unique and elemental nature of each instrument combined with binaural beats help create mental states that empower the test taker.

Binaural beats (syncopated rhythms used to reach a desired mental state more quickly) are used on specific tracks and interspersed throughout some of the music tracks. Alpha beats are used for a sense of ease, and beta beats for alertness. Both types of beats are embedded in our audio material to bring you into a calm and alert state, and maximize the effectiveness of the music and words. Gerard Oster's groundbreaking article about binaural beats in Scientific American began bringing this technology more into the mainstream in 1973.

If you burn a CD or make an audio tape recording, use your voice to follow the intensity of the music. Listen to the contours, dynamics, tempo, and emotional content of the music, and read in conjunction with the emotionality of the music, i.e. read with emotional intention.

Because music and sound become helpful mnemonic devices in memory enhancement and retrieval, we created the Full Potential Audio GMAT program, which helps students walk through many of the exercises described in this book in order to achieve their highest goals. There are over thirty highly effective techniques set to music and binaural beats that are designed to enhance your mental retention, concentration, and relaxation so you can perform your best. The audio is driven by an improvised sound score designed specifically towards the goal of each meditation and visualization exercise, and packaged with carefully explained exercises, test specific directions, and scientifically proven mental enhancement techniques. You can listen to a sample of our Full Potential Audio course on our website, www.testprepny. com. We've also included a free download of a full track for people who have purchased this book. This can be found on the website, as well.

__Yoga and Pilates__

Ophra Wolf, dancer and owner of Force and Flow Integrated Bodywork in Brooklyn, NY, recommends a regular mind-body movement practice such as Yoga and/or Pilates. Both Yoga and Pilates share the underlying principle that the coordination of breath and movement helps to relax the nervous system, focus the mind, and heighten awareness of the present moment. These modalities differ slightly in the type of movements involved, but both can be easily performed at home with nothing more than a little bit of floor space. The proof is in the pudding. The Journal of Alternative and Complementary Medicine reports that in a 12-week yoga study, researchers found patients with greater improvements in mood and anxiety than a metabolically matched walking exercise.[27]

Movement practices such as Yoga and Pilates are grounded in the simple observation that the mind and the body are not separate entities. Our awareness is necessarily embodied, and the more alert, relaxed, and flexible our bodies are, the more alert, relaxed, and flexible our awareness can be. The movements of Yoga and Pilates involve a conscious engagement of the entire body, and a focused attention to detail, waking up and toning our body and mind in preparation for those moments in which we need every cell of our body to be present and on-task. There are a variety of approaches to Pilates and many types of Yoga—Hatha, Iyengar, Vinyasa, Kundalini, Ashtanga and Anusara are just a few of the popular styles—and the best way to find out what approach is best for you is to speak with an instructor. Regardless, doing a little bit every day—whether it be in the morning, as a break from sitting at the desk, as a warm up for a test, or as a winding down at the end of the day—will give the best results.

Here is a simple exercise you can try on your own—remember, the focus is coordinating the breath and the movement. Stand barefoot with your feet at hip width and the arms relaxed at the sides of the body, and feel the weight of your body evenly balanced on the entire surface of your feet.

Take a moment to relax all the muscles in the body—let the feet soften, then the calves, the thighs, the hips, the abdomen, back and chest, the front and back of the neck, and jaw and all the little muscles in the face. Now, as you take a deep inhalation, raise your arms straight above your head and circle them, rooting down through your feet and energizing all the way through your fingertips.

As you exhale, circle the arms back down as you bend at the waist and drop your torso over your legs. You can bend your knees if you need to, making sure that your hips stay over your heels and not behind them. Hang for one to three deep breaths, allowing your head to hang heavy and your body to increasingly relax with every exhalation. Then bend your knees, and on an inhalation circle your arms to the sides and all the way overhead as you straighten up to standing. Once your weight is balanced on your feet again, exhale to circle the arms back to the sides of the body, returning to your starting position. You can repeat this cycle as many times as you like. When you finish, take a moment to stand quietly and sense both the body and the space around you, noticing any changes in quality.

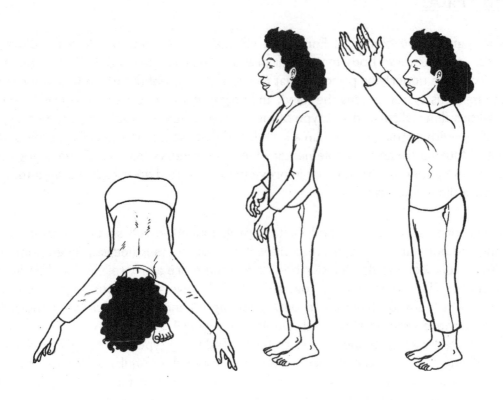

Mastering your mind in the quiet of peaceful surroundings is great practice for learning to do so under pressure. But once you're under pressure, you've got to up your game to get your fear reflexes under control. Tevis Trower founded New York-based work effectiveness consultancy Balance Integration to provide tools to help top executives do exactly this.

Having applied the following tools with high-performers in best practice organizations ranging from Morgan-Stanley to the NYPD, Tevis knows that decision making under stress can be optimized no matter the situation. Whether finding your seat in a test room or walking into a challenging meeting, you can stimulate a relaxation response and enhance your decision making ability by grounding your awareness in what is tangible and real, rather than giving in to a nervous system that has been triggered into adrenaline-producing mode by anticipatory fear. Think of it this way: in a moment of fear, the limbic and reptilian brain sends panic signals to your executive functions, saying, "Run, fight, get out of Dodge, you're about to die!" Adrenaline is sent through the body, shortening your breath and speeding up your pulse, preventing the executive function from doing what it does best: process subtlety and make nuanced decisions. By shifting your awareness into your actual, real state of wellbeing in a moment of stress, you separate your thinking from the fear stimulus so the nervous system can regain equilibrium.

Here's how you do it: notice the next time you're triggered and make it your "target practice." Whether at school, work, home, or just while navigating transactions in life, pay attention to how you respond to contentious moments or unpleasant (yes, even potentially disastrous) surprises. We each have our own way of responding to stress, so being an expert on yours will take you a long way towards mastering it. Physical responses you might notice can include a pounding heart, short breath, clenched muscles, a feeling of urgency, hot or cold skin, sweat, or a rush of blood to your face. Mental responses can be rushing thoughts, and inability to pay attention, frantic eye patterns, bottom-lining, and extreme negative emotions such as rage, blame, etc. When you notice yourself in this state, whether triggered by a professor, coworker, or the teller at the bank, you've got a perfect moment to practice:

1. Notice the state—what is happening? Scan your body for your particular stress responses, both physical and mental. By knowing your own response pattern, you'll be able to identify it and, with practice, be less handicapped by it.

2. Decide to shift your mind out of the state of alarm and into wellbeing. Yes, simply decide. Like taking a child's hand away from a hot stove and back into safety, shift your mind into immediate evidence of your own wellbeing.

3. Start by asking whatever part of your physical body has become most clenched to relax—for some of us it will mean unclenching our hands, for others it may be rolling back the shoulders, while still others may find their strongest physical response to fear to be clenched glutes. Based on your pattern, feel yourself relax those areas as you take slow, deep breaths.

4. Soften your eyes, tongue and forehead, and breath deep.

5. Shift your awareness to monitor your breath's rhythm. Invite yourself to relax your body around your breath, starting with relaxing your nostrils, keeping ease in your jaw and throat, and inviting a sense of ease down into your belly.

6. Now relax your mental response with a neutral statement about the truth of the situation, shifting into long-view thinking rather than being crippled by fear about the possible outcomes of the situation. This statement might be something along the lines of: "This moment has me triggered by fears of how others will judge me, but I am really perfectly okay," or, "I am triggered by wanting things to be exactly how I want them, but I am actually fine."

This target practice allows you to circumvent the habit of generating panic (i.e. survival function) through your thoughts, and assess each moment honestly, allowing you to respond with your executive functions intact. Let any area of your life serve as your laboratory to learn about your own stress response, and let it put you, the expert, on your path to grace under pressure.

Now that you've been introduced to these techniques and balanced lifestyle choices to aid in your study, list 3 things you're going to use in the next two weeks, and schedule them in your calendar.

1.

2.

3.

SECTION II

PREPARATION: A MAP TO SUCCESS

CHAPTER ONE

SETTING YOUR SCHEDULE

In the first part of this book, you learned how to play the inner game—you learned how to recognize and adjust the attitudes, emotions, and beliefs that powerfully shape your performance. With this knowledge in hand, you are now ready to prepare yourself for the outer game—to manage your schedule and the physical facts defining your genetic and environmental background. This section is about taking a snapshot of what your life looks like and where you're at with your priorities, setting up a schedule, and then establishing goals. The Appendix includes information about the timing of when to take the GMAT, as do the resources on our website.

THE WHEEL OF LIFE

It's likely that as you prepare for the GMAT, you'll have to reprioritize and make sacrifices. Change sometimes leads to imbalance. We know balance is a critically important factor to managing your stress, and being the most effective and efficient test taker. On the next page is a Wheel of Life diagram to help you become aware of what your life balance looks like right now. Each segment of the wheel represents one area of your life.

Too often, we think of our lives as divided into two parts, work and home, professional life and personal life. That way of thinking leads to a life out of balance. We want our professional lives to be infused with the same joy as our personal lives; we want to experience the same creative urge in our personal lives that we often experience in our professional lives.

This wheel of life, based on the archetypal Tibetan symbol, then, is not neatly divided into two parts, but spins through the emotional, intellectual, spiritual, and physical aspects of our lives. There is no correct way to divide up the time we spend on various parts of the wheel—instead, the wheel is a tool for understanding our individual values and priorities.

In the following exercise, assign a value to each segment of the wheel in terms of how it relates to where you are right now. If you don't relate to a particular segment, substitute your own header that has relevance.

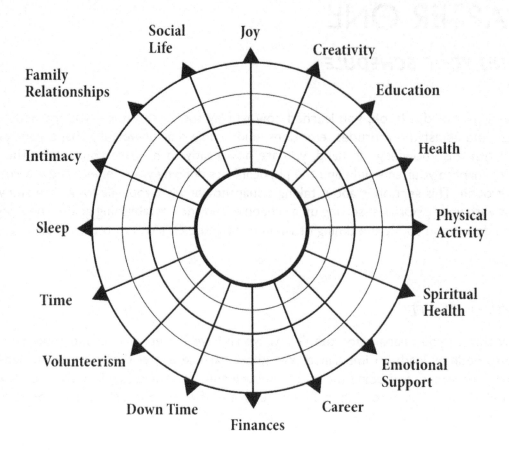

Exercise II.1.1. Your Values on the Wheel of Life

Consider each section of the wheel. For each one, ask yourself these questions: How satisfied am I with this area of my life? Am I putting as much time, energy, and attention into this area as I would like, or is it affected by my preparation for this test? The center of the wheel is 0 and means you are totally dissatisfied; the outer edge is 10 and represents full satisfaction and achievement.

Decide your degree of satisfaction from 0 to 10 in each of these areas, and mark it on the relevant spoke. Now draw a line to join your degree marks together. How balanced is your life? Which areas make you happy, satisfied, and fulfilled? Which areas need improvement and some bolstering up?

Put in where you're at on a scale of 0–10, and identify what makes it positive or negative now, where you'd like to be, and how you think you can 'get' to where you want to be:

Joy

Positive

Negative

What needs to change/how would you like it to be?

What could you do to change it short term or long term:

Creativity

Positive

Negative

What needs to change/how would you like it to be?

What could you do to change it short term or long term:

Education

Positive

Negative

What needs to change/how would you like it to be?

What could you do to change it short term or long term:

Health

Positive

Negative

What needs to change/how would you like it to be?

What could you do to change it short term or long term:

Physical Activity

Positive

Negative

What needs to change/how would you like it to be?

What could you do to change it short term or long term:

Spiritual Health

Positive

Negative

What needs to change/how would you like it to be?

What could you do to change it short term or long term:

Emotional Support

Positive

Negative

What needs to change/how would you like it to be?

What could you do to change it short term or long term:

Career

Positive

Negative

What needs to change/how would you like it to be?

What could you do to change it short term or long term:

Finances

Positive

Negative

What needs to change/how would you like it to be?

What could you do to change it short term or long term:

Down Time

Positive

Negative

What needs to change/how would you like it to be?

What could you do to change it short term or long term:

Volunteerism

Positive

Negative

What needs to change/how would you like it to be?

What could you do to change it short term or long term:

Time

Positive

Negative

What needs to change/how would you like it to be?

What could you do to change it short term or long term:

Sleep

Positive

Negative

What needs to change/how would you like it to be?

What could you do to change it short term or long term:

Intimacy

Positive

Negative

What needs to change/how would you like it to be?

What could you do to change it short term or long term:

Family Relationships

Positive

Negative

What needs to change/how would you like it to be?

What could you do to change it short term or long term:

Social Life

Positive

Negative

What needs to change/how would you like it to be?

What could you do to change it short term or long term:

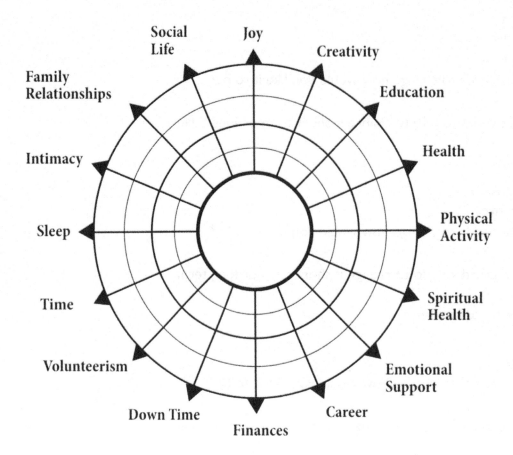

Social Life   Joy

Creativity

Family Relationships

Education

Intimacy

Health

Sleep

Physical Activity

Time

Spiritual Health

Volunteerism

Emotional Support

Down Time

Career

Finances

Exercise II.1.2. Re-evaluating Your Wheel of Life

Now answer these questions, in writing or to yourself.

1. Are you surprised by any of the responses you gave in the previous exercise? Forget about the GMAT for a moment: are there any aspects of your life that simply seem out of balance to you? What are they?

2. How can you re-adjust your life so that the aspects you value are more prominent? Color in the parts of the wheel (above) that you would like to be stronger. For example, if you want to devote more time to your career, fill in the spoke all the way to the outer limit. If you want to devote less time to your career, only fill in the first segment of that spoke.

3. What can you do to make these aspects of your life stronger? What can you let go of to free up your time and energy? Use the space below to write instructions to yourself:

PERSONAL:

In the future, I will spend less time _____

In the future, I will spend more time _____

PROFESSIONAL:

In the future, I will spend less time _____

In the future, I will spend more time _____

OTHER:

In the future, I will spend less time _____

In the future, I will spend more time _____

WEEKLY SCHEDULE

Now that you have a better sense of your personal priorities, you have to face a new challenge: how will you manage your wheel of life in the next three to twelve months as you work hard to study for the GMAT and jump through the hoops of the MBA application process? Where will you find the extra time and energy without disturbing the balance you have reached in your wheel of life?

Finding balance is an important key to success. Too often, test takers believe they have to throw their lives out of balance to study for a test. They cut out time with friends and family, stay up too late, and abuse their bodies—all to study for a test.

There's no doubt that studying for a difficult test like the GMAT takes a lot of time and hard work. If you throw your life out of balance, however, you will increase the stress you feel, as well as your anxiety. It is much more difficult to learn new concepts and to memorize new material when you suffer from high levels of stress and anxiety.

The secret to successful preparation is to find a new balance for this difficult period of your life. This balance will give you time to study, but won't deprive you of the aspects of your life that are most important to you.

To achieve this kind of balance you need a specific time management strategy, tailored to your personal wheel of life. You have 168 hours each week. What will you need to do each week to include study time? A good way to begin figuring it out is to block out the large chunks of time that are already committed: time to sleep, commute, and work, for example.

This weekly plan will be your guide. Return to it each week, both for guidance and to reevaluate whether you made the right choices or whether you need to modify your plans. You might find that you gain some time on some days, and have misjudged on others. Don't beat yourself up. Just figure out what will work out best for the following week. Sunday evening is a good time to look at the plan for the week ahead.

Exercise II.1.3. Daily Evaluation

St. Ignatius has a wonderful daily evaluation meditation, called *The Examen*, that is recited/contemplated each night. The following is an adaptation that could be helpful to add as a useful and insightful daily habit:

1. Become aware of the presence of something bigger than yourself. This could be a spiritual entity or nature. See yourself as part of life as a whole.

2. Review the day with gratitude. What have you done today that you feel good about, and that you're thankful for?

3. Pay attention to your emotional attachment. Does this serve you or not?

4. Prioritize. Choose one feature of the day and learn from it.

5. Look toward tomorrow. What does tomorrow bring, and are you ready for it?

Exercise II.1.4. Planning a Weekly Schedule

Find a calendar you will use. For some people, an old-fashioned weekly or monthly print calendar works best. Others might want to use the calendar that comes with your email program. If you use several devices (a smart phone, home computer, work computer) you may want to use a calendar that lives in the cloud, like the Google calendar.

Once you choose your calendar, put in the following can't-miss scheduled activities:

1. Diagnostic Test dates.

2. Social, family or professional obligations (weddings, birthdays, conferences).

3. Your class schedule, if you are a test taker; your work schedule, if you have a paid job.

4. Other scheduled events in your week (religious services, a volunteer job).

5. Meal times—make time for breakfast, lunch and dinner. Give yourself at least a half-hour for lunch and dinner—you need the break.

6. Time for physical exercise and fresh air!

7. Time for sleep—plan on at least 7-8 hours a night.

   Now put in the activities that reflect your values and current goals:

8. Time for study for the GMAT—each person is unique and comes to the test with different strengths and weaknesses. That said, the average recommended amount of time you should expect to study would be a minimal 2–2.5 hours per day/15–20 hours a week. If you are diligent and focused, you could see steady improvement doing 2/3rds of that. (In the pages that follow, we will give you a sample schedule for study.)

9. Time to complete school homework or job-related "home" work.

10. Time with friends/family/loved ones.

11. Down time: doing a hobby, watching TV/movies.

Take a look at your schedule. Is this schedule workable? Can you reasonably accomplish all the activities you set out to do? If not, rework it. You may want to ask a spouse or someone else close to you if this schedule seems workable. Don't forget to review the schedule once a week to change what doesn't work.

	Sunday	Monday	Tuesday
7:00	Get up – Cardio Exercise	Get up/Breakfast and Shower/Yoga **7:30 GMAT Study**	Get up/Breakfast and Shower 7:30 Cardio Exercise
8:00		Head to Work/Work	Head to Work/Work
9:00		Work	Work
10:00	Brunch with Friends		
11:00	**GMAT Homework**		
12:00			
1:00		Lunch/**GMAT review**	Lunch/**GMAT review**
2:00	Break 2:00–2:30/light lunch	Work	Work
3:00	**Diagnostic/Math**		
4:00			
5:00			
6:00	Break for Dinner	GYM	Dinner with Friends
7:00	**Go over Diagnostic**	Dinner	**GMAT homework**
8:00		**GMAT homework**	
9:00	9:30 Watch Television/		9:30 Down time
10:00	Talk on Phone/down time Prioritize for week	Open time	
11:00	**FP/Sleep**	**FP/Sleep**	**FP/Sleep**

	Wednesday	Thursday	Friday	Saturday
7:00	Get up/Breakfast and Shower 7:30 GMAT Study	Get up/Breakfast and Shower 7:30 GMAT Study	Get up/Breakfast and Shower 7:30 Exercise	FREE TIME
8:00	Head to Work/ Work	Head to Work/ Work	Head to Work/ Work	
9:00 –12:00				
1:00	Lunch/Shop or Organize House-hold Chores	Lunch/with friend	Lunch/**GMAT homework**	**FULL POTEN-TIAL (FP) Exer-cise**
2:00 – 6:00	Work	Work	Work	**GMAT home-work**
6:00	Household Chores Dinner	GYM Dinner	Dinner with Friends	Break for Dinner
7:00			**GMAT home-work**	OPTIONAL **GMAT home-work**
8:00	**GMAT home-work**	**GMAT home-work**		
9:00			9:30 Down time	
10:00	10:30 Downtime		Meet friends/ movie etc.	
11:00	**FP/Sleep**	**FP/Sleep**	**FP/Sleep**	**FP/Sleep**

Go to website to download these forms to create your schedule.

Notes:

CHAPTER TWO

MANAGING YOUR PHYSICAL ENVIRONMENT

In the last chapter, we focused on your personal time. Managing your time is an aspect of your "outer game" that you can definitely control. What about your physical space? You can't decide where to take the test, but you can decide where to study. You can also learn a set of tips for making the test-taking environment as comfortable for you as possible.

STUDY SPACE

There is a significant amount of research pointing to the importance of studying in the same physical space every day. As we saw in Section I, Chapter Seven, it is possible to program the mind to reduce stress. By sitting in the same chair at the same desk or table every time you study for the GMAT, you will find that you have more focus. You will, essentially, have been training your mind to click into "study" mode when you go to this place.

What makes a good study space? Try not to use a space that is reserved for some other critical aspect of your life. Studying in bed is a bad idea, for example, because whatever anxiety you might experience from studying will likely transfer to your attempt to sleep, and you may end up experiencing insomnia. Likewise, if possible, try not to study at your kitchen/dining room table. Your table is associated with food, which increases the chance you will snack too much if you study there. Eating is also often a social occasion, not one you want to associate with solitary study.

Some people benefit from a quiet study space; others do much better in a coffee shop, surrounded by noise and people. However, if you need a people-based environment, make sure it is one that contains no distractions. Do not go to a coffee shop where your friends hang out. If you are studying at home, make sure you will not be interrupted during your study session.

Whether you use it for study or not, it is important to have a quiet space where you can meditate, do yoga, and use the other techniques in Section I that promote and train our bodies to handle stress. That quiet place can be as simple as a small 2x3 throw rug that you pull out and sit on when you want some calm.

TEST SPACE

You do not have a choice of testing environments. The testing center where you take the test is often dictated by when you take the test and how early you register. However, if your schedule is flexible, or if you live in a large city where there are multiple testing sites, then do take a look at the test sites. You may find you can relax more if the test location is a place you are already familiar with. Plus, it is highly encouraged that you visit the test center before the test day. Learn the route to get there, and time it, so there are no surprises on the testing day. Prepare all required material the night before (identification, etc.), and don't be surprised when they pull out some CSI moves: you'll be handprinted and fingerprinted.

CHAPTER THREE

WHAT KIND OF LEARNER ARE YOU?

You control some aspects of the outer game, like your personal time and personal space. However, there are some parts of who you are that you can't change. Success depends on learning about yourself and building a study program that will match your needs.

Psychologists don't yet understand the mechanisms behind how we learn. What they do know is that people learn differently. Some of us are visual learners; some learn by listening and others by doing. In fact, how we learn maps to the five senses—most of us are visual (eyes), aural (ears), or kinesthetic (hands) learners, but a small percent of people actually learn best through smell or taste.

What kind of learner are you? Well, think about how you prefer to get directions when you plan to drive someplace new or take a trip. Would you prefer to listen to directions (aural)? Would you rather read a map or directions someone else supplied (visual)? Do you need to write down the directions in order to really feel you know where you are going, or even need to have someone go with you to the place in order to remember how to get there next time (kinesthetic)?

Did you answer more than one question with "yes"? Many of us combine more than one type of learning. For example, if you like to use a GPS, you may be both an aural and visual learner (listening to and reading directions). If you like to read a map and then write your own directions down, you may be both a visual and kinesthetic learner. One of the most common learning styles in our society is the "read/write" style, which combines visual and kinesthetic learning. Because it is so prevalent, we have used read/write as a separate learning category in the exercises that follow.

There is no right or wrong way to learn—what matters is understanding your learning style.

You can optimize your learning by adapting your study habits to accommodate your personal learning style. To begin with, you can use the questionnaire that we've supplied below to identify your personal style. (If you want to explore the concept more deeply, you can also speak to a specialist who deals with learning styles.)

Exercise II.3.1. What Kind of Learner Are You?

Below is a quick survey to give you a general idea of what kind of learner you are. This is not a scientific study, but it will help you identify your preferences and proclivities. Knowing how you learn and take in information is important because you can customize how you take in information and study, as well as learn the best way for you to retain and recall information. If you aren't currently engaging in a learning process that suits your style, you can be losing information—and time. So, get ready, set, GO!

Check the way you think you'd most likely respond. Then at the end, tally up the types indicated to identify your predominant learning style. NOTE: The letters indicate the predominant learning style (you use, or would use): Hearing, Seeing, Feeling or Read/Write. You can check off multiple circles with each statement given, however, only select two if the two answers are of equal relevance to your standard operational procedure.

1. You just got a new smart phone or tech gadget. To get started with it, you:

    ☐ Read the manual cover to cover (R/W)

    ☐ Call a friend or colleague and have them explain to you how to use it (H)

    ☐ Play around with it, thinking, "How hard could this be?" (F)

    ☐ Look for a step-by-step video or diagram online to show you (S)

2. You're finally on a vacation to a place you've wanted to visit for a long time. While you know the history and culture, you're unfamiliar with the terrain, the distances between places, and the layout of the towns you're visiting.   You don't have a GPS. Time is limited. When touring around in your rental car to visit sites, do you:

    ☐ Use a published map that you keep stashed in your backpack (S)

    ☐ Read and follow directions in a guidebook (R/W)

    ☐ Ask a local for directions (H)

    ☐ Drive around and to explore by yourself (F)

3. You and a friend are going to try cooking a very gourmet recipe for the first time. Do you:

    ☐ Google then read the recipe directions yourself (R/W)

    ☐ Have your friend read the directions out loud to you (H)

    ☐ Create the dish based on the ingredients you believe to be in there, noticing texture, color and taste as you go along (F)

    ☐ Use a visual how-to guide that illustrates the steps to create your dish (S)

4. You go to a restaurant where the food was not only cold but under cooked... and that was just the beginning. Do you:

☐ Leave in a huff, vowing never to step foot in there again (F)

☐ Complain to the server by pointing to each dish as if they were exhibits in a trial (S)

☐ Send a letter or email to management or post messages on a restaurant review site (R/W)

☐ Complain to your friends then give an earful to management over the phone (H)

5. You're thinking about buying a new vacuum. You:

☐ Go to the store to test drive some options (F)

☐ Look online for professional and/or actual consumer reviews (R/W)

☐ Ask the sales rep to explain the various models (H)

☐ Pick the one that looks the sleekest (S)

6. You've just heard a great, long quote that you are positive will come in handy. To remember it, do you:

☐ Write it out multiple times (R/W)

☐ Say it out loud over and over (H)

☐ Rehearse acting it out (F)

☐ Create diagrams and sketches to help understand the flow of it (S)

7. To prepare a once-in-a-lifetime experience for someone else (i.e. surprise party, engagement, etc.) would you prefer to:

☐ Read a book or DIY how-to article for directions (R/W)

☐ Look at pictures online that other people posted to see how they did it (S)

☐ Talk to someone who has prepared something like this (H)

☐ Head over to your local craft store and see what inspires you (F)

8. Your friend just gave you the most amazing gift and you're touched and overwhelmed. You:

☐ Send him or her an email, or write a thank you note (R/W)

☐ Call the person to thank them (H)

☐ Purchase flowers or buy a drink the next time you get together (F)

☐ Design a special card and send it to him or her (S)

9. You just returned from the tropical jungle to find a strange bump on your arm. Do you:

☐ Read up on your symptoms online to find out what it might be, and ways to deal with it (R/W)

☐ Go talk to a doctor (H)

☐ Diagnose it yourself and treat it based on your instincts (F)

☐ Look online for pictures of "skin bumps" to determine what you may have (S)

10. You're feeling stressed and anxious about your upcoming exam. To reduce your anxiety, do you:

☐ Purchase a self-help book about how to get over anxiety (R/W)

☐ Sign up for an exercise, meditation, or yoga class (F)

☐ Go to an art museum or movie (S)

☐ Sit back or lie down and listen to calm, relaxing music (H)

Write your totals here:

R/W _____

S _____

H _____

F _____

Go to surveys.testprepny.com/learning if you want to do this online.

Now that you have identified your primary learning style, you can take advantage of some of the following methods to accentuate your learning style and upgrade your study:

I SEE WHAT YOU MEAN. VISUAL: LEARNING BY SEEING

Visual learners learn through the sense of sight: using charts, maps, diagrams, and graphic representations to best glean, understand, and recall information.

To optimize study:

- Create charts and diagrams of everything you're learning. Make it as literal or abstract as you'd like, just keep it on paper so you understand your visual language.

- Use color-coding: for example, put frequently tested idioms in green; use red for expressions that are considered incorrect on the GMAT, etc.

- Use graphical symbols to remember concepts: for example, draw the circle-and-line "NO" symbol over examples of sentences that are considered wrong on the GMAT.

- Draw lines and arrows to show how parts of the sentences are interconnected (at least on your homework and the OG—remember the test is on a screen).

- Come up with your own visual symbols for key concepts. A key or a star works great. Suppose you wanted to decorate the margins of the Official Guide with simple, colorful visual symbols indicating the grammar rules tested by each question. What symbol would you put in the margin to mean Parallelism? Subject-Verb Agreement? Pronouns? It doesn't matter whether anyone else would understand why a particular symbol reminds you of a certain grammatical concept—what matters is that the symbols take on meaning for you, and that you're consistent with them.

- Translate key concepts from each of these chapters into a simple visual chart.

- Maximize the use of visual clues to find out what point is being tested in each question. Rather than trying to "hear" the original sentence in your head and listen for the mistake, you may want to look over the 5 answer choices first and see whether any patterns strike your eye.

- Create and use outlines and lists. Color code information.

- Write down what is on the board (if you're taking a class), online, in notes, or what people say.

- Create a PowerPoint presentation.

- Chart out sentences, readings, etc.

- Take notes, make lists.

- Watch videos demonstrations. Or make a simple video presentation and watch it.

- Outline reading and/or steps to do things; We're big fans of "to-do" lists.

- Use flashcards.

- Go to a quiet place to study (less distraction).

SAY WHAT? AUDITORY: LEARNING BY HEARING

If you find yourself saying, 'I totally hear you' when getting directions, then you likely learn best by your aural devices. Learners who excel at hearing are often effective communicators.

To optimize study:

- As you study the grammar rules that the GMAT tests, read both the correct and incorrect examples out loud, and identify the differences.

- When you solve a GMAT SC question, be sure to either read aloud or hear the sentence in your head.

- Study the steadfast grammar rules via examples and the idioms that the GMAT tests frequently by recording the list yourself, and then playing it back.

- Think of songs you know that have word patterns you need to remember for the GMAT. (For instance, one pattern—explained in Module 1—is exemplified by "If I were a rich man...". One idiom that's frequently tested is repeated over and over in a song from the musical "Oliver Twist", the one that goes "Consider yourself at home / Consider yourself part of the family").

- If you're having trouble remembering a rule, put it in the form of a rhyme. Take it one step further and imagine your favorite musician telling it to you.

- Use word association to remember things.

- Record lectures (if you're taking a GMAT class).

- Watch video demonstrations (or tape your class).

- Record facts and information.

- Participate in discussions with a study buddy.

- Tape record notes after writing them.

WALKING YOUR TALK! KINESTHETIC LEARNING BY DOING.

Are you empathic? Like doing things? You're likely a learner who learns by DOING. Kinesthetic learners are those who learn through experiencing and/or doing things. They are often tactile and experience things by movement. These learners prefer to move around rather than sit still with a book or study aids. Some people even learn through muscle memory. For some of these learners, even music can be a powerful aide for memory because of how it makes them feel!

To optimize study:

- Interact with the material physically: Use your finger to point to important clues in the sentence or to trace the connections between parts of the sentence. Cover up parts of long sentences with your hand as you can focus on other parts.

- Get up frequently during your study session and walk around the room, still thinking about what you've been learning.

- Study in short blocks.

- Imagine that you're the teacher of a GMAT class. Stand up in front of your imaginary audience and explain the material you've just studied. Use gestures. If you're really entrepreneurial or just want to have fun, start a meet-up group to teach and share the information with others.

- Study with others. In fact, find a study buddy and trade off teaching each other the material covered.

- Use memory games.

- Use flash cards to memorize—and carry them with you.

- If you find you are having trouble remembering something, pair it with a physical activity like standing on one foot or squeezing your wrist. Attaching the information this way makes it easier for many people to remember.

READING/WRITING

You're lucky if you learn this way: it's the dominant way we've been taught in the US for the last, um, forever. Reading/Writing learners prefer to take in information through the medium of the written word. In some ways, people who prefer reading/writing have it the easiest on GMAT SCs, since reading accurately and thinking about how a sentence should be written are what the test is all about. Rather than just tell you to rest on your laurels, though, we have a few suggestions.

To optimize study:

- Obviously, read every page of this manual.

- Write out key concepts in your own words.

- Write your own example sentences and sample questions.

- Write outlines of the chapters and review them. Write flashcards for idioms you need to memorize, and review them frequently.

You may find that your optimal learning mode spans more than one category. For more information about these types of learners and more, see Howard Gardner's work. He is the pioneer on multiple intelligences, and identified learning styles.

If you feel you've received this number in error, circle back and retake the survey.

Exercise II.3.2. A Moment of Self Reflection

Write down some of the techniques that you'll now use as a result of this evaluation and study suggestions.

CHAPTER FOUR

THREE KINDS OF ENGLISH LEARNERS

Are you getting ready to start learning some grammar? Great! We are almost there. But before you dig into the Sentence Correction portion of the GMAT, you need to know some things about what the GMAT is testing, and think about the best way to approach it. Again, your background and experience, your "outer game," is a critical part of this preparation.

You cannot go back and change how you first learned English or how you were educated through high school and college. What you can do is recognize what kind of English speaker you are, and how your current knowledge of English affects your ability to perform at the highest level on the GMAT.

The GMAT tests **formal written English**. Formal written English is different from everyday conversational English. You may have been born in the United States; you may be praised for your large vocabulary; you may be an able to talk anyone into anything: none of that means that you are an expert at formal written English.

Formal written English is the kind of English that is used in legal contracts, academic books, and certain "intellectual" magazines. Because the GMAT tests formal written English, there may be some cases in which the "best" answer may not <u>sound</u> any better to you than the "wrong" answer. In fact, in some cases, the "wrong" answers will be deliberately designed to sound normal and reasonable by <u>the standards of everyday conversational English</u>. However, they will break one or more rules of formal written English. You may think, "There's nothing wrong with that sentence" because it sounds all right. This is why you need to be on your toes to look for specific rules that may be broken. You can't always trust your ear.

First, take this quiz:

QUIZ: How Familiar Are You with Formal Written English?

Instructions: Read the following sentences, paying special attention to the underlined portion in each one. Put a check next to the sentences that sound OK to you—even if "OK" means, "Sounds like something you'd see in a book, not something you'd hear every day." Put a minus sign next to each one that sounds odd or ungrammatical (in or around the underlined part). Be honest.

1. Never have I heard such a thing.

2. So determined was he to succeed that he invested every penny of his fortune in the endeavor.

3. Had I known that there was a problem, I could have addressed it.

4. It's essential that he be there on time.

5. Only once did I mention it to him.

6. Few people knew of the tragedy, for the president's aides had decided to keep it a secret.

7. He said but one word: "Rosebud."

8. Should any problem arise, don't hesitate to tell me.

9. The volatile businessman was widely believed to have grown up in a tough neighborhood.

10. The senator has two offices, one of which is located in his home state.

11. That Rhode Island is not, in fact, an island comes as a surprise to some people.

12. The nation devastated by the bombings, the Prime Minister strove to offer some comfort to his people.

13. Controversies over genetically modified foods are particularly intractable in that the parties to the controversy typically have vastly different levels of scientific expertise.

14. The more than 36 million people living in California represent an astonishing diversity of ethnicities, languages and religions.

15. The man arrested for burglary was found to be an upstanding citizen.

Number of Checks:_____   Number of Minuses: _____

SO, HOW WELL DO YOU KNOW GMAT-STYLE ENGLISH?

So, how well do you know formal written English? The answer will depend on your background. Formal written English is still sometimes taught in high school English classes, but nowadays, many schools emphasize other priorities (and many people don't pay very close attention in high school English class anyway).

Some people, especially those who read a lot, will find that they have already picked up a feeling for the tone and style of formal written English (even if they didn't know that that is what it is called); others will find that what is considered "correct" in the formal written style sounds odd to them because it differs from the English used in everyday conversation. It's worthwhile to take a few moments to think about how you experience formal written English.

In our experience, learners come in three types:

1. **Native speaker with an ear attuned to formal written English.** If you grew up reading a lot, and/or if you like to read non-fiction and more "intellectual" magazines, you may already have a gut feeling for what sounds smoother, more polished, or "more correct" according to the standards the GMAT is testing. Your strategy for mastering the Sentence Correction section will be to build on the instincts you already have. You can trust your ear a lot of the time, though you still need to memorize the specific rules that the GMAT tests, as well as practice quickly identifying the stereotypical tricks and traps of the SC section.

2. **Native speaker with less familiarity with formal written English.** If you don't like to read very much, or if you tend to read only websites, popular fiction, or heavily technical material, you may not have developed an intuitive feeling for the structures and patterns of formal written English. Some of what the GMAT considers correct may strike you as very old-fashioned, stilted or simply weird. For learners in this group, the strategy is different. You can trust your ear sometimes, but not very often; you need to focus on memorizing rules and applying them almost as if you were studying a foreign language. In particular, you have to get used to the idea that what strikes your ear as 'wrong' may nevertheless be the choice the GMAT is looking for. You can draw on your knowledge as a native speaker to a limited extent, but you need to make a serious, focused effort to memorize the patterns that the GMAT is testing.

3. **Non-native speaker of English.** Non-native speakers often wonder whether they have any hope of scoring well in Sentence Correction. Clearly, native speakers have an advantage in this area. However, if you are a non-native speaker, the news isn't all bad. You will need to focus on memorizing rules and applying them without relying on your ear, but at times you may find the job easier than do the learners in category 2. Native speakers who aren't familiar with formal written English are often misled by their ears. They think that because something sounds right to them, it is right. For some native speakers, it's hard to think about it any other way. Non-native speakers know that they can't trust the judgment of their ears, so they're able to get down to the business of memorizing rules more efficiently.

To play this outer game, you need to learn the rules of grammar that the GMAT tests, and apply them even when a sentence doesn't sound all that bad to you. You also need to pay attention to wording that sounds awkward, weird, or "not the way anyone would say it." You have to find a balance between listening for what sounds right and applying specific rules of grammar.

Now, Let's Check your score from the Initial Quiz:

<u>All 15 checked</u>; no minus signs: Excellent! You are very familiar with formal written English. You still need to know which rules are tested on the GMAT, and you will need to practice problem sets so that you can tackle the questions quickly and efficiently, but in many cases you will be able to trust your ear to decide which choice is right.

<u>12-14 checked</u>; no more than 3 marked with a minus: You're pretty familiar with formal written English. You still need to study the rules (especially rules pertaining to the sentences you thought were wrong), but when you can't remember which rule applies, you will probably be able to trust your ear.

<u>8-11 checked</u>; 4-7 marked with a minus: You have only a partial working knowledge of formal written English. You need to study the rules and, in some cases, trust the rule you've memorized rather than rely on your ear.

<u>4-7 checked</u>; 8-11 marked with a minus: You have had only limited exposure to formal written English. You can polish up your awareness of it, but you should expect to rely on rules much more than on your ear.

<u>Fewer than 4 checked</u>; more than 11 marked with a minus: You don't seem to be very comfortable with formal written English, and probably haven't had a lot of chances to get used to it. You will need to memorize rules and trust them rather than your ear most of the time. The good news is that it is possible to become more comfortable with formal written English through practice. If you work at it, even the sentences that sound awkward to you now will sound normal.

CHAPTER FIVE

READY, SET, GO!

If you have read this far, you now know that test preparation means much more than studying the content of a test. To truly prepare yourself for a high-stakes test like the GMAT Sentence Correction, you have to play both the inner and outer game. The inner game is all about learning to deal with stress, changing behaviors that cause failure in the testing room, and learning how to condition your mind and body to be open to learning.

The outer game focuses on those aspects of your life that happen in your physical environment. That includes balancing test preparation with the busy life you already lead, along with understanding the tools you bring to the test, especially your learning style and your past educational experiences. It's all about learning how to manage what you cannot control to achieve the optimum result.

The next section of this book will feel very different. The focus is on content, content, content. The pages are full of grammatical rules and the emphasis is on results. Make sure to take your inner and outer game with you as you work through these modules. If you begin to feel stressed, look back to Section I—fire that inner critic! Remap your behavior! Meditate! Exercise!

Be sure to use the optimal learning techniques we reviewed to ensure that the information you are processing sticks. Use the mandalas and optical illusions interspersed through the next section to open your mind to new material. Hypnotize yourself into digesting new facts. Listen to your body and emotions.

Most importantly, keep to your schedule and refer to the goals you set back in Chapter 2 each day. Remind yourself why you are studying for this test—keep your eyes on the prize, which is not the test itself, but the life and career you desire. Remind yourself that you can do it—you can reach your full potential!

Exercise II.5.1. Remember your Goals

Return to Exercise I.2.3. Read over the goals you wrote down then. Using your new knowledge about your learning style, remember those goals now.

If you are visual, draw a picture of success—it may be a graph or a drawing or a list—but create something you can look at each day.

If you are aural, compose a song/rhyme about your goals, or play your favorite music and read your goals out loud—either way, record it and play it every day.

If you are kinesthetic, create a dance, make a sculpture, or if you have an outdoor space, create a path you can walk to remind yourself of your goals each day. If you have a study buddy or meet up group, teach the material to someone else.

If you prefer to read/write, then rewrite your goals in a clear style and post them above your desk.

This is your personal mantra. No matter how difficult studying grammar rules may be, you will constantly remind yourself of your goal. Now, let's get started!

SECTION III

EXECUTION: THE JOURNEY

EXECUTION

You have laid the groundwork and created your map to success. It's now time to start on your journey toward mastery of the GMAT's Sentence Correction questions.

As you go through this section, you will find mandalas and optical illusions that have been put into these pages in order to refresh and reset your mind. Any time you feel yourself getting fuzzy, take a physical break—get up, walk around, drink some water—and then focus on a mandala when you sit back down. The combination of physical and mental exercise will help bring your energy back and help you concentrate.

You may feel yourself becoming anxious as you work through some of the more difficult exercises here. If that happens, take a break and use one of the techniques we reviewed in the first Section—take a few minutes to meditate, or return to the exercises in 1.6 and reframe your negative thoughts. If you have been practicing self-hypnosis (Section 1.5), put yourself into a trance in order to diminish your stress.

PRACTICE TEST

The first step towards your preparation is to take a practice test. You may have already taken a practice test or you may even have taken the GMAT Sentence Correction already in a test setting. If so, you don't need to retake a test now. If you haven't yet taken a practice test, you get access to two when you sign up for the GMAT on the official website, mba.com. We also have a diagnostic test on our site, www.testprepny.com.

Why take a test before you begin studying? You take this first practice test to get a basic familiarity with the task ahead and to get a baseline score. It's ok if the score is low! The whole point of studying is to raise your score.

Make sure you take the practice test in a setting similar to the actual test. Use a timer and do not go over the time limit. Do not stop the test in the middle to take a break. You need to go through the experience of this particular test.

Score yourself as soon as you finish taking the test. Then, go immediately to Section 1, Chapter 2 and set a goal for yourself. Don't spend time focusing on the test you just took—focus instead on your goal for the test you will take, the test that will count. Keep your mindset on the future. Afterwards, give yourself a pat on the back and take the night off.

HOW TO STUDY FOR SENTENCE CORRECTION

The key to excelling on the Sentence Correction test is understanding the formal written English grammar that underlies each of the test questions. To help you understand and practice this grammar, we have organized your study into 10 modules. The first 6 modules cover the major areas that are most frequently tested on the GMAT. The next 4 modules cover the details that can mean the difference between a decent score and a great score.

 **Top Priority**

For each of the first 6 modules, there is a Top Priority item. The Top Priority items serve a few different functions, depending on where you are in your test taker preparation.

- If you are a test taker who is getting a low score and you have almost no time left to prepare, Top Priority items are the most essential elements to master. Learn these, and then, if you have time, circle back to the other items in each module.

- If you are a test taker who is getting a good score, the Top Priority items may address skills that you have already more or less mastered. However, you should nevertheless complete some harder practice questions in each of those categories and, especially, make sure that you can quickly identify errors in these categories, since these are generally the types of questions on which it is possible to pick up points and make up a lot of time.

- If you are a test taker who is getting a high score and believe you are adept at the Top Priorities, you should take a timed test of a set of "typical" practice items. Better yet, time each item and see if you are wasting precious seconds on items that you should be able to handle quickly and mechanically. Some modifier errors, for example, can be identified so quickly that a test taker can find the correct answer choice in 15 seconds or less. Time saved by quickly eliminating choices that break the Top Priority rules is time that can be used to think through the harder questions.

Mastering Top Priority techniques doesn't guarantee a high score. These are the skills that constitute the "floor"—if you cannot master these techniques, you are guaranteed to lose points. To get a top score, you need to master all of the material in this manual.

Symbols:

More Practice:

Grab a clue:

Take Notice:

OG Box: Herein, you'll find questions from the GMAT's Official Guide for further practice.

Here is a list of the Modules that follow, along with the skills you can expect to learn and the Top Priority items.

MODULE 1: SUBJECTS AND VERBS

Skills:

1. Identifying the subject of a sentence accurately

2. Determining whether the subject is singular or plural, and whether the verb agrees

3. Correctly matching subject to verb despite a great deal of intervening verbiage

4. Identifying inconsistencies in verb tense

5. Identifying misuse of present or past perfect

6. Recognizing when present perfect is required

7. Recognizing when present or past subjunctive is required

8. Recognizing correct and incorrect verb forms in conditional and counterfactual sentences

9. Recognizing other situations in which plural and singular can be confused

 Top Priority: Recognizing subject-verb agreement mismatches.

MODULE 2: PRONOUNS

Skills:

1. Identifying appropriate antecedents for *they* and *it*

2. Making sure that *it* and *this* are not used to sum up entire clauses or vague concepts

3. Using *that* and *those* correctly

4. Correctly differentiating between *who* and *whom*

5. Checking for consistency in pronoun use

6. Knowing the difference between *do so* and *do it*

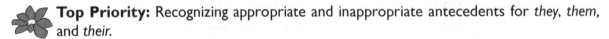 **Top Priority:** Recognizing appropriate and inappropriate antecedents for *they, them,* and *their.*

MODULE 3: MODIFIERS

Skills:

1. Recognizing dangling modifiers, including subtle instances and misplaced appositives

2. Recognizing "squinting" or otherwise unclear or misplaced modifiers

3. Recognizing errors in relative clause formation (especially the use of *where* as an all-purpose connector, and *which* with no referent)

4. Differentiating between modifiers that must modify the subject and those that are not so restricted

5. Correctly placing *only*

6. Differentiating adverbs from adjectives

 **Top Priority:** Recognizing dangling modifiers at the beginning of a sentence; using *which* correctly.

MODULE 4: COMPARISONS

Skills:

1. Recognizing apples-and-oranges comparisons

2. Recognizing unclear and ambiguous comparisons

3. Correctly using *like* and *as*

4. Recognizing errors in formulations *as X as* and *more X than Y*

5. Differentiating *less* and *fewer*

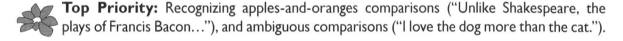 **Top Priority:** Recognizing apples-and-oranges comparisons ("Unlike Shakespeare, the plays of Francis Bacon…"), and ambiguous comparisons ("I love the dog more than the cat.").

MODULE 5: PARALLELISM

Skills:

1. Recognizing correctly and incorrectly formed lists

2. Checking paired expressions for parallelism

3. Avoiding traps in which it is difficult to identify the grammatical parts of speech used in a list

4. Recognizing errors involving fragments of verb phrases ("They have and will continue to insist…")

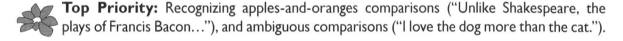 **Top Priority:** Recognizing correctly and incorrectly formed lists; checking paired expressions for parallelism.

MODULE 6: IDIOMS

Skills:

1. Recognizing idiomatic expressions that are considered correct or incorrect on the GMAT

 Top Priority: Learn the most commonly tested idioms on the GMAT.

The next four Modules are more advanced, detailed subjects that you will also need to master to get a top score.

MODULE 7: CLAUSES AND CLAUSAL CONNECTIONS

Skills:

1. Ensuring there is an independent clause (including being careful about semi-colons)

2. Knowing when to use *if* or *whether*

3. Recognizing when to use a shell noun such as *the fact/theory that* as opposed to a gerund ("the theory of Claudet's having executed the sculptures…")

MODULE 8: SPECIAL ISSUES OF MEANING

 Note that some meaning issues are covered under Misplaced Modifiers

1. Recognizing wordiness and redundancy

2. Specific meaning issues

MODULE 9: DICTION

1. Word choice

2. Using *-ing* forms vs. established nouns

MODULE 10: HALLMARKS OF FORMAL WRITTEN ENGLISH

1. When it is appropriate to use inverted word order

2. When participles should be followed by infinitives

3. Recognizing clausal subjects beginning with *that* ("That the supply of oil is finite…")

4. The use of infinitives and participles as modifiers in formal written English—"a population to be tested," "a man selected for his judgment," etc.

5. Formal uses of articles

OVERALL STRATEGY FOR GMAT SENTENCE CORRECTION

Knowing how to approach each test question is not only necessary for taking the test—it's also a critical skill you need to study for the test. As you go through the exercises in the modules that follow, you should practice your test-taking technique. There are a couple of possible techniques you can use. Choose the one that best fits your learning style:

TECHNIQUE ONE:

1. Read the sentence and see if anything sounds wrong to you.

2. Pay particular attention to the underlined section. If there are elements in it that depend on their relationship to things outside the underlined section—such as a verb that has to agree with a noun that isn't underlined—look and see whether those elements are correct.

3. If nothing seems wrong with the original version, glance at the 5 answer choices to see what is being tested. Usually, there's a split between two possibilities. For instance, 2 out of 5 may begin with "have" while 3 out of 5 begin with "has." In that case, they're clearly testing subject-verb agreement. Look at the sentence in terms of the primary concept that's being tested (there will probably be more than one).

4. Narrow down the answer choices by figuring out what exactly is being tested and eliminating the other set of answers. For example, if subject-verb agreement is being tested and the subject is singular, you can eliminate all the answers that begin with "have," which is a verb that agrees only with a plural subject. You now should be looking at just 2-3 answers.

5. Look for evidence to sort out which of the remaining items is best. What other concept is being tested?

6. Mentally "plug" your answer into the original sentence to make sure it fits smoothly with no mistakes.

TECHNIQUE TWO

1. Read the answer choices first. Identify the grammar rules that you believe are being tested. For example, if some answers begin with "has" and others with "have", you can assume subject-verb agreement is being tested.

2. Read the original sentence in order to decide which set of answers is correct for this sentence. For example, if subject-verb agreement is being tested and the subject is singular, you can eliminate all the answers that begin with "have", which is a verb that agrees only with a plural subject. You now should be looking at just 2-3 answers.

3. Identify the difference(s) between the remaining answers—decide if a second concept is being tested.

4. Reread the original sentence to decide which answer is correct.

No matter which technique you use, you need to remember which answers you have eliminated. Now that the GMAT is given on the computer, there is no way to mark up the testing paper. Instead, many test takers find it helpful to write the letters A B C D E on their scratch pad, going downward, and then cross off the letters of choices that are eliminated.

GMAT TRICKS

The techniques we just described may seem straightforward until you try them. You should be aware that the GMAT will try to trip you up in a few different but predictable ways.

First, The GMAT Sentence Correction test will tend to target the differences between spoken English and formal written English. In preparing for the test, you should focus on becoming aware of the differences between formal and informal English, and how the GMAT writers try to turn the differences into traps.

Second, the GMAT Sentence Correction testers will often try to slow you down by adding a lot of unnecessary complexity, including simply increasing the length of sentences. Test sentences are often (though not always) based on factual statements about the real world—scientific discoveries, historical events, artists, writers, musicians, etc. The writers frequently load on the details just to get you bogged down in interesting and/or confusing trivia: unfamiliar names, startling scientific claims, lists of strange species of plants and animals, dates, places, etc. When you read these sentences, you want to strike a balance in your reading:

Rule 1. **You need to read enough of the non-underlined part to know whether the underlined part is correct, but you don't want to get bogged down in long non-underlined sections that can't possibly help you answer the question.** When you read a sentence, your attention should be directed primarily toward the underlined part first. The underlined portion will usually give you a clue about what you need to look for, depending on whether it contains a pronoun, a present-tense verb, a piece of an idiom, etc.

You do need to read enough of the rest of the sentence to know what should go into the underlined portion, but you often don't need to read every detail. If the non-underlined portion has a long "introductory" section that includes a lot of trivia, it may have little or no bearing on the underlined part of the sentence. This is especially true if a semi-colon separates the parts of the sentence. A semicolon has almost the same force as a period, so the material on one side of the semi-colon can exert very little influence on the material on the other side. For example:

The Era of Good Feelings was an eighteen-year period in United States history in which the Federalist Party ceased attacking the president and partisan bitterness abated; the end of the Era began with the bitterly contested presidential election of 1824, <u>which Andrew Jackson alleged to have been stolen.</u>

   a. presidential election of 1824, which Andrew Jackson alleged to have been stolen

   b. 1824 presidential election, which was alleged to have been stolen by Andrew Jackson

   c. election of the president of 1824, which Andrew Jackson alleged stolen

   d. presidential election of 1824, an election which Andrew Jackson alleged had been stolen

   e. presidential election of 1824, an election by which Andrew Jackson alleged had been stolen

The correct answer is (d), as the discussion of the use of "which" and of modifier placement later on in this manual will make clear. The important point here is that everything that comes before the semi-colon is absolutely irrelevant to the task of answering the question.

A time-effective way to tackle this question would be to look at the underlined portion first, lightly skim the part of the sentence just before it so that you have some general idea of what you're looking at, and simply ignore the material before the semi-colon. You won't learn anything about the Era of Good Feelings this way, but you'll answer the question far more quickly than if you laboriously slog through every line. **Remember: Look at the underlined part first.** If the sentence is long and rambling, don't read all of it unless you have to.

Rule 2. **There are certain Sentence Correction questions that by their very nature never require you to read more than a few words of the non-underlined part of the**

sentence. We will point these out as we go over the different grammatical rules. Suppose you see a question like this:

<u>Unlike the climbing abilities of every other animal in the family Felidae,</u> the cheetah almost entirely lacks the ability to climb, but it rarely needs this skill as it is by far the fastest-moving animal on earth and therefore can depend on its fantastic speed to chase down prey.

a. Unlike the climbing abilities of every other animal in the family Felidae

b. Unlike every other animal in the family Felidae

c. As compared to the agility of other animals of the Felidae family

d. Unlike the skill at climbing which other members of the Felidae family have

e. As contrasted with the impressive climbing ability found in the rest of the Felidae family

Comparison sentences of this type are discussed in detail in Module 4. Once you review this topic, you will see that it only makes sense to compare two things of the same category, so comparing cheetahs to other animals in the Felidae family, as in (b), makes sense. Comparing animals to climbing abilities, as in the other four choices, doesn't. There's no need to read the entire sentence to the end to answer the question; you simply need to read far enough to make sure that the subject of the sentence is "the cheetah." Reading as far as "the cheetah almost entirely lacks the ability to climb" is sufficient to be sure of what you're dealing with; the rest is just a waste of time.

Rule 3. **Look for the 3-2 split either as a first step, or as soon as you've identified something wrong with the original version.** As mentioned, although the GMAT Sentence Correction usually tests at least two grammar points per question, you can often simplify matters by looking at the answer choices to determine the primary point being tested. For example, even without seeing the full original sentence, you can tell from the answer choices below what important grammar point is being called into question:

a. its members derive benefit from this policy in several ways

b. its membership benefits from the policy in numbers of ways

c. their members receive benefit from such a policy in several ways

d. their membership benefits from the policy in number of ways

e. its members benefit from this policy in several ways

If you were confronted with this question, your first priority should be to determine whether "its" or "their" is correct. You would then be left with either 2 or 3 choices to consider.

Rule 4. **Some types of mistakes allow you to eliminate answer choices instantly.** If you notice that an answer choice has a mistake in subject-verb agreement, or that it uses an expression that is never correct on the GMAT (such as "whether or not"), you should stop reading it immediately and simply cross it off.

Some people have the habit of reading every answer choice all the way to the end, even if they've found a mistake; you want to avoid that time-waster and instead develop the habit of eliminating a choice as soon as you find a mistake. The GMAT never allows exceptions when it comes to rules of grammar. The only time to look back to an eliminated choice is if you think you may have mis-read it. If you are sure that four out of five answer choices have outright grammatical errors, you should not hesitate to cross them off and pick the remaining choice, even if it sounds very awkward to you.

Rule 5. **You need to develop the skill of reading lightly.** It's true that there are times when you need to understand the sentence well enough to make sure that your answer choice makes sense in terms of not just grammar but also meaning—but even then, this doesn't mean you need to sit and ponder all the details. A long list of species names, for instance, may be nothing but padding designed to slow you down. It's enough for you to get that you are reading a list of plants or animals; don't stop and think about whether you recognize all of them. If they give you a date, it may have some relevance to determining which verb tense to use, but otherwise, don't focus on it. You do need to basically understand the sentence, but you usually don't need to dig into the meaning in great detail.

The key to a great score on the GMAT Sentence Correction is finding a balance. Sound familiar? In Section II, we focused on finding a balance between your personal and professional life, between studying as hard as you can for this test and taking the time to nourish your body, mind, and spirit. It should be no surprise that in taking the test itself, you also need a sense of balance. You need to balance out the need to understand the meaning of each sentence with the need to go fast.

As with life-balance, test-taking balance requires planning and practice. With practice, you'll learn to recognize the kinds of questions that require very little attention to the non-under-lined part, and those that require that you read everything carefully. This is a skill that comes only through familiarity with the material, which is why this book has so many exercises, and why we encourage you to do as many of the official GMAT questions as you can get your hands on. With practice, you learn to zero in on what's important and let the "fluff" slide by without bogging you down.

Trust the rules: Since the GMAT is computer adaptive, if you're getting all (or almost all) the questions right, you will be pulling some pretty hard questions later in the test. Some people imagine that the hardest questions test obscure idioms, and so they spend a great deal of time memorizing phrases. In our experience, while idioms can be helpful, it isn't true that high-level Sentence Correction problems are one big idiom hunt. The questions at the highest level tend to involve sentences that are more confusing than normal because all of the answer choices appear very similar, and all the choices seem notably awkward.

That is, if you're getting a very high score on the verbal section, as you get to the last few questions there's a stronger likelihood that your first reaction to a sentence may be, "All five choices sound weird, and it's hard to see much difference between them." This is when you need to rely even more firmly on the rules you have studied; it's likely that some of the choices break the more advanced grammatical rules (or break a basic rule in a less obvious way), and you have to read carefully to find the one that doesn't.

Finally, be proactive: Too many test takers approach Sentence Correction questions with the attitude, "Who knows what they might test? I'll just look for mistakes." That won't work if you want to get a high score. To reach your full potential, you need to think first in terms of the things that the GMAT tends to test. Certain grammatical rules tend to be tested over and over.

You should also keep in mind that "the basics"—the most fundamental rules of grammar, which dominate the low-to-medium questions—can still come into play even when you're pulling very high-level questions. We have seen with our own eyes that even on the very last question, when the test taker has gotten every item right so far and is now pulling high-level questions, some answer choices may still include mistakes in very basic rules of grammar. There is never a point on the test at which you can safely forget about "the basics."

In Sections I and II we suggested you prepare for the test by first planning for, and practicing, your inner and outer game. We suggested you set goals, understand and release your stress, and optimize your ability to learn. We helped you create a map to success by setting a workable schedule, finding the right kind of study space, and understanding how you learn. In the same way, you need to plan and practice grammar rules so that you can read test questions proactively, searching for the points being tested, and keeping in mind the list of issues that are most likely to be tested.

Imagine you are on a journey to climb Mt. Everest. You have practiced on lesser mountains for days, assembled your team, planned your route, packed your bags. Now, even as you make the ascent, you need to anticipate the cliffs and gulleys that lie ahead. Instead of allowing the *Sentence Correction component* to test you, the modules that follow will help you conquer the test.

Module 1: Subjects and Verbs

MODULE 1: SUBJECTS AND VERBS

1.1 TOP PRIORITY: SUBJECT-VERB AGREEMENT

You must be able to quickly spot what is wrong with sentences like these:

- The recent outpouring of complaints from both students and parents have prompted administrators to promise to reform the system.

- The company's board of directors—concerned by the recent rash of product safety lawsuits—have issued a new set of guidelines to managers.

- From the ashes of thousands of burned books and the pulp of rotted English textbooks grow the "ghetto palm" known to botanists as Ailanthus altissima.

The problem in each of these sentences is subject-verb agreement. A present tense verb has an "s" on the end if the subject is a singular noun (like *cat* or *democracy*), or a third-person singular pronoun—*he, she* or *it*. It doesn't have an "s" if the subject is plural.

Example:

Many economists believe that <u>the recent increase in mortgage failures indicate that the economy</u> will take a long time to recover.

    a. the recent increase in mortgage failures indicate that the economy

    b. the recent increase in mortgage failures indicates that the economy

    c. the recent increase in mortgage failures are indicators that the economy

    d. the recent increase in mortgage failures are indicative that the economy

    e. the recent increase in mortgage failures is indicative that the economy

The subject of the verb *indicate* is not *mortgage failures* but *increase*. (If this wasn't obvious to you, be sure to do exercise 2 below). (A), (C), and (D) have mistakes in subject-verb agreement—the verbs are plural. That narrows our choices to (B) and (E). (E) is awkward, so (B) is the only remaining choice.

Questions involving subjects and verbs are very common on the GMAT. If you haven't studied grammar since high school and aren't sure you remember what subjects and verbs are even in simple sentences, do the supplemental Basic Grammar Review exercise in the appendix. There are also exercises below to practice identifying subjects in more complex sentences.

Because subject-verb agreement is so commonly tested on the GMAT, we can essentially guarantee:

YOU WILL GET A QUESTION INVOLVING SUBJECT-VERB AGREEMENT ON THE GMAT.

In fact, you will probably get two or three.

 GRAB A CLUE: You can tell that a question is focused on subject-verb agreement if it has a present tense verb (a verb that *might* require an "s"). If you see that 3 of the answer choices have verbs with "s" and 2 have no "s" (or vice versa), you can be certain that verb agreement is being tested. Even when you don't see such an obvious warning sign, be on the lookout for subject-verb agreement— the GMAT likes to test it a *lot*.

To solve Sentence Correction questions involving subjects and verbs, there are a couple of steps that you need to carry out.

STEP 1: IDENTIFY THE SUBJECT

GMAT sentences will often use complex noun phrases as subjects to make it difficult to be sure which noun the verb is supposed to agree with. However, each complex subject includes a *simple subject*—the noun at the core of the subject—which is what the verb should agree with. A little practice will make it fairly easy to identify the subject.

Here's a simplified illustration:

> A *picture of a lighthouse hangs in the hallway.*

The complete subject is **a picture of a lighthouse**.

The simple subject is **picture**.

After all, what is it that's actually hanging in the hallway—a picture or a lighthouse?

Let's take a more complex example:

> *Recent reports of an increase in the cost of oil have caused anxiety among consumers.*

What is the simple subject?

The complete subject is **recent reports of an increase in the cost of oil.**

The simple subject—the core of the subject—is **reports**, not *increase* nor *cost*, so the verb is plural.

Contrast with this sentence:

> *The increase in the cost of oil, which has been documented in several recent reports, has caused anxiety among consumers.*

The complete subject is **the increase in the cost of oil, which has been documented in several recent reports.**

The simple subject is **increase**, so the verb is singular (takes an "s").

STEP 2: *DETERMINE IF THE SUBJECT IS SINGULAR OR PLURAL*

Important rules to know:

- <u>Each</u> and <u>every</u> are always singular: "each book is," not "each book are."

- If two nouns are joined with *and*, you add them together to make a plural subject (as in "A dog and a cat <u>are</u> in the kitchen"). <u>Don't</u> add the nouns together when they are joined with "together with" or "as well as" (as in "John, together with Mary, <u>is</u> coming to the party").

- If two nouns are joined with *or* or *nor*, the verb agrees with the second one: "Either the cat or the dogs are here," "Either the dogs or the cat is here."

- When the subject noun phrase begins with a quantity expression such as *some* or *half*, the noun determines whether the subject is singular or plural: "Some of the <u>people are</u> here," "Half of the <u>cake is</u> missing."

- A noun clause is always singular. A noun clause is a noun phrase that starts with a question word and includes a verb—for example, "what we need to do" or "who could have done such a thing." Phrases like these are always singular:

  Who could have done such a thing remains a mystery ("remains," not "remain"—the subject is singular).

  What we need to do is search for a new approach ("is," not "are").

- The phrase "a number of" is an expression meaning "some," so the subject is plural. The phrase "the number" is singular. For example, "A number of people are coming" is plural, but "The number of people in the room is 37" is singular.

Exercise 1: Imagine that each of these noun phrases is a subject and decide whether the verb should be singular (should take an "s") or plural (no "s"). (Additional exercises can be found on the website, testprepny.com)

the boys in that room	singular	plural
people in Rome	singular	plural
half of that book	singular	plural
all of the children	singular	plural
the girls under the tree	singular	plural
the cat and the dog	singular	plural
The United States	singular	plural
a number of reasons	singular	plural
half of those people	singular	plural
someone	singular	plural
the lion, as well as the tiger	singular	plural
neither of the two candidates	singular	plural
the reason that they went	singular	plural
all of the information in those books	singular	plural

Exercise 2: Determine which noun is the simple subject—in other words, which noun the verb should agree with (the verb you need to think about is underlined)—and correct any mistakes you find in verb agreement by changing the form of the verb. Circle the simple subject. Put corrections right into the sentences. (Additional exercises can be found on the website, testprepny.com)

1. The exact reason that so many people overeat during the holidays <u>are</u> difficult to determine.

2. Complaints about inconveniences and delays at the airport <u>have</u> reached unprecedented levels.

3. Due to unforeseen complications, negotiations between management and the union <u>is</u> expected to drag on much longer than previously anticipated.

4. The very last thing the reclusive multi-millionaire said in the moments before he died <u>was</u> "Rosebud."

5. The fact that so many people persist in activities that they know to be bad for their health and/or safety <u>is</u> a puzzle to some psychologists.

Exercise 3: Check for errors in subject-verb agreement. (Additional exercises can be found on the website, testprepny.com)

1. The firefighters' union, after long and tortuous negotiations, have agreed to a compromise.

   Subject: _____ Verb: _____ Agreement: Yes No

2. The principle of "innocent until proven guilty," often invoked in both real-life trials and television legal dramas, is not always properly appreciated by juries.

   Subject: _____ Verb: _____ Agreement: Yes No

3. The famous Victims' Bill of Rights, a topic of much controversy and editorializing, after much delay and protracted negotiations, have finally been adopted.

   Subject: _____ Verb: _____ Agreement: Yes No

4. A number of test takers, despite strenuous objections from the school board, has decided to stage the play *Bat Boy: The Musical.*

   Subject: _____ Verb: _____ Agreement: Yes No

5. The recent report of increased costs—though still not fully confirmed and in fact dismissed by some analysts—are stirring concerns among some investors.

   Subject: _____ Verb: _____ Agreement: Yes No

The subject doesn't always come at the beginning of the sentence. In the construction "There is/are…", the word *there* serves as a placeholder, the real subject which determines verb agreement comes after the verb:

There is <u>only one way</u> out of this situation.

There are <u>several people</u> waiting in the lobby.

There are also several types of phrases which can appear at the beginning of the sentence and require the subject to come after the verb. This kind of "inversion" (verb-before-subject word order) is far more common in formal written English than in everyday conversation, and if you're not familiar with it, you need to get used to it so that it doesn't surprise or distract you. The types of phrases that trigger inversion are

- Negative expressions such as "never" and "not once".

- Expressions beginning with "only," such as "only in the evening".

- Comparative expressions with "so" and "such," as in "So original was he that…".

- Expressions of location, such as "Between Holland and France" or "On the Left Bank".

For example:

Between Holland and Belgium lies France.

At the bottom of the page was a surprising footnote.

So perplexing was the problem that the greatest scientists in the field worked on it for years.

Such an inventive composer was he that his compositions set a new standard of musical excellence.

Never in my life have I heard such nonsense.

Only once did he consider divulging the truth.

Only after the war ended did the winery find the funding to expand.

Exercise 4: Find and underline the subjects in the following sentences. (Additional exercises can be found on the website, testprepny.com)

1. Out of the most recent series of debacles has come a new appreciation of the importance of internet security.

2. Only now are any of the people involved in the incident ready to talk to the press.

3. From one of America's forgotten small towns comes an unforgettable story of love and friendship.

4. Not until relatively recently have people realized that the tonsils perform an important function.

5. Only in the past week has the full extent of the damage become clear.

Exercise 5: Identify the subject of each underlined verb. (Additional exercises can be found on the website, testprepny.com)

1. The company's rather unconvincing denial of the rumor <u>was</u> both brief and incoherent.

2. The problems not yet identified in the software <u>could delay</u> the release.

3. A technique for making tougher sails for sailboats that sail under harsh conditions <u>was</u> the key to the success of the company.

4. Rumors of a new settlement agreement <u>came</u> as a surprise to the striking workers.

5. The recent discovery of the fossil of a fish with four working, paddle-like legs <u>helps</u> to establish the sequence by which fish developed into amphibians.

6. The significance of the fossils of *ambulocetus*, the so-called "walking whale," which in many ways resembled modern whales except for the presence of two hind legs, <u>cannot be</u> overstated.

7. Any claim for damages resulting from negligence or misuse <u>must be</u> accompanied by substantial documentation.

8. The ideal of a perfect society in which all of the inhabitants achieve their full potential <u>has</u> never been realized in actual practice.

NUMBER CONSISTENCY

In addition to making sure that verbs are marked singular or plural to agree with subjects, make sure that other nouns in the sentence are consistent in number so that the sentence makes sense:

> **CORRECT:** The workers were divided into three teams, all focused on <u>different aspects of the same problem</u>.

> **INCORRECT:** The workers were divided into three teams, all focused on a <u>different aspect of the same problem</u>.

The word "each" shifts the focus from a plural group to the individual members of the group, so that subsequent nouns will typically be singular:

> **CORRECT:** The manager assigned the workers to three teams, <u>each assigned to a different office</u>.

> **INCORRECT:** The manager assigned the workers to three teams, <u>each assigned to different offices</u>.

For more practice

OG, 12th edition, Questions: 40, 95
OG, 13th edition, Questions: 3, 6, 7, 14, 16, 30, 53, 55, 61, 70, 79, 81, 83, 108, 126, 129, 133, 140

1.2 VERB TENSES

In addition to looking at verb agreement (for present tense verbs), you also need to keep an eye on the <u>tenses</u> of verbs—that is, the difference between "Sam is eating", "Sam ate", "Sam has eaten", and so forth.

The good news is that it's not easy for the test creators to construct a sentence that requires the use of a specific verb tense, so there is only a limited number of ways in which the GMAT writers can try to trick you.

There are a few important rules to keep in mind:

1. Make sure the verb tenses stay consistent throughout the sentence.

2. Watch out for the distinction between simple present and present progressive.

3. Use present perfect, which means a form like *has done* or *have done* or *has been doing*, if the word *since* appears.

4. Don't use present perfect if the sentence specifies the time when the action was completed.

5. Past perfect ("had done") should be used only when it describes an event that happened before another time in the past.

1.2.1 MAKE SURE THE VERB TENSES ARE CONSISTENT

If a verb is underlined in a Sentence Correction question, make sure that the verb tense used fits with the rest of the sentence. If the rest of the sentence is in the past, the underlined verb shouldn't be present tense, and vice versa.

> **INCORRECT:** At the beginning of the movie, the girl is living in Africa, but at the end, she was in Australia.

> **INCORRECT:** John left home at age 8 because he wants to join the circus.

If there's a difference in verb tense between the underlined verb and the rest of the sentence, it should be because the sentence is actually talking about two different time periods.

1.2.2 WATCH OUT FOR THE DISTINCTION BETWEEN SIMPLE PRESENT AND PRESENT PROGRESSIVE

The GMAT sometimes tests the distinction between the simple present and the present progressive tenses. *Simple present* describes something that does not have a limited time frame, such as something that is always or generally true, or an action that is repeated habitually, as in these examples:

1. The moon <u>exerts</u> a gravitational pull on the earth.

2. Wisconsin <u>is known</u> for its dairy industry.

Present progressive describes an action that is happening in the immediate present and is not expected to go on indefinitely:

1. The board of directors <u>is currently considering</u> a new strategy.

2. Scientists involved with the project <u>are examining</u> the feasibility of a new approach.

The GMAT may test the distinction by incorrectly using present progressive to describe something that can reasonably be expected to go on indefinitely, or by using simple present to describe a time-limited activity that is described as current, as in these examples:

1. The company has long had a commitment to developing new blood pressure medications, and in fact <u>now conducts a study of one promising new drug</u>.

2. The length of the year is determined by the speed with which <u>the earth is orbiting the sun</u>.

3. In keeping with its mandate to investigate problems before they grow too large to handle, <u>the committee gathers data from three troubled neighborhoods this week</u>.

You will know that the GMAT is testing this distinction when the answer choices vary between simple present and present progressive. The correct choice will depend on the time frame described by the rest of the sentence and/or clues provided by the tenses of other verbs in the sentence.

1.2.3 USE PRESENT PERFECT IF THE WORD 'SINCE' APPEARS

 GRAB A CLUE: Be on the alert when you see the word *since*. If it means *from the past until now* (not *because*), check verb tenses immediately.

When the word *since* is used to mean *from a certain time up until now,* the present perfect verb tense is strictly required. (When *since* means *because,* it doesn't require a particular verb tense.)

'Present perfect' has verb forms like "has done" and "have done," as in "I have been living here for 3 years" or "Someone has eaten all the cookies". This tense is always used when the writer wants to convey that something began in the past and continues up to the present moment. Think about the difference in meaning between these two:

They have been married for 20 years.
They were married for 20 years.

In the first sentence, they're still married. In the second sentence, they're divorced, or perhaps one of the people is deceased.

Because one of the main meanings of the present perfect is "began in the past and continues until now", it is the ideal tense to use with *since,* as in "Since 1988, the soda pop factory in that town <u>has employed</u> more than one thousand people." It is incorrect to use either simple present or simple past in this instance, because English has this verb form that fits the meaning of since so perfectly. Compare the following examples:

CORRECT:

Since last year, everyone has been wondering whether the factory will reopen.

Since 1990, SUVs have become extremely popular.

Since Jim came home from Europe, he has been studying for the SAT.

INCORRECT:

Since last year, everyone is wondering whether the factory will reopen.

Since 1990, SUVs became extremely popular.

Since Jim came home from Europe, he studies for the SAT.

1.2.4 DON'T USE PRESENT PERFECT IF THE SENTENCE SPECIFIES THE TIME WHEN THE ACTION OCCURRED

 GRAB A CLUE: Pay close attention when you see present perfect verb forms: *has done, have done, has been doing, have been doing.* Make sure the tense is used correctly.

The entire point of the present perfect tense is to comment on how some action contributes to the <u>present</u> situation. The present perfect is most often used to talk about an action that is still going on; if it describes an action that's finished, it had better be an action that was recently finished and that is directly relevant to the present (for example, "I'm not hungry because <u>I have just eaten</u>"). If you remember this, it's easier to remember why it's incorrect to use present perfect if the sentence specifies when the action was completed, as in this example:

INCORRECT:

At a summit meeting held last May, the leaders of seventeen nations have reached an agreement to limit the amount of carbon produced by industry.

The correct form would be the simple past, "reached."

1.2.5 DON'T BE FOOLED BY INCORRECT USAGE OF THE PAST PERFECT

 GRAB A CLUE: Watch out when you see the verb form *had done* or *had been doing*. It's often used incorrectly on the GMAT. Make sure it's used correctly if you select that answer.

The past perfect verb tense—"had done"—is often used as a distractor (incorrect answer choice) on the GMAT. The past perfect is correctly used only to indicate that an event occurred before another past event, or before some specified time in the past, as in these examples:

> Long before the major European powers set out to explore the world, the Chinese had already mapped a great deal of the globe.

> By the time Mozart was 8, he had already written several significant pieces of music.

If the sentence simply states that something happened in the past, the simple past tense should be used:

> Microsoft <u>launched</u> (**not** "had launched") a new operating system last year.

> Agatha Christie's fame comes from the fact that she <u>wrote</u> (**not** "had written") a large number of popular mysteries.

On the GMAT, you will sometimes see the past perfect tense used when there is no justification for it. The GMAT writers are testing to see whether people will choose the answer with the past perfect just because it sounds exotic or impressive. You should select the past perfect only when the meaning of the sentence justifies it.

Exercise 6: Use of the Perfect Tenses. For each of the sentences below, decide whether each verb is in the correct tense. If a verb has the wrong tense, cross it out and correct it. (Additional exercises can be found on the website, testprepny.com)

1. Ever since the Great Depression, which gave FDR the political mandate he needed to enact the sweeping reforms of the New Deal, the majority of Americans thought of Social Security as an indispensable safety net.

2. When the prospectors and speculators known as the 49ers poured into California at the start of the Gold Rush, they had brought with them little beyond their clothes, their prospecting tools and their dreams of instant riches.

3. At the recently concluded meeting, the board has decided to focus on overseas expansion for the foreseeable future.

4. Archaeologists have recently discovered that the Maya had had a more complex writing system than is commonly believed to be the case.

For more practice

OG, 12th edition, Questions: 23, 47, 90, 139
OG, 13th edition, Question: 3, 14, 16, 23, 40, 47, 50, 70, 71, 72, 77, 89, 90, 128, 135

1.3 THE SUBJUNCTIVE

Read the following paragraph, paying particular attention to the underlined phrases. Do the verb forms sound correct to you?

It is essential that each person <u>be well-informed</u> about the issues of the day, as the first requirement of a democracy is that each citizen <u>vote</u> for the leadership he or she prefers—a task which proves impossible if the citizenry lacks the information needed to determine what the key issues are and what the aspiring leaders propose to do about them.

The underlined verbs are in the <u>present subjunctive</u> mood. The present subjunctive is used to describe an action that is considered necessary but which may or may not happen. It usually follows an expression of necessity, such as "It is imperative that…", "It is essential that…", or a verb such as "demand," "insist", or "suggest." The examples below are typical:

- It is essential that he be there on time.
- She demanded that the doctor explain the diagnosis more clearly.
- I suggested that he avoid eating sweets.
- It is imperative that she take the medication exactly as prescribed.

The form of the present subjunctive is the bare verb— no "s" on the end, no past tense marking. Notice the differences in meaning between the subjunctive and the indicative (a normal present or past-tense verb):

1. It's important that he be there. (Subjunctive: We don't know if he'll be there for sure, but he definitely should be there.)

2. It's important that he's there. (Indicative [not-subjunctive]: He is there, and that fact is important for some reason.)

3. She insisted that John be at the party. (Subjunctive: She told John, "You'd better be at the party!" We don't know if he actually showed up or not.)

4. She insisted that John was at the party. (Indicative [not-subjunctive]: People were arguing over whether or not John was at the party, and she insisted, "Yes, he was!")

GRAB A CLUE: Warning signs that a GMAT question is probably focused on the subjunctive include these: an expression of necessity ("It is essential...", "Inspectors demanded...", "On condition that..."), present or past tense verbs in some answer choices, and the word "should" in one of the answer choices.

'Should' is the incorrect choice in a sentence that requires the subjunctive.

British speakers take note: The use of *should* in this context is now considered correct in written British English, which has mostly dropped the use of the subjunctive; however, the GMAT is written by Americans, and so *should* will not be the credited answer. Many Americans are now also picking up the use of the word *should* in place of the subjunctive. This is a prime example of the mismatch between Everyday Conversational English and Formal Written English (what the GMAT wants). The choice with *should* is the trap, and the choice with the subjunctive will be correct. (This doesn't mean that an answer with *should* is always wrong on the GMAT. It means only that if you see *should* and an expression of necessity, you should be on your toes and thinking about whether the sentence needs the subjunctive.)

For example, suppose you see a question set up like this:

blah blah blah demanded that the company refund customers' money blah blah blah

a. the company refund customers' money

b. the company should refund customers' money

c. the company refunds customers' money

d. the company refunded customers' money

e. the company ought to refund customers' money

You have two clues that the GMAT may be looking for the subjunctive: there is an expression of necessity ("demand"), and choice B includes the word *should*, which is the classic trap that the GMAT sets for those who are less than fluent with the subjunctive. The correct answer here is A, which uses the subjunctive form.

Exercise 7: Subjunctive. Choose the best answer for each item below. (Additional exercises can be found on the website, testprepny.com)

1. Confident of its strategy despite an unprecedented spike in the rate of customer complaints, the Beatlejuice company has made the bold decision to ignore the growing chorus of critics who demand <u>that the product in question must be recalled</u>.

   a. that the product in question must be recalled

   b. that the product in question will be recalled

   c. that the product in question be recalled

   d. that the product in question should be recalled

   e. that the product in question ought to have been recalled

2. The members' organization that had insisted for months that the museum <u>increase hours and reduce admission fees</u> was soundly disappointed by the recent decision by the museum's board to cut back hours and raise fees instead.

   a. increase hours and reduce admission fees

   b. increases hours and reduces admission fees

   c. ought to have been increasing hours and reduced admission fees

   d. increased hours and reduced admission fees

   e. should increase hours and reduce admission fees

THE PAST SUBJUNCTIVE

The past subjunctive is used in statements employing *if* to indicate that something is only imaginary—not a real possibility. For example, "If I had a million dollars…" The past subjunctive is mostly not a problem to deal with on the GMAT, because it looks exactly like the past tense for all verbs except one: the verb *to be*. The subjunctive of *to be* is *were*—never *was*. For example:

- If I were you, I would stay home. (Not "If I was you…")

- If he were king, he would be a tyrant. (Not "If he was king…")

- If I knew the answer, I would tell you. (Past subjunctive *knew* looks just like past tense; nothing special to remember)

- If he actually called me, I would be astonished. (Past subjunctive *called* looks just like past tense; nothing special to remember)

 GRAB A CLUE: If some answer choices have the sequence "If… was…" and others have "If… were…" then the sentence is looking for the past subjunctive.

All you have to do is remember "If I Were a Rich Man" (note that it's not "If I Was a Rich Man"), and you should be able to handle the past subjunctive. For example:

The company soundly denied rumors of an imminent merger with its largest competitor; a company spokesman said that <u>if the rumor was true, it would indicate</u> a massive lapse in judgment on the part of the board of directors.

 a. if the rumor was true, it would indicate

 b. if the rumor were true, it would indicate

 c. if the rumor was true, it would have been indicating

 d. if the rumor was true, it should have indicated

 e. if the rumor were true, it would have been indicative that

The correct answer is (b).

Exercise 8: Increasing Familiarity with the Present Subjunctive. (Additional exercises can be found on the website, test-prepny.com)

Below is a collection of sentences and paragraphs drawn from various sources on the Internet. Find all the examples of subjunctive verbs that you can (some have more than one; you should find a total of **9** verbs). If the subjunctive feels new or unfamiliar to you, read these over more than once; you may even want to read them out loud. Your goal is to get used to this construction and recognize that, from the point of view of traditional written English (the kind of grammar the GMAT tests, and which some professional editors still insist on), the subjunctive is correct in these contexts. If it sounds odd to you, read the sentences again until it doesn't sound odd.

1. In front of a glass-enclosed display case outside the American Consulate here, clusters of Chinese gather silently to read material that the Chinese Government has demanded be removed.

2. I'd link to the brawl, but the NBA demanded that youtube.com remove all clips of the incident.

3. Previously, Mr. Bancroft has insisted News Corp. pay $66 a share—$6 more than it is offering—to the family in order to win his support for the transaction.

4. "From day one, I thought it was essential that everyone touch the project and get engaged in it."

For more practice

OG, 13th edition, Question: 54

You need to be careful about verb forms whenever the word "if" appears in the sentence. There are three constructions that can be confusing: the present hypothetical, the present counterfactual and the past counterfactual. Look at the difference between these three sentences:

I don't know how much money I have, but <u>if I have enough money, I will buy a car.</u>

I don't have any money, but <u>if I had enough money, I would buy a car.</u>

I didn't have any money, but <u>if I had had enough money, I would have bought a car.</u>

There are two common mistakes that native English speakers make in using these constructions, and both are sometimes tested on the GMAT.

Mistake #1: Mixing the three types of constructions. Speakers are sometimes sloppy when it comes to keeping the three types of constructions separate. In conversation, they sometimes mix the pieces of the three constructions. They may use the construction that means "possible but not certain" when talking about something that is impossible. They may also use the form that is appropriate for the present counterfactual (something not possible now) when they're talking about the past. This kind of mixing is considered incorrect on the GMAT.

INCORRECT: If the company can secure enough capital, it would expand its operations.

CORRECT: If the company can secure enough capital, it will expand its operations *or* If the company could secure enough capital, it would expand its operations.

INCORRECT: If I had known you were here yesterday, I would invite you over.

CORRECT: If I had known you were here yesterday, I would have invited you over.

Mistake #2: Using "would have" in the "if" part of the sentence. Many speakers use "would have" to set up the condition, as in "If I would have known what was going on, I would have acted differently." This is becoming common usage in many parts of the U.S., but it is still non-standard and is considered wrong on the GMAT.

INCORRECT: If I would have known about it, I would have done something.

CORRECT: If I had known about it, I would have done something.

Exercise 9: Identify any mistakes in the verb forms in these sentences. (Additional exercises can be found on the website, testprepny.com)

1. If I would've known that you were coming, I'd have baked a cake.

2. Had I but known about the problem, I could have done something.

3. The birds in the local area will not return if nothing were done about the cat problem.

4. If John knew about the problem last year, he would have taken care of it.

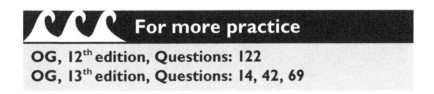

For more practice

OG, 12th edition, Questions: 122
OG, 13th edition, Questions: 14, 42, 69

MODULE 2: PRONOUNS

MODULE 2: PRONOUNS

2.1 TOP PRIORITY: YOU MUST BE ABLE TO QUICKLY SPOT WHAT IS WRONG WITH SENTENCES LIKE THESE:

- In Holland, they eat a lot of fish.

- The company announced today that they would begin a new round of layoffs within the next month.

- Anyone who wishes to apply for the position should submit their documents by the end of the week.

The words *they, them,* and *their* are pronouns. A pronoun is a special kind of noun: it needs another noun to make clear who or what it refers to. In the sentence "The stockholders said that *they* would support the proposal," "they" refers to the stockholders. The noun that the pronoun depends on in this way is called the antecedent.

 GRAB A CLUE: Whenever you see the words *they, them,* or *their,* the first thing you should do is check to make sure they're used correctly.

Be alert whenever you see the words they, them, or their.

Any time a GMAT sentence has the words *they, them,* or *their,* there must be a plural antecedent. This is another area in which conversational English is very different from formal written English. In everyday conversation, all of the sentences listed above would sound natural and unremarkable. On the GMAT, none of them would be credited. Because there is such a large gap between "what sounds OK in everyday conversation" and "what is considered correct on the GMAT," this is a favorite area for the GMAT to test. We can almost guarantee that you will see this point tested on the real GMAT.

Be careful: words such as *company, government, army, society, Japan, France,* or *the United States* are <u>not</u> plural antecedents. Even though they describe entities made up of large numbers of people, they describe each one as a singular entity.

CORRECT:

The government announced today that it will support the colonization of Mars.
The company's board of directors has made its position very clear.

INCORRECT:

The government announced that they will make skateboarding illegal.
The company reaffirmed that they will cooperate with investigators.

In addition, a noun phrase with the words *each* or *every* cannot be the antecedent for *they.* Recall that *each* and *every* are always singular; a plural pronoun such as *they* cannot refer back to them. In everyday conversation, it's common to hear sentences like "Everyone who wants to be in the band should bring their instrument." But on the GMAT, that sentence would be incorrect. (The most likely credited answer would be something like *Everyone who wants to be in the band should bring an instrument* or *Everyone who wants to be in the band should bring his or her instrument*. The use of *his* rather than *his or her* would also technically be correct, though the GMAT writers might try to avoid usage that is now commonly seen as sexist.)

Exercise 10: Determine whether the pronoun has an appropriate (plural) antecedent. (Additional exercises can be found on the website, testprepny.com)

1. Due to recent shortfalls in sales, the company has announced that they will have to lay off a number of workers.

2. Apparently convinced that they would have to act quickly to avert a strike, several top managers called for renewed negotiations.

3. Unlike companies in Japan, in the United States they have to pay the costs of workers' healthcare.

4. Announcing that contract negotiations had fallen through, the union declared that they were highly likely to call for a temporary work stoppage.

5. In Russia, unlike the United States, they frequently eat lemons with salt.

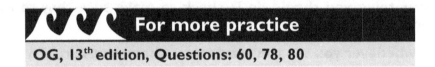

For more practice

OG, 13th edition, Questions: 60, 78, 80

In addition to the rules for the words *they*, *them*, and *their*, you need to learn the rules that cover other pronouns such as *he, him, his, she, her, it,* and *its*, as well as the distinction between *who* and *whom*. The word *this* is also used as a sort of pronoun in conversational English, but this usage is considered incorrect on the GMAT; we will cover this point in detail below.

Native English speakers, beware: you usually can't trust your ears when it comes to pronouns; you need to memorize all the rules covered in this section and rely on them. Non-native speakers should take heart and master the rules, because questions that test pronouns are usually questions on which a native grasp of "what sounds right" isn't required—in fact, thinking about "what sounds right" may just mislead a test taker who hasn't learned the rules. A non-native speaker who studies the rules has a realistic chance of doing as well as a native speaker when it comes to pronouns.

For all test takers, the appearance of a pronoun such as *it*, or *they*, or the word *this* standing alone (as in *This is a problem* or *This means...*), should immediately draw your attention. There's a high likelihood that some of the answer choices will have a mistake in the use of the pronoun, so you should use the pronoun clue to eliminate wrong answer choices as quickly as possible.

GRAB A CLUE: The words *it* and *they* are so often used incorrectly on GMAT SCs, if you see either one, this should be the very first thing you check.

One of the tricks the GMAT frequently pulls is to have a mismatch between a pronoun in the underlined portion of the sentence and an antecedent in the non-underlined part (or vice versa). People sometimes fall into this trap because they are thinking about their answer choice only in terms of one problem that they're trying to solve, and forget to make sure that everything goes together. Where you see pronouns in the sentence, it's essential that you mentally fit the pieces together and make sure that the whole sentence works. If the pronoun *it* appears in the sentence, make sure that it has a singular antecedent; if *they* appears, make sure the antecedent is plural.

Exercise 11: Decide which of the two choices should fit into the blank in the sentence. (Additional exercises can be found on the website, testprepny.com)

1. The cheetah (*Acinonyx jubatus*) is an atypical member of the cat family—unique in terms of speed, _____.

    a. while lacking climbing abilities, they are placed in their own genus, *Acinonyx*.

    b. while lacking climbing abilities, it is placed in its own genus, *Acinonyx*.

2. Fairies are generally described as tiny humans with wings, having magical powers and _____ which humans are strictly forbidden to enter.

    a. living in their own land, a place

    b. living in its own land, a place

3. The mandibular third molar (commonly known as the wisdom tooth) is the <u>tooth</u> located distally (away from the midline of the <u>face</u>) from both the <u>mandibular second molars</u> of the <u>mouth</u>, at the extreme posterior of the <u>permanent teeth</u>;

    a. they usually appear between the ages of 16 and 25

    b. it usually appears between the ages of 16 and 25

For more practice

OG, 12th edition, Questions: 1, 86, 91, 124, 139
OG, 11th edition, Questions: 25, 84, 93
OG Verbal Review, 2nd edition, Questions: 16, 19, 21, 40, 43, 48, 70
OG Verbal Review, 1st edition, Question: 74

2.3 MAKE SURE THAT THE PRONOUN 'IT' HAS AN ANTECEDENT

In everyday conversational English, we often use the pronoun *it* to sum up complex concepts, even when there is no specific antecedent. This is another example of divergence between spoken English and formal written English, so you should be on your toes. The GMAT frequently tests this point. The following examples would all be considered incorrect:

> If you cannot keep your balance on a windsurf board, it's an indication that the board is too small.

> The company decided to lay off several thousand people, but it wasn't because of a lack of money.

> A lot of people have lost money in the last few months, and it isn't going to get better any time soon.

In each case, the pronoun *it* lacks an antecedent—a noun that specifies what *it* refers to. In the first example above, it's clear that the speaker intends the word *it* to mean something like "the fact that you cannot keep your balance", but there is no noun for the word *it* to refer back to. This kind of "summarizing" usage of *it* is considered incorrect in formal written English. On the GMAT, the most common way to fix the problem is to insert a phrase in place of *it*:

> If you cannot keep your balance on a windsurf board, the difficulty is an indication that the board is too small.

> The company decided to lay off several thousand people, but this decision wasn't a result of a lack of money.

> A lot of people have lost money in the last few months, and the economic situation isn't going to get better any time soon.

In some cases the best fix on the GMAT will be a very different phrasing of the sentence. For example:

INCORRECT: Although Vicodin can be addictive, it can be avoided through careful monitoring of dosage.

BETTER: Addiction to Vicodin can be avoided through careful monitoring of dosage.

There is only one set of exceptions to the rule stating *it* requires an antecedent: sentences in which *it* serves as a "dummy subject." These include sentences such as the following, which do not have any errors:

> It is difficult to learn to ice skate like an Olympic champion.

> It is clear that there was nothing more anyone could have done.

> It has come to our attention that some of the expenditures have not been fully accounted for.

These sentences are different from the problematic sentences described earlier. In each of these cases, the word "it" is functioning as a kind of "place holder" for a clause that comes later in the sentence, which we've underlined in the following examples. The clause that comes later is, in a sense, the real subject of the entire sentence, and "it" is only standing in for it temporarily. This point becomes clearer if you think about the fact that the sentences could have been written like this:

> <u>To learn to ice skate like an Olympic champion</u> is difficult.

> <u>That there was nothing more anyone could have done</u> is clear.

> <u>That some of the expenditures have not been fully accounted</u> for has come to our attention.

These versions of the sentences are grammatical, but they don't sound like normal, everyday English. Speakers usually prefer to put the word *it* in the subject position and let it "stand in" for the heavy, complex clause that comes later. The word *it* is linked to the clause, as we can see if we think about each of the sentences:

> <u>It</u> is difficult to learn <u>to ice skate like an Olympic champion.</u> (What is difficult? To learn to ice skate like an Olympic champion.)

> <u>It</u> is clear <u>that there was nothing more anyone could have done.</u> (What is clear? That there was nothing more anyone could have done.)

> <u>It</u> has come to our attention <u>that some of the expenditures have not been fully accounted for.</u> (What has come to our attention? That some of the expenditures have not been fully accounted for.)

When *it* serves as a "dummy subject" or place holder in this way, this does not present a problem from the standpoint of GMAT English. **There is a problem with *it* only when *it* is being used to refer to something that was only vaguely described or alluded to. In other words, *it* is a problem if it is not being used as a dummy subject "holding a place" for an upcoming clause, but rather refers to something that is never clearly stated by any noun.**

Exercise 12: Decide whether *it* is used correctly (from the standpoint of formal written English) in each of the following sentences. (Additional exercises can be found on the website, testprepny.com)

1. If the groundhog doesn't see his shadow, it means that winter will soon be over.

2. It's obvious what the President will have to do.

3. When the rains fall for three weeks without let-up, it can lead to dangerous mudslides in the mountains.

4. The stars appear to twinkle, but it's only because of atmospheric disturbance.

5. It has now been established that human activity is an important cause of global warming.

For more practice

OG, 12th edition, Questions: 47, 71, 78, 86, 89, 101, 112
OG, 11th edition, Questions: 4, 110
OG Verbal Review, 2nd edition, Questions: 34, 64, 105

2.3.1 A MINOR RULE: BE CAREFUL IF THE ANTECEDENT IS POSSESSIVE

One minor rule of traditional grammar is the restriction on possessive antecedents. The rule is controversial even among grammarians, and is no longer tested on some other tests such as the SAT; it is unlikely to come up on a real GMAT, but the GMAC does make reference to the rule in its explanation of the answer for one official question (Verbal Supplement, question #86). It's prudent, therefore, to take a moment to review the rule, but we do not recommend that you devote a great deal of time to mastering it.

The rule is that a possessive noun (a noun that ends with apostrophe "s," such as *Sally's*, *Cathy's*, or the *corporation's*) can serve as an antecedent only for a possessive pronoun (such as *his*, *her*, *its*, or *their*), not for a subject or object pronoun. In other words, these sentences would be considered incorrect:

INCORRECT: <u>F. Scott Fitzgerald's</u> first novel was so brilliant that <u>he</u> was immediately hailed as an important new voice in literature.

INCORRECT: <u>The bank's</u> liquidity problems were so severe that <u>it</u> was forced to file for bankruptcy.

INCORRECT: <u>The woman's</u> daughters decided that <u>she</u> should move into an assisted living facility.

The rationale is that the possessive noun is technically no longer a noun—by being made possessive, it has been transformed into a kind of adjective. It therefore cannot be the antecedent for a subject or object pronoun, but it can serve as the antecedent for possessive pronouns (which presumably are also a kind of adjective). These sentences would therefore be considered correct:

CORRECT: <u>F. Scott Fitzgerald's</u> first novel was so brilliant that it seemed <u>his</u> future as a literary icon was already established.

CORRECT: <u>The bank's</u> liquidity problems were so severe that <u>its</u> board of directors filed for bankruptcy.

CORRECT: <u>The woman's</u> daughters decided that <u>her</u> problems warranted a move to an assisted living facility.

This rule is mentioned very rarely in official materials from GMAC, and is in fact, not accepted as a valid rule of English grammar by many grammarians. You should make a mental note of it, but GMAT experts disagree on how likely it is that you will need to apply this rule on an actual GMAT.

2.4 WATCH OUT WHEN 'THIS' APPEARS WITHOUT A NOUN

 GRAB A CLUE: If you see the word *this* without a noun (as in "This has caused problems"), watch out!

The use of the word *this* is another area in which conversational English is different from the kind of formal written English tested on the GMAT. Once again, native speakers will need to study the rule and ignore their ears. In formal written English, the word *this* should always have a noun together with it. In everyday speech, the rules for using *this* aren't nearly as strict. We often use *this* as a sort of pronoun to refer back to something that has been vaguely hinted at or described in a roundabout way, so that the listener has to figure out what *this* refers to by interpreting a whole sentence. This kind of usage would be considered imprecise and therefore would not be credited on the GMAT. Notice the difference between the incorrect and correct sentences in the following pairs:

INCORRECT: Heating oil has become very expensive, and <u>this</u> is a huge problem for residents of New England.

CORRECT: Heating oil has become very expensive, and <u>this development</u> is a huge problem for residents of New England.

INCORRECT: Astronomers recently declared that Pluto is not a planet; <u>this</u> came as a shock to many people.

CORRECT: Astronomers recently declared that Pluto is not a planet; <u>this announcement</u> came as a shock to many people.

INCORRECT: The moon is not actually made of green cheese, but <u>this</u> was apparently not clear to some naïve people.

CORRECT: The moon is not actually made of green cheese, but <u>this fact</u> was apparently not clear to some naïve people.

INCORRECT: Many people imagine that the flow of electricity is like that of water, but <u>this</u> is not an accurate model of what is actually going on.

CORRECT: Many people imagine that the flow of electricity is like that of water, but <u>this analogy</u> is not an accurate model of what is actually going on.

In each incorrect sentence, the word *this* is used in an imprecise way. Of course, those sentences may not sound imprecise to you, because in spoken English this usage is common—and that is why the GMAT is likely to test this distinction. Notice that the correct version of each sentence provides a noun that pins down the concept that *this* refers to.

> *The*
> *fastest   way   to*
> *learn anything is to imitate*
> *a role model. Think about how*
> *you learned to walk, speak, write the*
> *alphabet and tie your shoes. In the early*
> *years, learning by imitation dominates. ...*
> *Imitating what you admire in others and*
> *want to acquire for yourself requires becom-*
> *ing their student, not their judge and jury.*
> *As a student of the assets of human nature,*
> *you are now ready to spot the best of*
> *what anyone has to offer. Enjoy!*

Cramer, KD, and Wasiak, H.[58]

Exercise 13: Decide whether *it* or *this* is used appropriately in each of the following sentences. If there is a mistake, correct it (you may need to do some serious revision of the sentence). (Additional exercises can be found on the website, testprepny.com)

1. Another major bank announced plans for a merger today; this stirred up fresh speculation about future changes in the financial sector.

2. If you are repeatedly late in paying your credit card bills, it will have a negative impact on your credit rating.

3. Though many people feel a craving for carbohydrates in the winter, this response to cold weather is not universal.

4. Though some people were surprised to hear that the new movie had done so well at the box office, it didn't come as any surprise to those who had seen the work in previews.

5. Columbus was not, in fact, the first white person to journey to North America, but this wasn't proven until the remains of ancient Viking settlements were found by archaeologists.

6. It has often been observed that, when all is said and done, there is a great deal more said than done.

7. If one studies just a couple of hours each day, it will add up to a considerable time investment after just one month.

8. The announcement of massive layoffs came as a surprise to many people, but to some analysts, this development was a long-overdue response to an obvious problem.

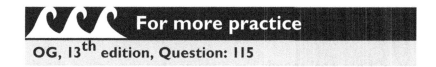

For more practice

OG, 13th edition, Question: 115

When the GMAT uses *it* in a comparison, there's often a problem. Usually the word *it* will incorrectly limit the comparison to a single, specific item, or otherwise make the comparison awkward or nonsensical. For example:

> **INCORRECT:** The General Accounting Office estimates that this year's GDP will be 1.3% lower than it was last year.

What does *it* refer to? Logically, it seems it must refer to "this year's GDP." Therefore, the sentence is saying that the GDP for this year will be 1.3% lower this year than the GDP for this year was last year. A better version:

> **BETTER:** The General Accounting Office estimates that this year's GDP will be 1.3% lower than last year's.

You should also watch out for antecedents of *it* that simply don't make sense, as in "While the term *decimation* is often understood to mean a complete massacre, it is actually a situation in which one out of ten people is killed." The term *decimation* isn't any kind of a situation; it's a term. Therefore, it doesn't make sense to say "it is a situation." A better version would be, "… it actually describes a situation in which one out of ten people is killed."

Exercise 14: Decide whether *it* makes sense in each sentence below. If it doesn't, correct the sentence (you may need to make significant changes). (Additional exercises can be found on the website, testprepny.com)

1. Thanks to modern agricultural techniques, the current crop of alfalfa is much healthier than it was just ten years ago.

2. A rock from space that crashes on the earth's surface is a meteorite, but if it merely enters the atmosphere but doesn't hit the ground, it is a meteor.

3. The concept of clean coal sounds like a major step forward in the fight against global warming, but in fact it doesn't exist yet.

4. Federal regulations that were put in place after the Great Depression ensure that the modern banking system is much healthier than it was in the early 20th century.

5. The economic situation that the nation currently faces is much more serious than it was in the 1980s.

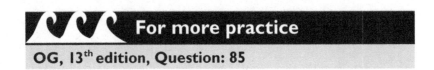
For more practice

OG, 13th edition, Question: 85

GRAB A CLUE: Be alert when you see the word *that* or *those* used in comparisons, as explained below. Make sure the word is used correctly.

When a sentence makes a comparison of two similar things—similar enough that some of the same words would be used to describe both things—writers often use the words *that* or *those* to avoid repeating some of the words. For example, a writer could pen the rather repetitious sentence "The production of the play in 1993 wasn't as good as the production of the play in 1939." It's neater and more economical, though, to write "The production of the play in 1993 wasn't as good as that in 1939." The word "that" stands for "production of the play."

Here are a few more examples:

The effect of honey on blood sugar levels appears to be less dramatic than **that** of regular white sugar ("that" stands for "the effect…on blood sugar levels").

In an effort to determine whether Pixar truly rules the world of animation, the five best animated movies from Pixar were compared with **those** from its most prominent rivals ("those" stands for "the five best animated movies").

There are two common ways that GMAT sentences may contain mistakes in the use of *that* or *those*. There may be a mismatch in number between the noun that *that* or *those* is standing in for, or there may be no noun for those words to stand in for in the first place. Let's look at each of these traps separately.

Mismatch of number: The word *that* or *those* can be used to stand in for a noun, but there has to be an original noun or noun phrase **somewhere else in the sentence** so that we know which word(s) are being replaced by *that* or *those*. The original noun has to agree in number with either *that* or *those*: if the original noun is singular, only *that* can be used, and if it is plural, only *those* is correct. Even if the local phrase *that* or *those* appears in seems to require singular or plural, the sentence won't be correct if there's a mismatch between *that* or *those* and the original noun.

CORRECT: During the lead-up to the American Revolution, <u>supporters of the King</u> who lived in Boston were harassed much more often than were <u>those</u> who lived in New York.

INCORRECT: During the lead-up to the American Revolution, <u>any supporter of the King</u> who lived in Boston was harassed much more often than were <u>those</u> who lived in New York.

CORRECT: The <u>venom</u> of the tarantula is much less toxic than <u>that</u> of some other large spiders.

INCORRECT: The <u>venom</u> of the tarantula is much less toxic than <u>those</u> of some other large spiders.

In the second pair of sentences, notice that it might seem more logical to use *those*, because now we're talking about the venom of many different kinds of spiders. Nevertheless, *that* is required, to go with the original noun *venom*. A similar rationale applies to the next pair:

> **CORRECT**: The <u>cost</u> of proton therapy is far less than <u>that</u> of the various alternatives.

> **INCORRECT**: The <u>cost</u> of proton therapy is far less than <u>those</u> of the various alternatives.

That or *those* with no noun at all: GMAT sentences sometimes try to trick you by using the word *that* or *those* when there is no original noun to refer to. These sentences are usually complex, and the GMAT writers take advantage of the complexity by throwing in an unnecessary *that*. For example:

> So difficult and costly was the restructuring, with so many unknown variables, that analysts monitoring the situation had no expectation <u>that</u> the company would outlast that of its competitors.

What does the underlined *that* in the sentence refer to? There is no noun that would have to be repeated if 'that' weren't there. It doesn't make any sense, and should be taken out. Here's another example:

> Medical ethics guidelines mandate that plastic surgeons who provide elective surgery with no tangible health benefits disclose the worst possible outcomes rather than merely showcase those of the best.

What does *those* in this sentence refer to? You might think it's *the outcomes*. Let's test that idea by putting *the outcomes* into the sentence in place of the word *those*:

> Medical ethics guidelines mandate that plastic surgeons who provide elective surgery with no tangible health benefits disclose the worst possible outcomes rather than merely showcase the outcomes of the best.

The difficulty now is that "the best" is obviously short for "the best outcomes," so the end of the sentence means "the outcomes of the best outcomes." It doesn't make sense.

Remember to mentally "plug in" the word or phrase that *that* or *those* is supposed to be standing in for, to make sure it sounds right and makes sense.

Let's look at one more example:

> **INCORRECT**: Unlike the standard treatment for metastatic cancer, the new treatment does not use fluorouracil as the radiosensitizing chemical agent to enhance the radiation effects, but rather uses <u>that</u> of gemcitabine.

What does *that* mean here? To figure out what it stands for, we need to find a phrase "NOUN of NOUN", parallel to "that of gemcitabine", so that we can tell which noun *that* is standing in for. But there isn't any such phrase. Once again, the use of *that* doesn't make sense.

On the GMAT, you should especially watch out for mistakes with *that* in sentences that involve comparison of numbers. For example:

> In 1880, 107,000 Chinese immigrants came into the United States, a number double that of 1870's.

What could *that* refer to here? If you read it as *number*, the sentence reads, "...a number double the number of 1870's," which is clearly wrong. A better version would avoid *that*:

> In 1880, 107,000 Chinese immigrants came into the United States, twice as many as in 1870.

Exercise 15: Decide whether the word *that* or *those* is used correctly in each of these sentences.

1. The illustrations by Roberts are more evocative than those by Townsend.

2. At 2008 fuel prices, battery powered buses are more economical than those of diesel or gasoline powered buses.

3. In an electric vehicle, gasoline is indirectly replaced by whatever is being used to generate domestic electricity, reducing dependence on that of foreign commodities.

4. Last year, the number of applicants to the fellowship program reached 78, double that of the previous year's.

5. The plot twists at the end of the movie were in some ways less surprising than those at the beginning.

For more practice

OG, 12th edition, Questions: 92
OG, 13th edition, Questions: 20, 85

2.7 WHO VERSUS WHOM

 GRAB A CLUE: If the answer choices include some with *who* and some with *whom*, focus in on that distinction.

We know for a fact that the distinction between *who* and *whom* is still being tested on the GMAT, despite the lack of examples in the current edition of the Official Guide. You may not get a question on *who* vs. *whom* in your exam, but if you do, it will probably be a high-level question that will help make the difference between a very good score and a stellar score.

The distinction between these two words confuses some people because *whom* is not used often in everyday speech. The difference is actually simple, though. It's a matter of the distinction between subjects and objects, so let's quickly review that first. The subject of the sentence is the noun that the verb agrees with. In a normal active-voice sentence, the subject is the person who's doing something. The object, in contrast, is the one that gets done too. For example:

The <u>cat</u> [subject] bit the <u>dog</u> [object].

The <u>woman</u> [subject] read the <u>newspaper</u> [object].

<u>Colonel Ketchup</u> [subject] stabbed <u>Professor Prune</u> [object].

The next thing to be aware of is that in English, most of the pronouns have different forms depending on whether the pronoun is serving as the subject or the object. The different forms are shown in this chart:

Subject Pronouns	Object Pronouns
I	me
you	you
he	him
she	her
it	it
we	us
they	them

Native speakers almost never think about this, of course—they just use the form that sounds right—but "what sounds right" actually depends on whether the pronoun is the subject or object of the verb.

You can hear the distinction if we compare some sentences that sound right with a few that don't sound so good. In the first group of sentences below, the subjects are all subject pronouns, and the objects are all object pronouns, so the sentences sound correct:

<u>I</u> saw <u>him</u> at the post office.

<u>He</u> kissed <u>me</u> on the doorstep.

<u>She</u> hired <u>him</u> immediately.

<u>We</u> took them <u>home</u>.

<u>They</u> threw <u>us</u> out at midnight.

Now look at what happens if we use the wrong forms. If you're a native speaker or a fluent non-native speaker, the sentences below will probably sound pretty bad to you:

<u>Me</u> saw <u>he</u> at the post office.

<u>Him</u> kissed <u>I</u> on the doorstep.

<u>Her</u> hired <u>he</u> immediately.

<u>Us</u> took <u>they</u> home.

<u>Them</u> threw <u>we</u> out at midnight.

For ordinary pronouns, any competent speaker can hear which form is right, at least in a basic, everyday sentence. The distinction between *who* and *whom* is <u>exactly the same distinction</u>.

Who is the subject form, and *whom* is the object form. In other words, using *who* when you should use *whom* is the same kind of mistake as using *he* when you should use *him*.

So why is it so hard to hear when you should use who and when you should use *whom*? Because the English language is undergoing a process of change, and the object form *whom* is actually dying out. We don't use it in everyday speech very often, so it's hard to hear when the rules of formal written English require it. For example, both sentences of the following pair may <u>sound</u> right, but only one is correct in formal written English:

CORRECT (though we don't talk this way):
Whom did you see?

INCORRECT (though common in speech):
Who did you see?

The word *whom* is required because the question is asking about the object of the verb. We would say "I saw <u>him</u>," not "I saw <u>he</u>," so *whom* is right.

In spoken English, the only time many native speakers of English feel the need to use *whom* is when it directly follows a preposition, as in certain old-fashioned expressions like "<u>For whom</u> the bell tolls" or "Do have any idea <u>to whom</u> you're speaking?" When it comes right after a preposition such as *for, to, from*, etc., the preposition seems to prod speakers into remembering that *whom* is required. The rest of the time, most people who aren't fluent in formal written English are likely to feel unsure when to use *whom*. (This is another area in which a non-native speaker can learn to apply the rules just as well as, or better than, native speakers who rely on their ears. If your first language has a pair of distinct forms parallel to the distinction between *who* and *whom*—and many languages do—you may even have a leg up.)

How can you be sure when to choose *who* or *whom* for a GMAT SC? You need to determine whether it's the subject or object of the verb. For example:

Police still don't know <u>who/whom</u> triggered the alarm.

Try rewriting the sentence just a little to make it a statement. Substitute the pronouns *he* and *him* for *who* and *whom* and see which one sounds better:

The police know he triggered the alarm. (OR)

The police know him triggered the alarm.

In some cases it's a little more challenging to decide which form to use, because if you <u>just</u> substitute *he* or *him* for *who* or *whom*, it still may not sound like English. Take our example from up above, "Whom did you see?" If you try to test whether that's right by changing it to "Him did you see," it sounds like a bad attempt at poetry. What you need is to figure out what role the *whom* or *who* plays in the sentence; do that by coming up with a version that is reworded as little as possible but still seems to mean basically the same thing. For instance, change "Him did you see" to "You saw him"—now it sounds like normal English, but it clearly means the same thing, whereas "He saw you" changes the meaning completely.

Sometimes the GMAT tests the who/whom distinction by using a relative clause—a modifier that looks like a question attached to the noun, as in "the man <u>who married my sister</u>." When *who* or *whom* appears in a relative clause, the choice of which to use is determined by whether it's the subject or object <u>inside the relative clause</u>, not by anything going on outside of it. For example:

I met the man <u>who invented a new kind of solar battery.</u>

Who is the subject of "invented," so it's the right choice. Take another example:

The man <u>whom my sister married</u> turned out to be a very odd fellow.

Whom is the object of "married," so it's the right choice here.

The way to test which is correct is to ignore the noun that the relative clause is attached to, and just re-word the relative clause itself as a test sentence. For example, in this case ignore "the man" and just look at "whom my sister married":

my sister married him

my sister married he

When you're dealing with a relative clause, ignore the part that comes before *who* or *whom* and just focus in on the relative clause itself. When you're dealing with a sentence that involves multiple verbs, don't ignore any part of the sentence, but just change the *who* or *whom* to *he* or *him* in the usual way. Then see if you need to rearrange things a little to get something that sounds like English. Let's try two examples.

1. The police did not know who/whom was responsible for the break-in.

Would you say "The police did not know he was responsible" or "The police did not know him was responsible"? It's the first one, so "who" is the right form – it's the subject of "was responsible."

2. The police did not know who/whom to blame for the break-in.

This one is a little trickier. You may already have a feeling that who/whom in this case is functioning as the object of "blame", but if you're not sure, you can try making test sentences. The problem is that "The police did not know he to blame" sounds bad, and so does "The police did not know him to blame." So change it just enough to make it sound like English, trying to keep the meaning as close as you can—how about "The police did not know whether to blame him"? That's pretty close, whereas if we try to make something like "The police did not whether he to blame", we still don't have English. We can be pretty confident that we're dealing with the object of the verb "blame" (and we are), and therefore it should be "whom."

Here's one more that is a bit trickier:

The politician who/whom most historians believe to be responsible for the outcome was a freshman senator at the time.

This is an example of a relative clause. Remember that you should ignore the noun that the relative clauses is attached to ("politician") and just think about the relative clause itself. We get "most historians believe him to be responsible for the outcome." That sounds correct, whereas "Most historians believe he to be responsible" isn't correct. So the right form is *whom*.

Exercise 16: Decide whether *who* or *whom* is correct in each sentence. (Additional exercises can be found on the website, testprepny.com)

1. No one knows who/whom first invented the alphabet.

2. Isabella was thrilled to meet the woman who/whom was believed to have painted the portrait.

3. Despite numerous attempts to determine who/whom was responsible for the debacle, the investigation never yielded any fruit.

4. Whoever/whomever is eventually found to have authorized the decision will have a great deal of explaining to do.

5. The person to who/whom the letter is addressed must sign for it.

2.8 WATCH OUT FOR 'DO IT' VERSUS 'DO SO'

When one is comparing actions or talking about repeating an action, *do so* is preferable to *do it*. Consider the following examples:

1. Some senators oppose giving federal aid to cash-strapped corporations, because they believe that to do it only encourages corporate executives to take unnecessary risks.

2. Some people do not see the value in having regular checkups, and think that doing it is an unnecessary expense.

3. The nations of the world must work together to address global warming; failure to do it will have catastrophic consequences.

In each of these cases, the GMAT would consider "do it" to be awkward and unclear, since there isn't an antecedent for *it*; the credited choice in each of these would be "do so." So remember, regardless of what Nike—or its advertising agency—might want you to think, don't "just do it"—just "do so."

For more practice
OG Verbal Review, 2ⁿᵈ edition, Questions: 62, 76

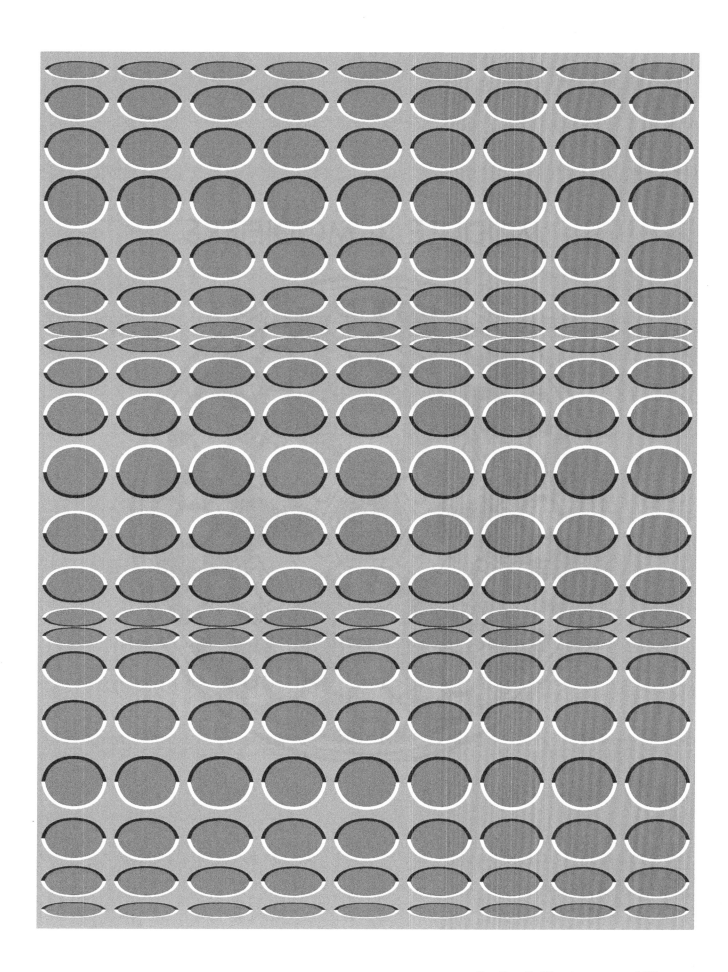

MODULE 3: MODIFIERS

MODULE 3: MODIFIERS

3.1 TOP PRIORITY: DON'T LET MODIFIERS DANGLE

You must immediately spot what is wrong with sentences like these:

- A creative genius of wit and style, Sondheim's musicals have won many awards.

- When evaluating fine wines, cabernets are often appreciated for their complex flavors.

- Often cited as a favorite of many critics, the fans chose <u>Pride and Prejudice</u> as the best Jane Austen novel of all time.

Though the sentences look different, the problem with each of these is the same: each begins with a dangling modifier.

First let's get clear about what modifiers are. The basic components of a sentence are a verb and the nouns that go with it—the subject and object(s). A very simple sentence such as <u>I gave John the book</u> consists of nothing more than a verb and three nouns. None of those are modifiers. Sentences more complicated than that one, though, typically have any number of **modifiers**: words or phrases that provide additional information. Modifiers tell you things about when/where/how/why, beyond the basic "who and what" that you get from the subject and object(s).

Here are some examples to give you the general idea (the modifiers are underlined):

> <u>Shocked by the news</u>, John sent off some <u>urgent</u> e-mails.

> <u>Driving to work</u>, Cynthia saw snowmen <u>dressed up as characters from a Tolkien novel</u>.

> <u>Outside the courtroom</u>, reporters waited <u>anxiously</u>.

> <u>Because he's such a nice guy</u>, Sam does <u>volunteer</u> work <u>for a charity</u>.

> <u>At least once a month</u>, Sally likes to go shopping <u>at the thrift stores</u>.

A modifier is considered "dangling" if it isn't properly connected with the word or phrase it modifies. SCs that have dangling modifiers at the beginning of the sentence are extremely common on the GMAT. If you learn to identify these patterns quickly and reliably, you will be able to answer these SC questions very easily. You should aim to identify the most common types of dangling modifiers <u>very</u> quickly. In some examples we have seen in official material, it is possible to identify the dangling modifier and find the one answer choice that fixes it in just under 15 seconds. The time you save by identifying a dangling modifier quickly can be applied to harder questions.

SCs that test modifiers most commonly involve phrases that have a gerund (an *–ing* word), or a passive participle (a word like *broken, stolen, shocked, exhausted*). If a phrase like that comes at the beginning of the sentence, **the person or thing described by the modifier must be the subject of the sentence.**

These are examples of modifiers used correctly (not dangling):

> <u>Lying down for a nap</u>, <u>he</u> discovered that the couch was covered with cat hair.

> <u>Utterly exhausted</u>, <u>the team</u> decided to wait til morning before attempting the summit.

> <u>Frozen with fear</u>, <u>the thief</u> decided it was better to surrender than to risk getting shot.

> <u>Upon arriving at the skating rink</u>, the girl decided to warm up with some simple moves first.

When one of these modifiers is "dangling," that means it's not describing the subject of the sentence. These sentences all have dangling modifiers:

> Lying down for a nap, his first shock was finding out that the couch was covered with cat hair ("shock" can't be lying down for a nap).

> Utterly exhausted, it would be advisable for the team to wait til morning before attempting the summit (*it* isn't utterly exhausted).

> Frozen with fear, the thief's impulse was to run ("impulse" isn't frozen with fear, the thief is—but "impulse" is the subject).

> Upon arriving at the skating rink, the warm-up began with some simple moves ("the warm-up" didn't arrive at the skating rink).

ALL OF THOSE SENTENCES WOULD BE CONSIDERED WRONG ON THE GMAT

The same rule applies if the sentence starts with a noun that essentially provides an alternate description of the subject. A noun phrase used in this way is known as an <u>appositive</u>, and when it appears at the beginning of a sentence, it must modify the subject:

> A lifelong environmental activist, Sally once spent a week protesting logging in the Amazon. (*Correct: Sally is a lifelong environmental activist.*)

A videogame addict, John once forgot to eat for a week. (*Correct: John is a videogame addict.*)

A lifelong activist, the protester had attended hundreds of demonstrations over the years. (*Correct: the protester is a masterful card player.*)

An amazingly skilled composer, Mozart's compositions achieved immediate fame. (*Incorrect: Mozart's <u>compositions</u> weren't an amazingly skilled composer.*)

A passionate idealist, there was no way that the lawyer could refuse the case. (*Incorrect: "there" is not a passionate idealist.*)

A lifelong activist, the protester's arrest came as a shock to him. (*Incorrect: "the protester's <u>arrest</u>" isn't a lifelong activist.*)

Native speakers especially should take note that phrases that look like dangling modifiers are wrong on the GMAT. This is true even if they are well-worn expressions that are used in everyday conversation so often that it's hard to believe that the GMAT would insist on reading them as dangling modifiers in the first place. For example:

INCORRECT: Based on the evidence so far, we can conclude that the murderer was a kleptomaniac.

INCORRECT: Taking everything into consideration, this form of cancer isn't the worst one out there.

These sentences start with familiar phrases that are hard to read as dangling modifiers, but the GMAT would insist that they are. In other words, *we* aren't based on the evidence and *this form of cancer* isn't taking everything into consideration. The GMAT requires that you read these sentences that way (as unnatural as this may feel to a fluent speaker), and recognize that they're technically incorrect.

The only definite exception to this rule is the idiom "According to...," which does not have to be read as modifying the subject of the sentence. Some test prep manuals claim that any well-known idiom of this type is an exception to the dangling modifier rule, but this has not been borne out by our research.

 GRAB A CLUE: Whenever you see an SC item begin with an *–ing* phrase, a phrase based on a past participle (*-ed* or *–en*), or a noun phrase followed by a comma (as in "A widely respected expert, blah blah blah"), your first priority should be to check and to see whether the question is testing for dangling modifiers.

Note:

The rule requiring the modifier to refer to the subject of the clause applies when a modifier comes before the clause. When a modifier beginning with a gerund (an *–ing*) comes after a clause, it doesn't have to refer to the noun that it's closest to. Instead, it can be understood to modify the subject of the clause or the action

described in the clause, or both. Typically it describes a secondary action that takes place simultaneously with the action described in the clause. It does not have to be read as modifying the noun that comes just before it (and in fact, generally speaking it cannot be read that way). For example:

The hippopotamus ran through the house, smashing furniture as it went.

The modifier "smashing furniture as it went" clearly describes something the hippopotamus did, not the house. This is correct usage.

You should also note that a prepositional phrase that comes at the beginning of the sentence does <u>not</u> have to describe the subject of the sentence. These sentences would all be correct:

In his most famous work, F. Scott Fitzgerald explored the ways that desire can warp a person's behavior. (OK, and doesn't mean that F. Scott Fitzgerald was in his most famous work.)

In addition to sculpture, Leonardo Da Vinci was a master of painting, engineering, and anatomy. (OK, and doesn't mean that Leonardo Da Vinci was in addition to sculpture.)

On top of the cake, the chef placed a tiny figurine of a unicorn. (OK, and doesn't mean the chef was on top of the cake.)

To summarize: The requirement that a modifier at the beginning of a clause describe the subject applies to these types of phrases; therefore you should be careful when you see a sentence beginning with any of these, all of which are common on the GMAT:

Modifiers using an –*ing* form

Modifiers using past participles

Appositives (noun phrases)

Comparative phrases such as *Like X...* or *Unlike X...* (these are covered extensively in the next module)

Exercise 17: Decide which of these sentences have dangling modifiers. For those that are incorrect, write corrected versions (there is more than one way to correct each of the incorrect ones). (Additional exercises can be found on the website, testprepny.com)

1. Born in Frankfurt, Germany, Frank and her family moved to Amsterdam in 1933, after the Nazis gained power in Germany.

2. Long unknown to most people, researchers have discovered a new composition by Mozart.

3. Using a variety of sophisticated techniques, archaeologists have been able to establish the age of the artifacts with reasonable certainty.

4. Struck by the remarkable coincidence, the reporter asked whether he could do a feature story on the recently reunited triplets.

5. Though outraged by the situation, there was nothing the lawyer could do.

For more practice

OG, 12th edition, Questions: 25, 56, 61, 79, 110, 135
OG, 11th edition, Question: 72
OG Verbal Review, 2nd edition, Questions: 9, 11, 57, 59, 106, 111, 113
OG Verbal Review, 1st Edition, Question: 38

3.2 WATCH OUT FOR BADLY PLACED MODIFIERS LATER IN THE SENTENCE

In addition to the more obvious and common examples of dangling modifiers at the beginnings of sentences, the GMAT often tests more subtle examples of bad modifier placement. Consider the following examples:

1. Ambiguous: The author described how the war began in three dense chapters. (Sounds as if the war began in three dense chapters.)

   Better: In three dense chapters, the author described how the war began.

2. Ambiguous: The main character is skating on page 33 of the novel. (Sounds as if page 33 is a flat surface on which the character is skating.)

   Better: On page 33 of the novel, the author describes the main character ice skating.

3. Ambiguous: The theater is so large that it is best to watch the actors with binoculars. (Should one use binoculars to see the actors, or should one make sure to watch the actors who have binoculars?)

   Better: The theater is so large, it is best to use binoculars to watch the actors.

4. Ambiguous: Many people don't realize that it is possible to see several moons circling Jupiter without a telescope. (Can one see the moons without using a telescope, or can one see the moons that don't have a telescope?)

   Better: Many people don't realize that one does not need a telescope to see several moons circling Jupiter.

5. Ambiguous: The police inspector explained how the killer carried out the murder by using a diagram on a blackboard. (Was the murder committed with the use of a diagram?)

   Better: Using diagram on a blackboard, the police inspector explained how the killer carried out the murder.

The key to handling these kinds of questions is to compare the answer choices and determine whether one arrangement of the phrases is less ambiguous than the others.

 GRAB A CLUE: If the sentence has a lot of modifiers and more than one version of the sentence sounds perfectly good to you, check for subtle problems with modifier placement, such as those shown in the examples above.

For more practice

OG, 12ᵗʰ edition, Questions: 26, 56, 105, 107, 111
OG, 11ᵗʰ edition, Question: 120
OG Verbal Review, 2ⁿᵈ edition, Questions: 33, 79, 83, 105, 109, 110, 111
OG Verbal Review, 1ˢᵗ edition, Question: 21

3.3 MAKE SURE RELATIVE CLAUSES ARE WELL-FORMED

Relative clauses are modifiers of a particular kind: they are clauses (phrases with a subject and a verb) that modify nouns. In these examples, the relative clauses are underlined:

The man <u>who lives next door to me</u> collects antique muskets.

The last thing <u>I want to do</u> is get in your way.

That movie about elves, <u>which I finally saw last week</u>, was pretty offbeat.

Relative clauses often (but not always) begin with question words such as *who* or *which*, or with the word *that*. These function to connect the relative clause to the noun. For example, in "The man *who* lives next door to me", the word *who* refers to the man and makes clear what role the man plays in the relative clause (*who* is the subject of the clause <u>*who* lives next door to me</u>). There are a few rules you should be aware of concerning the choice of connecting words.

3.3.1 USE 'WHO' TO REFER TO A PERSON.

"Which" should never be used to refer to a person.

CORRECT: the man <u>who</u> lives next door to me

INCORRECT: the man <u>which</u> lives next door to me

The same rule applies to *that*—even though many speakers, in everyday speech, use *that* as a connecting word to refer to a person, it's considered wrong in GMAT-style English to do so. This distinction is definitely still being tested on the GMAT. The correct choice in this kind of sentence is "who."

CORRECT: the man <u>who</u> lives next door to me

INCORRECT: the man <u>that</u> lives next door to me

> ### For more practice
> **OG, 12th edition, Question: 63**
> **OG, 13th edition, Questions: 29, 33, 40, 65, 67, 73, 86, 87, 90, 102, 105, 113, 123**

3.3.2 WATCH OUT FOR 'WHICH'

 GRAB A CLUE: Sit up and take notice whenever you see the word *which* on the GMAT. It may not be an error, but you should immediately check to make sure.

Be careful when you see the word *which* on the GMAT. In everyday conversational English, we often use *which* to summarize an entire clause or situation:

My friend was three hours late for dinner, which totally ticked me off.

On the GMAT, that would be incorrect—the word *which* is summing up the entire clause ("my friend was three hours late for dinner"). By the rules of formal written English, a relative clause using *which* should modify only the noun it is attached to. In other words, that sentence would be correct only if the speaker meant that somehow <u>dinner</u> ticked him/her off—just dinner, not the whole situation. Because of the large difference between casual conversational English and formal written English on this one point, the GMAT seems to test this frequently, especially in the higher-level questions. Therefore, you should always be on your toes when you see the word *which*; it may in fact be acceptable usage in a particular case, but you have to read carefully and think about the usage to make sure.

> It's OK to use *which* as a connecting word if the relative clause describes the noun that *which* is attached to, like this:

> My friend cooked a delicious dinner, *which* consisted of salmon, broccoli and rice pudding.

> Here the dinner consisted of salmon, broccoli and rice pudding, so the sentence is OK.

> It's also OK to use *which* to refer to a complex noun phrase:

> I recently bought a picture of a lighthouse, *which* I hung in the hallway. (The picture was hung in the hallway, not the lighthouse—but the complete noun phrase is "picture of a lighthouse" so it's OK.)

You simply can't use *which* to "reach back" into the sentence and summarize the entire situation described by the clause. You also can't use *which* if there isn't any noun at all, as in this sentence:

> My friend is incredibly smart, *which* makes me envious.

Since it doesn't make sense to say "smart makes me envious," this sentence would be considered wrong on the GMAT. But again, it would sound perfectly normal and natural in everyday speech, making this type of usage a perfect target for the GMAT test writers. The bottom line is, when you see *which*, be alert!

In many (though not all) cases, the best re-write for a bad use of "which" would be a construction with an –ing modifier after the clause, since modifiers with –ing are allowed to modify the whole clause rather than just the noun:

INCORRECT: My friend drove straight through a red light, which scared me half to death.

CORRECT: My friend drove straight through a red light, scaring me half to death.

In other cases, the best re-write for a bad use of *which* would be a noun that sums up the idea that needs to be described:

INCORRECT: The government cracked down on the striking workers, which only inflamed the situation.

CORRECT: The government cracked down on the striking workers, an action that only inflamed the situation.

INCORRECT: Analysts have pointed out a number of instabilities inherent in the current business model, which prudent investors will want to take into consideration.

CORRECT: Analysts have pointed out a number of instabilities inherent in the current business model, instabilities that prudent investors will want to take into consideration.

Exercise 18: Mark each of these sentences as OK or Wrong with respect to the use of the word *which*. Fix the ones in which *which* is used incorrectly (there will usually be more than one way to fix it). (Additional exercises can be found on the website, testprepny.com)

1. He spent two months' pay on a diamond ring, which cost a fortune.

2. He spent two months' pay on a diamond ring, which made me angry.

3. There were several factors which contributed to the debacle.

4. There were several factors nobody had taken into consideration, which shows that the so-called leadership wasn't really paying attention.

5. There are huge cracks forming in that dam, which indicates that the town will soon be in danger if something isn't done.

6. There are several dogs on that plane, which ought to be illegal.

7. There are huge cracks forming in that dam, which wasn't very sturdy to begin with.

8. There are several dogs on that plane, which is scheduled to take off in an hour.

9. The congressman is running for reelection, which he promised he wouldn't do.

10. He ran 25 miles, which the doctor had told him would be dangerous.

For more practice

OG, 13th edition, Questions: 35, 43, 101, 102, 103

3.3.3 KNOW THE DISTINCTION BETWEEN 'WHICH' AND 'THAT'

There is another rule involving *which* to be aware of, though for this rule, the wrong answer choices are more likely to involve the word *that*. The rule has to do with the distinction between relative clauses that provide necessary information, and those that provide extra, parenthetical information. Here is an example of the contrast:

a. The barn is designed for elephants that weigh over 3000 pounds.

b. The barn is designed for elephants, which weigh over 3000 pounds.

Sentence (a) says that the barn isn't for all elephants—it's only for the ones that weigh over 3,000 pounds. The relative clause "that weigh over 3000 pounds" is needed in order to make it clear which elephants are meant. Sentence (b) says that the barn is for all elephants, and then adds a comment that elephants (in general) weigh over 3000 pounds. The comment isn't needed in order to make it clear which elephants are meant; if it were deleted, you would still understand that the barn is designed for elephants in general. If you read the sentences out loud, you may hear the difference in tone; in (b), the phrase "which weigh over 3000 pounds" sounds as if it's in parentheses.

The two kinds of relative clauses are punctuated differently. Relative clauses that are necessary to make the noun phrase clear, as in (a), are not set off with a comma. Relative clauses that merely add an extra comment, as in (b), are separated from the main clause by a comma (or sometimes by a dash or by parentheses).

There is one additional difference between the two types, and the GMAT may test it. Relative clauses that merely provide an extra comment <u>cannot</u> use the connecting word *that*. If they modify a thing, they must use the word *which* (if they modify a person, of course, they must use the word *who*). Note the contrast:

CORRECT: The protagonist lives in Newton, which is a small town in Massachusetts.

INCORRECT: The protagonist lives in Newton, that is a small town in Massachusetts.

A simple rule of thumb is that if the relative clause is separated from the noun by a comma, it is probably an "extra comment" relative clause, and so it should not use the word *that*.

3.3.4 BE CAREFUL WHEN USING 'WHERE' IN RELATIVE CLAUSES

 GRAB A CLUE: The word *where* is usually incorrect on the GMAT—but study the explanation below so you can tell whether it's correct or incorrect.

In everyday conversational English, we frequently use *where* as a sort of catch-all connecting word in contexts in which it would take some thought to make a more precise choice. This kind of casual usage is considered incorrect on the GMAT, and as usual in cases of mismatch between spoken style and formal written style, the GMAT tests this point frequently. The following examples of correct and incorrect usage should give you the idea. Remember that once again, the "incorrect" versions may sound fine to you, because they reflect usage that is common in everyday speech; compare them to the correct versions to see what is required in formal written style.

INCORRECT: It was the kind of situation where you don't know who to trust or what to do.

CORRECT: It was the kind of situation in which you don't know who to trust or what to do.

INCORRECT: It was the kind of day where you wonder why you even bothered to get out of bed in the morning.

CORRECT: It was the kind of day on which you wonder why you even bothered to get out of bed in the morning.

INCORRECT: Congress, in its wisdom, came up with a plan where it was guaranteed that nobody would feel satisfied with the outcome.

CORRECT: Congress, in its wisdom, came up with a plan by which it was guaranteed that nobody would feel satisfied with the outcome.

INCORRECT: The first half of the movie was pretty good, but it had the kind of bizarre ending where you just sit there and wonder, "What was that all about?"

CORRECT: The first half of the movie was pretty good, but it had the kind of bizarre ending that makes a person wonder, "What was that all about?"

The only time when it is correct to use "where" to introduce a relative clause is when the clause is actually describing a location:

> **CORRECT:** Johnson never returned to the town where he had grown up.

> **CORRECT:** Several environmental groups have inspected the site where the wind farm is to be located.

> **CORRECT:** A small percentage of salmon do not, in fact, return to the locations where they were born.

For more practice

OG, 12th edition, Questions: 43, 102, 103, 104
OG Verbal Review, 1st edition, Question: 27

3.3.5 BE FAMILIAR WITH RELATIVE CLAUSES USING QUANTITY EXPRESSIONS

Relative clauses can start with more complex expressions of quantity, as in this example:

> He wrote several books, three of which were later made into movies.

> The correct form for these is this formula:

> QUANTITY EXPRESSION + "of" + "whom" or "which".

There are several variations which are all considered incorrect on the GMAT:

> **CORRECT:** He wrote several books, three of which were later made into movies.

> **INCORRECT:** He wrote several books, of which three were later made into movies.

> **CORRECT:** Johnson had four brothers, none of whom went to college.

> **INCORRECT:** Johnson had four brothers, none of who went to college.

> **CORRECT:** The General had three sisters, all of whom were also in the military.

> **INCORRECT:** The General had three sisters, two of them who were also in the military.

> **CORRECT:** The children saw a herd of elephants, several of which had long tusks.

> **INCORRECT:** The children saw a herd of elephants, several of them which had long tusks.

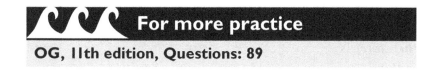

For more practice

OG, 11th edition, Questions: 89

3.3.6 REMEMBER THAT 'WHOSE' CAN MODIFY AN INANIMATE NOUN

A relative clause can begin with *whose* even if the noun it goes with refers to an inanimate object. Sentences like these sometimes throw test takers off, since most of us don't talk this way in everyday conversation. However, they are considered correct by the traditional rules of English grammar:

> **CORRECT:** The detective suspected that the car whose owner had disappeared was somehow involved in the murder.

> **CORRECT:** Detroit, whose industrial base declined with the loss of the auto industry, now seeks to put its economy on a new footing.

> **CORRECT:** The film whose ending most startled audiences was *The Sixth Sense.*

Another way to think about it is that "whose" is the possessive form for both "who" and "which." After all, there's no such word as "which's."

Although there are no questions that hinge on this point in the Official Guides, as of the time of the printing of this book, it has appeared as a trap in practice tests recently provided by GMAC. In the practice material, the trap the GMAT writers set is a simple one: the only version of the sentence that uses *whose* is the correct choice, and the incorrect versions avoid the use of whose but are unnecessarily wordy or incorporate various mistakes. The question is designed to trick test takers who would immediately dismiss the choice with *whose* and be forced to pick from among the other four. The key to avoiding this trap is simply to be aware that *whose* can be used to refer to inanimate objects.

Exercise 19: Decide whether the underlined word or phrase at the beginning of each relative clause is correct. (Additional exercises can be found on the website, testprepny.com)

1. The plan was an exceedingly complex one, involving multiple stages <u>where</u> no one was quite sure what he was supposed to do next.

2. There were several doors, only <u>one of which</u> led outside.

3. The first minute after the explosion was a time <u>when</u> no one knew what to expect.

4. Everyone in the room suddenly began applauding, <u>which</u> startled the cat.

5. The person to whom the letter was addressed realized that this was a situation <u>where</u> things could change in an instant.

6. The conference participants—<u>of which one</u> was a Nobel Prize winner—gathered outside the hotel for a group picture.

7. The company directors realized too late <u>that</u> the man that they had brought in was unsuited to the job.

8. The gallery-goers were astonished by the exhibition, <u>whose</u> creator was a 9-year-old child from the slums of Mumbai.

> *The best way out is always through.*
>
> Robert Frost[78]

 GRAB A CLUE: If you see the word *only* in a GMAT SC, your first priority should be to check to see if it's used correctly.

In everyday conversational English, speakers are not especially careful in deciding where to place the word *only*. They often put it in front of the verb, regardless of which phrase the word *only* is intended to modify. The following examples are typical of everyday speech—and all exemplify usage that might not be credited on the GMAT:

Spoken Style: The chairman of the company did not understand the question because he only spoke Korean.

Spoken Style: The junior partners didn't see the memo because it only went to the senior partners.

Spoken Style: The US Postal Service announced that, as a cost-cutting measure, it would only deliver mail five days a week.

Spoken Style: The latecomers were bewildered by the final scene, because they only saw the last one-third of the movie.

In conversational English, none of these would present any problem for comprehension, because the speaker would use his or her voice to emphasize the phrase that is to be modified by *only*. The end of the first sentence, for instance, would sound like "...he only spoke <u>Korean</u>." In formal written English, however, the sentence would be considered misleading. It could be read as meaning "He only <u>spoke</u> Korean" (i.e. he didn't write Korean, or read Korean). In formal written English, it should be rewritten like this, so that *only* appears just before the phrase it modifies:

Written Style: The chairman of the company did not understand the question because he spoke only Korean.

The second sentence could be read as meaning "The memo only went to the senior partners" (it didn't do anything else —e.g., it didn't shock them, didn't persuade them, didn't please them...). A better version:

Written Style: The junior partners didn't see the memo because it went only to the senior partners.

> *If you only care enough for a result, you will almost certainly attain it.*
>
> William James[79]

The third sentence could be read as meaning that the US Postal Service will only <u>deliver mail</u> five days a week (it won't do anything else—e.g., it won't sell stamps, won't administer post office boxes, etc.). A better version:

> **Written Style:** The US Postal Service announced that, as a cost-cutting measure, it would deliver mail only five days a week.

And the fourth sentence could mean that the latecomers only <u>saw</u> the last one-third of the movie (they didn't hear it). A better version:

> **Written Style:** The latecomers were bewildered by the final scene because they saw only the last one-third of the movie.

Exercise 20: Decide whether the placement of *only* makes sense (by the standards of Formal Written English) in each sentence; if not, move it to the right spot.
(Additional exercises can be found on the website, testprepny.com)

1. Jonathan didn't enjoy watching the movie because he only wanted to sleep.

2. The board of directors announced that it would only need to lay off 300 employees.

3. The novel is incredibly popular in Europe but so far is available only in German.

4. If you need anything, you only have to ask.

5. The governor's office announced that under the new rules, homeless people would only be allowed to stay in shelters for a maximum of three months.

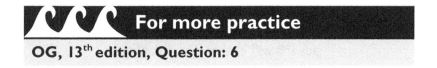

For more practice

OG, 13th edition, Question: 6

3.5 WATCH OUT FOR ADJECTIVES VS. ADVERBS

No one can possibly achieve any real and lasting success or get rich in business by being a conformist.

J. Paul Getty[81]

GMAT SCs sometimes test the distinction between adjectives and adverbs. The difference is fairly simple: Adjectives modify (that is, describe) nouns, whereas adverbs modify everything else: verbs, adjectives, and other adverbs. For example:

> He is an *intelligent* speaker. (Adjective modifying the noun speaker.)

> He spoke *intelligently*. (Adverb modifying the verb spoke.)

Most adverbs end in –*ly*.

The simplest way to learn what to watch out for is to observe a few examples of the kinds of incorrect usage that you may see on the GMAT. Most of the mistakes people make with adjectives versus adverbs come from rushing through the sentence and not reading carefully. Be alert for these mistakes:

An adjective form may be used where an adverb is needed, or vice versa:

> **INCORRECT:** The professor explained the concept clear. (Should be "clearly.")

> **INCORRECT:** The decline in the stock price was so gradually that it did not alarm investors. (Should be "gradual.")

You may also see a sentence in which the choice of adjective or adverb will change the meaning:

> a. The scientist announced his surprising recent results at the convention.

> b. The scientist announced his surprisingly recent results at the convention.

In (a), the results are both surprising and recent. In (b), the adverb "surprisingly" modifies the adjective "recent"—so what is surprising is not the results, but how recent they are. The choice of adjective or adverb will depend partly on what makes sense in the context. In general, errors involving the distinction between adjectives and adverbs are easy to catch if you slow down enough to read the answer choices carefully, and think about how the differences in wording change the meaning.

No road is too long for him who advances slowly and does not hurry, and no attainment is beyond his reach who equips himself with patience to achieve it

Jean de La Bruyèrey[82]

Finally, it should be noted that it is grammatically correct to use an adjective, not an adverb, to describe the state or condition of a thing that is "acted on." For example:

CORRECT: Traditional Japanese clothing can be packed flat. (Not "flatly.")

CORRECT: The police shot the criminal dead. (Not "deadly.")

CORRECT: Borscht should be served hot. (Not "hotly.")

CORRECT: The suitcase was quickly packed full. (Not "fully.")

For more practice

OG, 12th edition, Question: 40
OG, 11th edition, Question: 12
OG Verbal Review, 1st edition, Question: 33

"...Our deepest fear is not that we are inadequate. Our deepest fear is that we are powerful beyond measure. It is our light, not our darkness, that most frightens us. We ask ourselves, who am I to be brilliant, gorgeous, talented, fabulous? Actually, who are you not to be? You are a child of God. Your playing small doesn't serve the world. There's nothing enlightened about shrinking so that other people won't feel insecure around you. We are all meant to shine, as children do. We were born to make manifest the glory of God that is within us. It's not just in some of us; it's in everyone. And as we let our own light shine, we unconsciously give other people permission to do the same. As we're liberated from our own fear, our presence automatically liberates others."

Marianne Williamson[80]

MODULE 4: COMPARISONS

MODULE 4: COMPARISONS

4.1 TOP PRIORITY: MAKE SURE COMPARISONS ARE CLEAR AND SENSIBLE

You must quickly spot what is wrong with sentences like these:

1. Like many charities, contributions to Hope for Hooligans are used in part to cover administrative expenses.

2. Unlike the East Coast, people on the West Coast have to think about earthquakes.

3. People in California eat more granola than people in New York.

4. Last year, Acme corporation sold off more assets than its chief rival.

5. The company made as much money this year as 2009.

Some or all of these sentences may sound like normal, everyday English, but none of them would be credited on the GMAT. In conversational English, we often express comparisons in ways that are not fully precise; we rely on the listener to use common sense. In formal written English, comparisons have to be worded so that they're airtight; every imaginable ambiguity has to be avoided. This means that comparison sentences are another area in which simply relying on your ears may lead you into trouble. Once you study the patterns that the GMAT accepts or rejects, however, you can learn to quickly spot the important factors in comparison sentences. Often, SC questions that focus on comparisons can be answered very efficiently— saving you time that you can put to use on a harder question.

Let's look at what's wrong with the sentences above. They all make nonsensical comparisons, but in different ways. Whenever a sentence begins with "like" or "unlike," as in the first two sentences, the thing being compared to must be the subject of the sentence. In other words, sentence 1 is comparing "many charities" to "contributions." Sentence 2 is comparing "East Coast" to "people." These are apples and oranges comparisons. Logical comparisons compare two things of the same type—charities to charities, people to people, etc. Versions that might be credited on the GMAT would look like this:

1. Like many charities, Hope for Hooligans uses its contributions in part to cover administrative expenses.

2. Unlike people on the East Coast, those on the West Coast have to think about earthquakes.

When an SC begins with "like" or "unlike", you should <u>immediately</u> check to see whether the subject of the sentence is something that can logically be compared to whatever follows "like" or "unlike."

The remaining three sentences above also make illogical comparisons but in a slightly different way. They're ambiguous—you can tell what the writer means, but they can each be read in a way that makes no sense. Sentence 3, "People in California eat more granola than people in New York,"could mean that people in California eat both granola and people in New York, but of the two, they eat more granola. Sentence 4, "Last year, Acme corporation sold off more assets than its chief rival", could mean that among the assets Acme sold off was its chief rival. Lastly, in sentence 5, "company made as much money this year as 2009" raises the question "How much money did 2009 make?"

In short: a comparison must be worded so that it is clear what role each noun phrase plays in the comparison. If it is unclear what role the noun following "than" or "as" is supposed to be playing, you have to add an auxiliary verb (e.g. *does* or *do*) to clarify the sentence. These sentences could all be corrected like this:

> People in California eat more granola than *do* people in New York.

> Last year, Acme corporation sold off more assets than *did* its chief rival.

> The company made as much money this year as *in* 2009.

One more example. What's wrong with this one?

INCORRECT: Riding a bicycle is better exercise than rollerskates.

The sentence attempts to compare an object, rollerskates, with an activity, riding a bicycle. It's apples and oranges again.

CORRECT: Riding a bicycle is better exercise than rollerskating.

The bottom line: Comparisons must compare things of the same type, and they must be unambiguous. If there's another way to read the sentence which makes it unclear which two things are being compared (even if common sense would tell you which reading the writer meant), you need to add words to clarify what's being compared. Comparisons are tested very frequently on the GMAT, and sentences with mistakes of the kind illustrated in sentences 1-5 above are especially common.

GRAB A CLUE: If you see a sentence begin with *like* or *unlike*, or if you see the word *than* anywhere in the sentence, you should immediately focus on the comparison and make sure it's correct and unambiguous.

Exercise 21: Decide which of the following comparisons make sense and which need revision. (Additional exercises can be found on the website, testprepny.com)

1. Like Hemingway, Steinbeck's works are often assigned in high school English classes.

2. Unlike cottage cheese, yogurt contains a significant amount of calcium.

3. Unlike most other television dramas, the characters in this series change and evolve.

4. Unlike humans, dogs have a toxic reaction to chocolate.

5. Like cats, people should be aware that giving aspirin to dogs can be dangerous.

6. Fear of clowns is known as *coulrophobia*; like most phobias, it is difficult to explain where it comes from.

Exercise 22: Determine whether these comparisons are clear and make sense. If not, fix them. Remember that sentences that <u>sound</u> as if they make sense from the point of view of everyday conversational English may be considered ambiguous (and therefore wrong) on the GMAT. (Additional exercises can be found on the website, testprepny.com)

1. Surprisingly enough, David could eat a lot more than Goliath.

2. Sickle cell anemia is much more common in areas that are plagued by malaria than areas that aren't.

3. Though sucrose contains both fructose and glucose, high fructose corn syrup contains more fructose than sucrose.

4. This year's model doesn't weigh as much as last year.

5. Tea bags contain more caffeine than coffee grounds, but brewed coffee contains more caffeine than brewed tea.

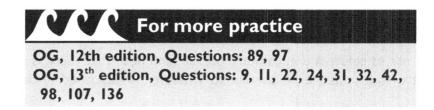
For more practice
OG, 12th edition, Questions: 89, 97
OG, 13th edition, Questions: 9, 11, 22, 24, 31, 32, 42, 98, 107, 136

GRAB A CLUE: If some answer choices use the word *like* and some use *as*, sort out which is correct.

The basic rule about when to use *like* or *as* in a comparison is very simple: use *like* if it is followed by a noun by itself, or use *as* if it is followed by anything else, such as a clause. Notice the contrast in these pairs:

Like a dog, that cat follows me wherever I go.

As a dog follows it master everywhere, that cat follows me wherever I go.

He eats like a horse.

He eats a huge amount, as does a horse.

Like corn, rice provides many essential nutrients.

As corn provides a number of important nutrients, so too does rice.

Like his father, he has pursued a career in waste management.

He has pursued a career in waste management, just as his father did.

Like most educated people of his time, Thomas Jefferson studied Greek.

Thomas Jefferson studied Greek, as did most educated people of his time.

To clear up one common cause of confusion, we need to make clear that the choice between "like" and "as" is <u>not</u> determined by the basic concept that the author wants to get across. That is, essentially the same situation could be described using either a construction with *like*, or one with *as* (although one way of doing it may sound more natural than another). Instead, the deciding factor is exactly which other words are used to form the comparison. This is why the like-versus-as distinction seems slippery at first. It's natural for a person to think, "Well, the comparison is kind of talking about the person—so that's *like*—but the point is what the person <u>did</u>—so that's *as*. But really it's more about the person, I think, so that would be *like*..." You can go around in circles like that for quite a while.

The key is to get away from thinking about "what the comparison is really talking about", and instead focus on the <u>words</u> that are used. If the comparison uses only a noun phrase, as in "Like most educated people of his time", then *like* is correct. If the comparison uses a whole clause or at least a verb, as in "As did most educated people of his time", then *as* is correct.

You should also use *as* before a prepositional phrase (and note that there is no requirement that the subject of the sentence be parallel to whatever is described in the prepositional phrase):

As in 2004, the campaign rhetoric has become very heated.

As in Athens, the citizens of Rome expected certain things from their leaders.

Here is one more set of examples to recap the rules (note that a couple of these are a bit wordy, so they aren't all equally good, but they are all <u>grammatical</u>):

Like his older contemporary Manet, Monet used a vivid, quick brush technique to create his masterpieces.

Monet used a vivid, quick brush technique to create his masterpieces, as did his older contemporary Manet.

As in any creative revolution, there were both leaders and followers in the Impressionist movement.

Exercise 23: Decide whether the use of *as* or *like* is correct in each sentence.
(Additional exercises can be found on the website, testprepny.com)

1. Like Monet, Manet is considered an Impressionist.

2. Just as St Francis did, St Claire embraced the concept of poverty as a spiritual discipline.

3. Like the works of Beethoven and Mozart have been, the works of Bach have been studied by musical theorists for centuries.

4. Many people feel like their lives are changing too rapidly for them to adjust.

5. As organic grain, which is subject to specific limitations on the use of fertilizers and pesticides, organic milk must meet rigorous standards of purity.

6. The day passed as a shadow.

OG, 13th edition, Questions: 66, 99

"Imagine that the whole world belongs to you. The birch trees in New Hampshire's White Mountains are yours, and so are the cirrus clouds in the western sky at dusk and the black sand on the beaches of Hawaii's big island. You own everything, my dear sovereign—the paintings in all the museums of the world, as well as the internet and the wild horses and the roads. Please take good care of it all, OK? Be an enlightened monarch who treats your domain with reverent responsibility. And make sure you also enjoy the full measure of fun that comes with such mastery. Glide through life as if all of creation is yearning to honor and entertain you."

Rob Brezsny[88]

4.3 A NOTE ON 'LIKE' VERSUS 'SUCH AS'

The distinction between *like* and *such as* is tested with some frequency on the GMAT. This is another distinction that is not often observed in everyday spoken English, so relying on your ear alone could cause you to miss it.

 GRAB A CLUE: When you see the word *like* used to give an example (as in "A man like him") check to see whether some answer choices use "such as" instead, and sort out which one is correct, as explained here.

According to the rules of formal written English, *like* is used only to make a comparison, <u>not</u> to give an example. Compare:

> A small country like Denmark needs strong alliances.

> A small country such as Denmark needs strong alliances.

The first sentence means only that small countries that are like Denmark—but not Denmark itself—need strong alliances. The second means that Denmark is an example of a country that needs strong alliances. In everyday spoken English, *like* is often used to give an example; in formal written English, this would be considered incorrect. Here's another example:

> **Spoken style (not credited on the GMAT):** The oncologist explained a number of common side effects of chemotherapy, like hair loss, nausea and rash.

> **Written style (credited on the GMAT):** The oncologist explained a number of common side effects of chemotherapy, such as hair loss, nausea and rash.

You can also separate "such" from "as", in these examples:

> A number of citizens who live near the sewage treatment plant have complained about such problems as noise, odor, and vermin.

> To prepare for a career as an illustrator, an artist must develop solid skills in such areas as anatomy, perspective, and color.

Finally, there is no such phrase as *such like*. Any answer choice with *such like* will not be the credited answer.

For more practice

OG, 12th edition, Question: 28
OG, 13th edition, Question: 138

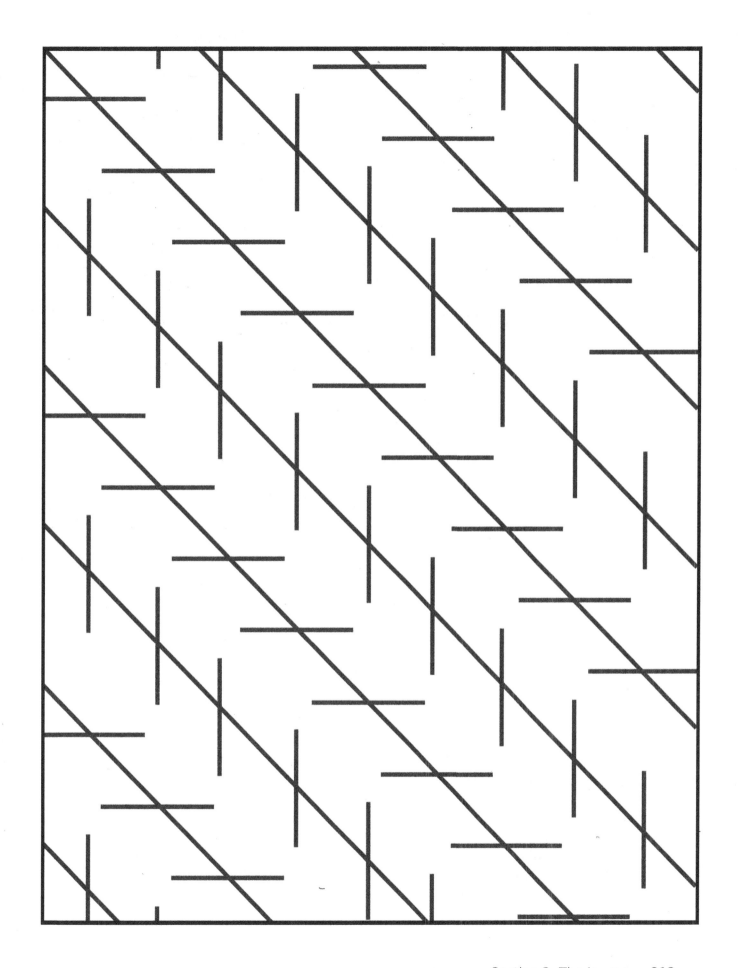

4.4 'THAN' VS. 'AS' AND OTHER PHRASES

GRAB A CLUE: Be aware whenever you see a comparison made with either *than* or *as*. Make sure the comparison is formed correctly.

Than is used for unequal comparisons (one person or thing is better, worse, larger, smaller, etc., <u>than</u> another thing). It should not be replaced with "as", "as compared to", "instead of" or "rather than":

CORRECT: The company's image would be far better served by this advertising campaign <u>than</u> by the other one.

INCORRECT: The company's image would be far better served by this advertising campaign <u>as</u> by the other one.

INCORRECT: The company's image would be far better served by this advertising campaign <u>as compared to</u> the other one.

INCORRECT: The company's image would be far better served by this advertising campaign <u>rather than</u> by the other one.

INCORRECT: The company's image would be far better served by this advertising campaign <u>instead of</u> by the other one.

'As' is used for equal comparisons (for instance, one thing is *as good as* another), in the pattern <u>as ADJ as.</u> Note that "as X as" is correct, not "so X as":

CORRECT: This dress costs <u>as much as</u> that one.

INCORRECT: This dress costs <u>so much as</u> that one.

However, there is a different expression, "not so much X as Y" which is a correct idiom. The two phrases X and Y must be parallel:

Some economists argue that the Great Depression was caused <u>not so much</u> by the stock market crash <u>as</u> by a confluence of other economic forces.

Be especially careful when the GMAT combines two comparisons, one unequal and one equal, using a *than* phrase and an *as* phrase. Frequently one of the phrases will have a word missing:

The couple wanted to find a house that was <u>as large or larger than</u> the one they had had before.

The second *as* is missing—the expression should be "as large as." In general, the correct choice for this kind of problem (when the A choice has a combination of "as ADJ as" and "more ADJ than") will use "at least":

The couple wanted to find a house <u>at least as large as</u> the one they had had previously.

Occasionally, however, the correct answer will include both complete phrases in the pattern "<u>as X as</u> or <u>more X than Y</u>."

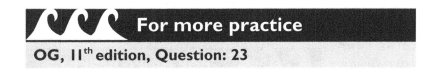

For more practice

OG, 12th edition, Questions: 4, 13, 76, 123
OG, 11th edition, Questions: 4, 30, 37, 76
OG Verbal Review, 2nd edition, Questions: 85, 87
OG Verbal Review, 1st edition, Questions: 36, 47, 75, 89

4.5 A FEW ADDITIONAL DETAILS OF WORDING

Fewer vs. Less: Use *fewer* when making a comparison involving count nouns (countable things like trees, people, books, etc.), and *less* when making a comparison involving non-count or mass nouns (e.g. water, gold, apathy).

More vs. most: Use *more* (or an adjective with an –er ending) to compare two things. Use *most* (or an adjective with an –est ending) to compare three or more things:

Of the two companies, Acme is the newer and the more successful.

Of the three companies, Acme is the newest and the most successful.

For more practice

OG, 11th edition, Question: 23

4.6 THE BOTTOM LINE: COMPARISONS MUST MAKE SENSE

The fundamental rule is that comparisons must make sense. In addition to the frequently tested, Top Priority patterns described above, there are other, more subtle errors that are sometimes tested on the GMAT. Consider these examples:

> Israel has a land area about the same as Massachusetts.

> Japan's population is larger than that of any island nation.

> Cleaning a rayon dress costs as much as a silk dress.

The first sentence appears to mean that Israel's land <u>area</u> is the same as Massachusetts in every way (e.g. the type of land, the plant life, etc.), not just size. The second sentence seems to be saying that Japan is not an island nation. The third sentence seems to be saying that the cost of merely cleaning a rayon dress is the same as the entire cost of purchasing a silk dress. These sentences would be better rewritten as follows:

> Israel has a land area about the same size as Massachusetts.

> Japan's population is larger than that of any other island nation.

> Cleaning a rayon dress costs as much as cleaning a silk dress.

The bottom line is that you need to assess comparisons to make sure they make sense. Sometimes the errors are subtle, but you can guess that something like this may be a factor when you can't find any more obvious mistakes. A good rule of thumb is that if an SC involving a comparison seems to have two correct answer choices, the odds are that one of them doesn't entirely make sense.

For more practice

OG, 12th edition, Questions: 89
OG, 13th edition, Questions: 43, 67, 85, 94, 136

MODULE 5: PARALLELISM

MODULE 5: PARALLELISM

5.1 TOP PRIORITY: YOU MUST BE ABLE TO QUICKLY IDENTIFY WHAT IS WRONG WITH SENTENCES LIKE THESE:

1. The board of directors announced today that it would cut spending in such areas as research, human resources, and combine several departments to save money.

2. The economic recovery has prompted investors to expand their portfolios, increase their investments in new ventures, and to engage in riskier short-term investments.

These sentences lack **parallelism**. The basic idea of parallelism is that any time different words or phrases serve the same function in a sentence, they should all be of the same grammatical type.

Let's take a simple example: "I like *swimming, surfing,* and *hiking.*" The words swimming, surfing, and hiking are all objects of the verb *like.* It's as if the speaker said "I like swimming and I like surfing and I like hiking", but without repeating "I like" over and over.

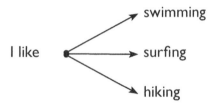

Any time two or more words go together to fit into the same "slot" in the sentence (like three nouns that together serve as the object of the verb), they must have the same basic shape, grammatically.

How might this example look if it were not parallel? Something like "I like <u>swimming</u>, <u>to surf</u> and <u>hike</u>." In this version, it's not clear that the 3 words or phrases are all supposed to fit into the same slot, as objects of *like.* It looks as if they're each trying to do something different.

In sentence 1 above, "research" and "human resources" are both nouns, but "combine" is a verb. The mistake in sentence 2 is slightly more subtle: "to expand", "increase", and "to engage" must be parallel, but "increase" lacks the word "to."

It's often possible to <u>hear</u> a mistake in parallelism, even if you aren't sure what's wrong—it sounds jarring, as if the parts of the sentence don't quite go together. Of course, on the GMAT the sentences will sometimes be cleverly constructed to make it harder to find the mistakes by ear. To get them all right, you need some awareness of what counts as parallel and what kinds of traps to watch out for. But before you focus on the harder cases, the first thing to do is to train yourself to recognize mistakes in parallelism that aren't so cleverly hidden, so that you have a good intuitive grasp of what you're looking for. Once you have a solid grip on what counts as a parallelism problem, you can move on to the trickier things you may see on the advanced GMAT questions. (We should also mention that the GMAT frequently includes questions with obvious mistakes in parallelism, so getting faster and more accurate at recognizing the "simple" ones is a good use of your time in its own right.)

Exercise 24: Underline all the parallel phrases in these sentences. Identify any mistakes in parallelism and suggest a re-write.

1. Shakespeare excelled at character, plot, dialogue and did amazing things with language.

2. Goats will eat just about anything: leaves, grass, paper, rags, and tree bark.

3. There are only two certainties in life: death and you have to pay taxes.

4. John liked visiting Aspen, where he enjoyed hiking, rock climbing, and skied.

5. The clever student excelled in math, in physics and gym.

5.2 WHEN IS PARALLELISM REQUIRED?

GRAB A CLUE: Parallelism can be an issue in many kinds of sentences, but you should be especially alert for problems with parallelism if you see the words *and*, *but*, or *or*, or if you see the paired expressions (explained further below) *not only... but also, both... and, neither... nor,* or *between... and.*

> *"There
> is a vitality, a life-
> force, an energy, a quickening
> that is translated through you into
> action. And because there is only one of
> you in all of time, this expression is unique.
> And if you block it, it will never exist through
> any other medium and be lost. The world will not
> have it. It is not your business to determine how
> good it is nor how valuable nor how it compares
> with other expressions. It is your business to keep
> it yours clearly and directly, to keep the channel
> open...whether you choose to take an art class,
> keep a journal, record your dreams, dance
> your story or live each day from your own
> creative source. Above all else, keep
> the channel open!"*

Martha Graham[93]

5.2.1 CONJOINED PHRASES

Sentence components must be parallel when they are joined with *and, but, so, or,* or *nor.* These are called "coordinating conjunctions"—connecting words that coordinate or bring together things that are all of the same type.

John bought *pizza and wine.*

Sally likes *skiing, swimming and arm-wrestling.*

The committee decided *that the park needed to be relandscaped and that the city would have to pay for it.*

The dog wants *fish or hamburger.*

When a list with "or" is negated by the word "not," you should not use any other negative words later in the list, but rather use words beginning with "any":

CORRECT: The guru does not eat beef, mutton, or any other kind of meat.

INCORRECT: The guru does not eat beef, mutton, or no other kind of meat.

CORRECT: A person trying to lose weight should not drink beer, soda, or anything else high in calories.

INCORRECT: A person trying to lose weight should not drink beer, soda, or nothing else high in calories.

Exercise 25: Decide which of the following sentences have mistakes in parallelism and correct them.

1. John ate pizza and drank wine, although the combination didn't taste very good.

2. The evil robot ate the pizza, the couch, the table, and drank wine.

3. Sally likes skeet-shooting, scuba-diving, windsurfing, and to lie on the beach afterwards.

4. The committee decided that the park needed to be re-landscaped and made safer at night.

5. The dog wants fish, hamburger, or to drink out of the toilet.

5.2.2 PAIRED EXPRESSIONS

Components must be parallel when they are joined by paired expressions—expressions that have two parts:

both... and...

not only... but also...

either... or...

neither... nor...

from... to...

The words or phrases that are combined by the parts must be parallel. Often, eliminating the non-parallel answer choices will narrow the choices down to only two, or even one.

 GRAB A CLUE: When you see the expression "not only...but also..." immediately look at the phrases that follow *not only* and those that follow *but also*, and eliminate all the parallelism errors. This might be all you need to do to find the right answer.

The following examples are parallel:

John may order *either beer or wine*.

Applicants must *not only submit a resume but also provide three references*.

The topics ran the gamut *from A to Z*.

The injured athlete could *neither jump nor run* for six weeks.

He ate *both eggs and fish*.

The train runs *from Detroit to Chicago* (not "up to Chicago").

Paired expressions to memorize:

not only... but also

not... but

both... and

either... or

neither... nor

from... to

between... and

just as... so

Exercise 26: Identify and correct any mistakes in parallelism in these sentences.

1. King Herod's reign over Judea from 37 to 4 B.C. is not remembered for justice but for its indiscriminate cruelty.

2. Listed in the 25-page will were not only some very unusual items but the deceased also left some choice comments about his heirs.

3. Disgruntled vacationers were informed that they could either submit their complaints for arbitration or, if they insisted, they would have to file a class action lawsuit.

4. The discovery of the archaeological site of ancient Troy was both a major accomplishment for the archaeologist and came as a huge shock to those who had always assumed that Troy was a Homeric myth.

5. The new corporate headquarters are either to be constructed in London or in Paris, at a cost of $300 million.

For more practice

OG, 12th edition, Questions: 56
OG, 13th edition, Questions: 4, 15, 21, 44, 56, 57, 64, 84, 86, 92, 93, 95

5.2.3 ELLIPSIS

When two ideas are compared in a sentence, it is often possible to leave out a few words in order to avoid repetition. This is called an *ellipsis*. For example, instead of saying "John can speak Japanese, and I can *speak Japanese* too", the speaker can skip two words and just say "John can speak Japanese, and I can too."

Full statement: John can speak Japanese, and <u>I can speak Japanese too.</u>

Ellipsis: John can speak Japanese, and <u>I can too.</u>

The word or phrase that is omitted must be the same as something that appeared earlier in the sentence. In this case, the omitted phrase is "speak Japanese."

In a way, this is the mirror image of the kind of parallelism we've discussed elsewhere. In the other cases of parallelism, two or more phrases together fill one slot in the sentence. Here, we have one phrase filling two slots: the phrase appears in the sentence only once, but it's understood to fill in a second slot as well. The sentence has to be constructed so that the same words can function in two places.

The GMAT is especially likely to test for parallelism by omitting part of a verb phrase. Consider the following example:

The baseball player insists that since the drug in question has never been banned, he <u>was not</u> and is not cheating.

What does "was not" mean? Clearly it means "was not cheating." You know because the phrase is partially parallel to "is not cheating", so "was not" is "was not cheating" with a word omitted. It's OK for the word to be omitted earlier in the sentence and appear later, or the writer could have done it the other way around, as in "he was not cheating and is not now."

In contrast, this sentence is wrong:

The doctor said the patient <u>has not</u> and <u>will not recover.</u>

What does "<u>has not</u>" mean? It must mean "has not recovered." But does the word "recovered" appear anywhere else in the sentence? No. The closest we have is "recover," and that won't work. The sentence would have to be read as "<u>the patient has not recover.</u>" This example would not be credited on the GMAT.

Another example:

John said he would clean the garage today, and so far he <u>has been.</u>

"<u>Has been</u>" what? It's supposed to mean "has been cleaning the garage", but the word "cleaning" never appears in the sentence. If we read the sentence according to strict rules of grammar, it would read "so far he <u>has been</u> clean the garage."

NOTE: On the GMAT, questions of this type often involve the verb *continue*. For example:

> The doctor said the treatment <u>is and will continue to work</u>.

You might think the obvious way to fix this is to say "The doctor said the treatment <u>is working and will continue to work</u>." That <u>would</u> fix the parallelism problem, but the GMAT will usually prefer a different solution. In this case, "The doctor said the treatment <u>will continue to work</u>" would be the better choice, because "is working" is redundant. Obviously, if the doctor is saying the treatment will <u>continue</u> to work, it must be working already.

The bottom line: Watch out for unfinished verb phrases and make sure that the "pieces" you need to complete the phrase are available elsewhere in the sentence, in **exactly the right grammatical form**. In some cases—especially when you see the verb "continue"—think about whether the better solution is not just to make the phrases parallel, but to cut out one of the phrases altogether.

Exercise 27: Decide whether the parallel phrases in these sentences are formed correctly. Fix any mistakes you find.

1. Economic analysts say that the recession has been and will continue to abate.

2. The mortgage crisis was predicted to hit bottom by mid-year, and it did.

3. Nuclear engineers testified that the plant was running at full capacity and had been for six months.

4. Union leaders promised to bring the strike to a rapid conclusion, and they have.

5. Local officials said that the dam was and is cracking due to the excessive pressure.

5.2.4 OTHER STRUCTURES THAT REQUIRE PARALLELISM

Equation: Sentences of the form "X is Y" are sometimes tested on the GMAT. X and Y must be parallel. Usually, the GMAT tests this by focusing on the distinction between gerunds and infinitives. A gerund is <u>not</u> considered parallel to an infinitive.

> **CORRECT:** <u>To know him</u> is <u>to love him</u>.

> **INCORRECT:** <u>Knowing him</u> is <u>to love him</u>.

X rather than Y: The expression "rather than" requires that the two things being compared be parallel. Determining which two things are being compared requires looking at the meaning of the sentence to see what makes sense. So long as the phrase following "rather than" is parallel to some phrase earlier in the sentence that describes whatever the second phrase is being compared to, the sentence will be grammatical.

> **CORRECT:** John wants to eat a hamburger rather than a hot dog. (OK because "hot dog" is parallel to "hamburger.")

> **CORRECT:** John wants to eat a hamburger rather than take protein pills. (OK because "take protein pills" is parallel to "eat a hamburger.")

> **INCORRECT:** John wants to eat a hamburger rather than drinking a milkshake. (Not OK, because "drinking a milkshake" isn't parallel to anything.)

Whereas X, Y: "Whereas" is used to introduce a clause that is contrasted with another clause. The two clauses should be parallel in structure in the sense that the main features of the word order and grammatical structure of the first clause should be reproduced in the second clause. The things that are being compared should be in essentially the same positions in both clauses. This makes the comparison clearer.

> **CORRECT:** Whereas in Germany the commercial production of beer is governed by strict laws intended to ensure purity, in the United States the beer industry is subject to much looser regulation.

> **INCORRECT:** Whereas in Germany the commercial production of beer is governed by strict laws intended to ensure purity, there is much looser regulation of beer production in the United States.

The correct version has the parallel phrases "in Germany... in the United states" at the beginnings of the clauses. The incorrect version expresses roughly the same ideas, but the clauses are not as fully parallel.

Here's another example:

> **CORRECT:** Whereas the primary risk factor for lung cancer has been identified as cigarette smoking, the risk factors for pancreatic cancer have not been clearly identified.

> **INCORRECT:** Whereas the primary risk factor for lung cancer has been identified as cigarette smoking, scientists still have not fully identified the risk factors for pancreatic cancer.

5.3 WHEN IS PARALLELISM NOT REQUIRED?

Parallelism is required when you are making a comparison (e.g. using "whereas" or "rather than", as explained above), or when you have two or more phrases filling one "slot"; for example, in the sentence "John loves chocolate and coconut", *chocolate* and *coconut* are both objects of the verb *loves*. In the sentence "John drinks chocolate and eats coconut", *drinks chocolate* and *eats coconut* are both verb phrases that go with a single subject. These are examples of two phrases filling one grammatical slot.

Parallelism is <u>not</u> required if the sentence doesn't have two or more phrases filling the same slot. For example, look at this sentence:

> John loves to eat chocolate, although the doctor told him last year that he should avoid it.

You don't need to worry about parallelism between "John loves to eat chocolate" and "the doctor told him last year that he should avoid it." These are two different clauses connected with *although*, and while each of them has to be internally well-formed as a standard English clause, there's no requirement that any elements within the two separate clauses be parallel.

One situation that often makes test takers worry (unnecessarily) about parallelism is the use of gerund phrases as clausal modifiers. To put it in simpler terms, if the writer uses an –ing phrase either to introduce the sentence or to add some information at the end, that's OK. You don't have to fiddle with things to try to make them parallel. Here are some examples of what we're talking about:

> *Coming back from the store*, John stopped off at the bank.

> The California Salton Sea is a lake accidentally created in 1905 when irrigation canals ruptured, *filling a desert basin*.

There's nothing in the –*ing* modifiers that needs to be parallel to anything else in the sentence.

WHAT COUNTS AS PARALLEL?

Parallelism requires that a series of phrases all be of the same grammatical type: all verbs, or all prepositional phrases, for example. It doesn't require that all the verbs bear the same tense, or that all the prepositions in a series be exactly the same. Here are some examples of series that are considered parallel:

> The industrious businessman <u>has already visited</u> Hong Kong, <u>is currently visiting</u> Taiwan, and <u>will be</u> in Istanbul later this week.

> John <u>runs</u> a small grocery store now, but <u>worked</u> as CEO of a large corporation until recently.

> The mouse ran <u>down the hall</u>, <u>up the stairs</u>, <u>around the bookcase</u>, and <u>under the bed.</u>

If a series begins with a noun phrase with *a* or *the*, the rest of the list may consist of just nouns, as in "The <u>cat</u>, <u>dog</u>, <u>rabbit</u>, and <u>raccoon</u> were all there." Or the word *the* may be repeated each time: "The cat, the dog, the rabbit, and the raccoon were all there." Either way is correct. What is not correct is to repeat *the* for some items on the list (after the first one) and not all of them.

Similarly, if a series begins with an infinitive ('to' plus a verb), the rest of the list may consist of just bare verbs without *to*, as in "He likes <u>to swim</u>, <u>run</u>, and <u>climb</u>." Or the word *to* may be repeated each time, as in "He likes <u>to swim</u>, <u>to run</u> and <u>to climb</u>." Either way is correct. What is not correct is to repeat *to* for some items on the list (after the first one) and not all of them.

Infinitives are <u>not</u> parallel to gerunds (*-ing* forms). "He likes <u>running</u> and <u>to swim</u>" is not parallel and would not be correct on the GMAT.

Infinitives are also not parallel to prepositional phrases. That is, even though an infinitive begins with "to", you can't consider it parallel to a prepositional phrase. (The GMAT has been known to test this point.) For instance, "The protester shouted for justice and to be released" would not be parallel.

Present and past participles can be parallel to each other. A present participle is a verb plus an *–ing* ending: *running, jumping, snoring,* etc. A past participle is a word like *broken, stolen, eaten, shot, killed, thrown, published,* etc. The past participles of many verbs look the same as the past tense forms of the same verbs, but that doesn't mean they are the same. You could think of them as a special kind of adjective made from a verb, as in *The watch stolen by gnomes* or *The man wanted by the police*. The two kinds of participles—present and past—are considered to be the same type of thing for purposes of parallelism, and the GMAT has been known to test this specific point. The following examples illustrate this kind of parallelism:

a. <u>Bleeding</u> from numerous paper cuts and <u>pursued</u> by rabid wolverines, the hero scampered towards safety.

b. <u>Assembled</u> from an astonishing range of sources and <u>covering</u> an equally impressive sweep of history, the 10-volume *History of Peat Moss* makes for riveting reading.

c. Lavishly <u>illustrated</u> by trained lemurs yet <u>costing</u> only pennies per page, this volume is one coffee table book that no home should be without.

5.4 THE TRAPS THE GMAT USES

Now that you know when things must be parallel and what counts as parallel, all that remains is for you to learn to navigate around the traps that the GMAT typically sets. On the actual GMAT, questions that hinge on parallelism will range from simple sentences with obvious errors to much more complex sentences in which it is difficult to tell which phrases should be parallel. There are four main ways the GMAT writers can make spotting the errors in parallelism tricky. Read the explanations and do the exercises to develop your skill in avoiding these traps.

5.4.1 FAILING TO CLOSE THE LIST

A GMAT sentence may have a sequence of phrases joined only with commas rather than with a closing connector such as *and, or, but, yet,* etc. **Avoid this trap** by reading the entire sequence and making sure that it ends with an appropriate final phrase. Don't be thrown off by any phrases that are added in to interrupt the sequence: read the sequence itself carefully and make sure it ends properly. For example:

> The moonrock known as armalcolite is named for the three astronauts who manned the Apollo 11 mission—Neil Armstrong, Buzz Aldrin, who was the second man to walk on the moon but was the first to take communion in a space capsule situated on the lunar surface and was also the first to urinate inside his spacesuit while standing on the moon, Michael Collins.

There's a mistake in this sentence, but it's hard to hear because the sequence of names is interrupted by a digression about Aldrin. Check the sentence by scanning along just the names: "Neil Armstrong, Buzz Aldrin, Michael Collins." Some people find it helpful to trace along with their finger on the screen and/or read the sequence out loud. You can hear that the word *and* is missing. The sentence should read:

> The moonrock known as armalcolite is named for the three astronauts who manned the Apollo 11 mission—Neil Armstrong, Buzz Aldrin, who was the second man to walk on the moon but was the first to take communion in a space capsule situated on the lunar surface and was also the first to urinate inside his spacesuit while standing on the moon, *and* Michael Collins.

Those with a background in literature may object that some of the most highly respected writers in the English language sometimes deliberately omit the connecting word at the end of

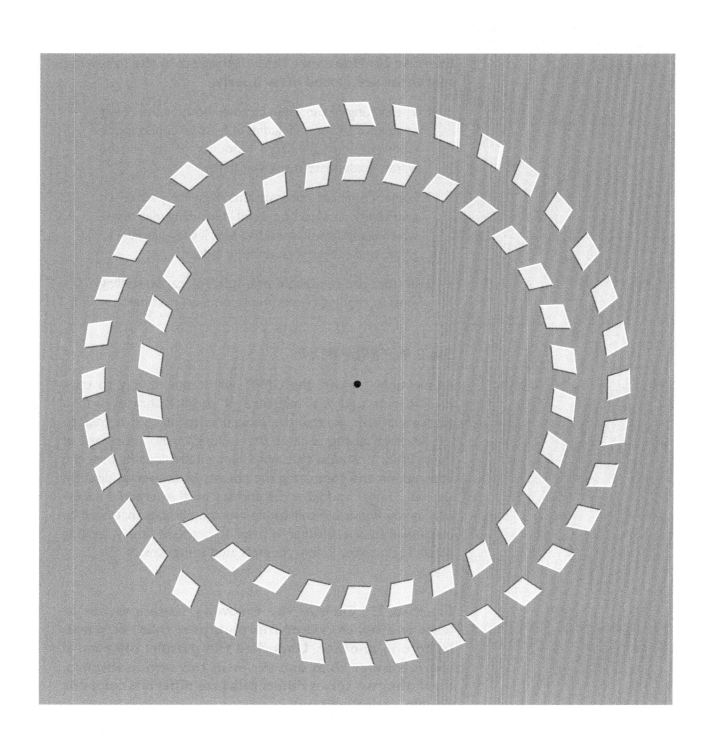

a list, in order to create a particular effect (a technique called asyndeton). However, Emily Dickinson and Ernest Hemingway aren't taking this test. The GMAT is testing standard written English, not literary art, and on the GMAT, failing to close the list properly is always a mistake.

Exercise 28: Make sure that all the lists in the following sentences are closed off properly.

1. The sinking of the Titanic came about as the result of several factors, including excessive speed, poor visibility, unusually large amounts of ice in the water, inadequate maneuverability.

2. Some common superstitions require people to avoid black cats, to be careful in handling mirrors—which bring seven years' bad luck if they break—to go around rather than under a ladder.

3. In the pre-television era, playing cards, telling stories, reading books were common pastimes.

5.4.2 INTERRUPTIONS

As mentioned above, the GMAT will frequently try to trick you by interrupting a sequence of parallel phrases with a phrase that isn't part of the sequence, to make it harder to tell whether all the phrases that belong in the series are of the right form. **Avoid this trap** by mentally skipping over the interruption and comparing the phrases in the series directly. Use your finger to follow the phrases on the screen if necessary. If you find it difficult to identify the phrases that need to be parallel to one another, it helps to practice simply locating parallel sequences in long, complicated sentences.

Exercise 29: Each of the following sentences has at least one set of two or more phrases that are parallel to one another. Underline the parallel phrases. If there is more than one series in the same sentence, mark the two series differently (use different colors or double-underline one).

1. The board of directors decided to diversify the company's product line, to hire a new marketing agency, and to plant spies in the competitors' factories.

2. A triathlon is a multi-sport endurance event consisting of swimming, cycling, and running, in immediate succession.

3. Joan of Arc reported that Saint Michael, Saint Catherine, and Saint Margaret told her to dress as a man, to take up arms, to drive out the English and to bring the Dauphin to Reims for his coronation.

4. Charged with instituting new cost-saving measures, the library committee decided almost immediately to increase overdue fines, an important source of revenue for the library, and to cut back on hours.

5. When the Californian's officers first saw the lights of an unknown ship on the horizon, they tried signaling her with their Morse lamp, but never appeared to receive a response.

6. How long the Titanic will remain on the ocean's floor is unclear; many scientists, including Robert Ballard, are concerned that visits by tourists in submersibles and the recovery of artifacts are hastening the decay of the wreck.

5.4.3 RED HERRINGS

The GMAT may use confusing sentence structure to trick you into thinking that one phrase should be parallel to another, when in fact it should be parallel to something else entirely. That is, if there are 3 phrases (A, B, and C), you may think that C should be parallel to A, when in fact C should be parallel to B. **Avoid this trap** by thinking carefully about the meaning of the sentence and making sure that the version of the sentence you pick makes sense. Think about how each phrase in the series connects with the rest of the sentence to make sure that the version you pick makes sense.

Example:

> The thousands of tons of ash from the supervolcano that erupted 75,000 years ago in Toba, Sumatra, killed three quarters of all plants in the northern hemisphere by blocking the light from the sun and <u>pushing mankind to the edge of extinction</u>.

Which version is preferable?

a. pushing mankind to the edge of extinction

b. pushed mankind to the edge of extinction

To answer the question, think about the <u>meaning</u> of each version and which one makes more sense. (a) would mean that the way that the supervolcano killed three quarters of all plants in the northern hemisphere was by both blocking light from the sun and pushing mankind to the edge of extinction. (b) means that the volcano killed three quarters of all plants in the northern hemisphere, and pushed mankind to the edge of extinction. Clearly (b) makes more sense.

Exercise 30: Choose one of the two versions of each underlined phrase. Pay attention to meaning to decide which one is correct.

1. The detective identified the murderer after interviewing several witnesses—some of whom were frightened and reluctant to talk—and <u>uncovered/uncovering</u> several important but previously unknown clues.

2. The startling profit and loss figures released by the board of directors sent stock prices plummeting, panicked investors into selling as fast as possible and <u>triggered/triggering</u> an SEC investigation.

3. Having overpowered its prey, a cat may deliver a lethal neck bite with its long <u>canine teeth</u>, thus either severing the prey's <u>spinal cord</u> with irreversible <u>paralysis</u> or causing fatal bleeding by puncturing the <u>carotid artery</u> or the <u>jugular vein</u>, or <u>asphyxiate/asphyxiating</u> the prey by crushing its <u>trachea</u>.

4. Some researchers believe that cats who bring prey to their owners are attempting to take care of them much as they would care for a sick or elderly cat, <u>bring/to bring/bringing</u> food to sustain them until they are well enough to hunt for themselves.

5. Soon after stepping out of the spacecraft onto the surface of the moon, Armstrong made photographic records of the lunar module so engineers would be able to judge its post-landing condition, <u>making/make</u> a panoramic sweep with the MESA TV camera, and then collected a contingency soil sample using a sample bag on a stick.

5.4.4 SOUND-ALIKES

GMAT questions that test parallelism often use words that could easily give the wrong impression as to which part of speech they belong to. For example, words that end in –ing could be present participles or nouns; the GMAT may present a series of –ing words to trick you into choosing a participle that also ends in –ing, when the correct choice is a noun. Words that end in –ed could be past tense verbs or passive participles; some of the answer choices will also have past tense forms, and others will have passive participles or even present participles.

Avoid this trap by reading the entire sequence carefully and ensuring it makes sense. Don't just assume that because a few of the words in the sequence end in –ing or -ed, all of them should.

Exercise 31: Decide which word in the underlined pair is correct.

1. The young entrepreneur accomplished many of his goals astonishingly early: by the age of twelve he had founded a successful business, set aside enough money for his retirement, met most of the major players in the industry, and <u>wrote/written</u> a best-selling book.

2. Investigators found signs of widespread fighting, killing and <u>destroying/destruction</u> at the battle site.

Exercise 32: Overall review of parallelism. Identify the errors (if any) in parallelism in the sentences below and correct them.

1. The source of the fire that killed the Mercury 7 astronauts was never determined but their deaths were attributed to a wide range of lethal design hazards in the early Apollo command module such as its highly pressurized 100% oxygen atmosphere during the test, many wiring and plumbing flaws, inflammable materials in the cockpit, a hatch which might not open at all in an emergency and even the flight suits worn by the astronauts may have been a factor.

2. After the capsule splashed down, Grissom began final preparations for egress, opening up the faceplate on his helmet, disconnected the oxygen hose from the helmet, unfastening the helmet from his suit, released the chest strap, the lap belt, the shoulder harness, knee straps and medical sensors.

3. Carnivorous plants employ a variety of traps to capture and digest insects: pitfall traps, flypaper, lobster pots, as well as sticky hairs.

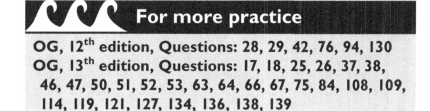

For more practice

OG, 12th edition, Questions: 28, 29, 42, 76, 94, 130

OG, 13th edition, Questions: 17, 18, 25, 26, 37, 38, 46, 47, 50, 51, 52, 53, 63, 64, 66, 67, 75, 84, 108, 109, 114, 119, 121, 127, 134, 136, 138, 139

MODULE 6: IDIOMS

MODULE 6: IDIOMS

6.1 TOP PRIORITY: THE MOST IMPORTANT IDIOMS

The terms *idioms* and *idiomatic* are used in two different but related senses. In some cases, when the correct answer on the GMAT is identified as a matter of "idiom" or being "idiomatic", it means nothing more than, "This is considered the most natural, elegant way to say it." In short: This is how English is.

In other cases, the term "idiom" when applied to the GMAT means a specific phrase that is considered correct, while very similar phrases are considered incorrect. For example, "different from" is considered to be the correct idiom on the GMAT, while "different than" is wrong. (This is not precisely the standard use of the term "idiom" in any context outside of the GMAT.)

 GRAB A CLUE: The idiomatic phrases in the list below come up frequently in official material, suggesting that they're likely to come up again on the real GMAT. Some of these are considered important enough by the GMAT writers that the entire question hinges on getting the idiom right. If you have only a small amount of time to prepare for the GMAT, you should memorize these phrases; first we give you the form the GMAT considers correct, then the version(s) that would not be credited on the GMAT. Whenever you see them in a question, you should use them to eliminate the wrong choices as quickly as possible.

1. **ability to do** Use this phrase rather than "ability for doing." For example:

   CORRECT: The company hopes to enhance its ability to compete.

   INCORRECT: The company hopes to enhance its ability for competing.

2. **acclaimed as** not "acclaimed to be"

3. **appear to be, seem to be** not "appear as" or "seem as"

4. **attribute** [effect] **to** [cause]

   Lady GaGa **attributes** her success **to** her previous experience writing songs for others.

   Doctors **attribute** many cases of coronary artery disease **to** a high-fat diet.

   In a passive construction, "attribute" will be used like this:

   [effect] **is attributed to** [cause]

   Lady GaGa's success **is attributed to** her previous experience writing songs for others.

Many cases of coronary artery disease **are attributed to** a high fat diet.

5. **claim to be able** not "claim the ability"

Scientists **claim to be able** to identify planets orbiting other stars.

Not: Scientists claim the ability to identify planets orbiting other stars.

6. **consider X Y**

Automatically reject any choice that uses the form "consider X to be Y" or "consider X as Y." For example:

CORRECT: I consider President Obama a good speaker.

INCORRECT: I consider President Obama to be a good speaker.

INCORRECT: I consider President Obama as a good speaker.

CORRECT: President Obama is considered a good speaker.

INCORRECT: President Obama is considered to be a good speaker.

INCORRECT: President Obama is considered as a good speaker.

7. **credit X with Y** (not "credit X for Y")

The passive form is "X is credited with Y"

8. **dated at** not "dated to be"

The pyramids are **dated at** 5,000 years old.

9. **different from**

Choose "different from" rather than "different than" or "different to."

10. **distinction between X and Y** not "distinction of X from Y" or "distinction X has from Y"

11. **equipped to do** not "equipped for doing"

12. **estimate** [something] **to be** [age] (often used in the passive voice)

Archeologists **estimate** the fossil **to be** 35 million years old.

The fossil is **estimated to be** 35 million years old.

13. **forbid X to do** not "forbid X from doing"

14. **known to be** not "known as being"

15. **mistake X for Y**

16. **prohibit X from doing** not "prohibit X to do"

17. **targeted at** not "targeted to"

18. **think of X as Y** not "think of X to be Y"

19. **try to do** this is the correct form, not "try and do." For example:

CORRECT: The corporation is going to **try to raise** the value of its stock by cutting costs.

INCORRECT: The corporation is going to try and raise the value of its stock by cutting costs.

20. **whether** Use the word "whether" by itself, not "whether or not". On the GMAT, the phrase "or not" is considered redundant with "whether" (since "whether" already includes the idea of uncertainty).

21. **with the aim of VERB-ing** or **aimed at VERB-ing** not "with the aim to"

22. **X is to Y what W is to Z** not "X is to Y like W to Z" or "X is to Y just as W is to Z"

You should also review the paired idioms:

not only... but also

both... and

neither... nor

not... but

from... to

between... and

just as... so

These are tested very commonly on the GMAT. See section 5.1.2 on parallelism with paired expressions.

For more practice

OG, 12th edition, Questions: 40
OG, 13th edition, Question: 4, 15, 21, 24, 28, 30, 34, 38, 51, 56, 57, 59, 62, 74, 76, 79, 81, 82, 95, 119, 122, 140

Exercise 33: Choose the version of each sentence that has no errors in the use of idioms.

1.
   a. The manager decided to try and improve morale, with the aim of increasing productivity.

   b. The manager decided to try to improve morale, with the aim to increase productivity.

   c. The manager decided to try to improve morale, with the aim of increasing productivity.

2.
   a. Rice is to Asia just like wheat is to Europe: the staple grain.

   b. Rice is to Asia what wheat is to Europe: the staple grain.

3.
   a. Benjamin Franklin is credited with proving that lightning is electricity.

   b. Benjamin Franklin is credited for proving that lightning is electricity.

4.
   a. Asian elephants are different from African elephants in several interesting ways.

   b. Asian elephants are different than African elephants in several interesting ways.

5.
   a. Though the fossils were originally estimated at 35 million years old, paleontologists have more recently dated them to be 47 million years old.

   b. Though the fossils were originally estimated to be 35 million years old, paleontologists have more recently dated them at 47 million years old.

   c. Though the fossils were originally estimated to be 35 million years old, paleontologists have more recently dated them to be 47 million years old.

   d. Though the fossils were originally estimated at 35 million years old, paleontologists have more recently dated them at 47 million years old.

6.2 DANGER! EXPRESSIONS THAT ARE (ALMOST) ALWAYS CONSIDERED WRONG ON THE GMAT

 GRAB A CLUE: Memorize these expressions; if they appear in a GMAT answer choice, immediately check to see whether you can eliminate that choice. Some of the expressions below are always wrong; others are wrong only if they are used with a particular meaning.

1. **liable to** (meaning "likely to")

Many native speakers are accustomed to using "liable" to mean "likely", as in "He's liable to lose his temper and do something foolish." This usage is considered non-standard in formal written English; choose "likely to" instead.

2. **the reason why/the reason is because/for the reason that**

All of these phrases are considered wordy or redundant, and therefore incorrect on the GMAT. Each of these examples would be considered wrong:

> The reason why so many people drink coffee every day has to do with the effects of caffeine on the brain.

> The reason so many people drink coffee every day is because they have become addicted to caffeine.

> Many people drink coffee every day for the reason that they are addicted to caffeine.

After the word "reason," you don't need any connecting word at all; in other words, the following sentence could be correct on the GMAT:

> <u>The reason so many people drink coffee</u> is that they enjoy the effects of caffeine.

In many cases, though, the GMAT will want a more concise version:

> Many people drink coffee because they enjoy the effects of caffeine.

3. **hopefully**

In modern conversational English, "hopefully" is often used to mean that the speaker hopes something is true, as in "Hopefully, he's feeling better by now." The GMAT follows the more traditional rule, according to which "hopefully" is used only to describe doing something in a hopeful manner. In other words, "John asked hopefully whether the mail had come yet" would be correct, but "Hopefully, the mail has come by now" would be incorrect—the mail isn't doing anything in a hopeful manner. In short: don't choose "hopefully" to mean that someone hopes something is true. For example:

> **INCORRECT:** The CEO said that hopefully, the economic forecast would improve by the end of the quarter.

> **CORRECT:** The CEO said that he hoped that the economic forecast would improve by the end of the quarter.

4. on account of

"On account of" is generally considered wordy and awkward on the GMAT; look for a simpler expression such as "because".

5. as to

Although "as to" may be correct in the context of a larger expression ("so X as to Y"—although as noted, the GMAT writers are giving mixed signals about the acceptability of that expression), it shouldn't be used as a substitute for "about" or "over." For example, "There is some concern as to the chance of an epidemic" or "There was a great deal of discussion as to the best course of action." In these contexts "as to" is wordy and vague. Choose a preposition such as "about" or "over" instead.

6. so as to

Do not choose the phrase "so as to" when the three words appear together as an unbroken phrase meaning "in order to" (which is also a phrase the GMAT doesn't like). The GMAT will prefer a simple "to" or "could."

INCORRECT: John sold his house so as to move to the East Coast.

INCORRECT: John sold his house in order to move to the East Coast.

CORRECT: John sold his house so he could move to the East Coast.

INCORRECT: The lion moves silently so as to catch its prey.

CORRECT: The lion moves silently to catch its prey.

7. as contrasted with

This formulation is always wrong. Choose "in contrast with", "in contrast to", or simply "unlike" instead.

8. being

The GMAT generally doesn't like the word "being", although this is not because there's anything intrinsically wrong with it. It's just that the GMAT Sentence Correction writers usually throw in "being" in a context in which it's unnecessary and wordy. They do it so often that many test prep instructors simply tell test takers, "Never pick *being*." This is too simplistic, however. It appears that in the last few years, the GMAT writers must have become aware that test takers were using this as a shortcut: items on recent practice tests on the official GMAC site included *being* in the correct answer, and so does one item in OG-11 and another item in OG-12. So rather than follow the simple-minded rule, "never pick *being*", test takers need to be aware of what is <u>usually</u> wrong with *being* in the way it appears in the GMAT, and pick an answer with *being* only when they're sure that it's right.

When is *being* wrong? Generally speaking, the incorrect uses of *being* fall into two categories. GMAT items often add *being* to a phrase that doesn't require it, especially when the implied meaning is *because*. For example, in the sentence "Being afraid of losing his job, John covered up his mistake", the word "being" isn't needed—you could say "Because he was afraid of losing his job, John…" or simply "Afraid of losing his job, John…" A good rule of thumb is, **if you can remove "being" without changing the meaning—that answer is wrong.**

Incorrect GMAT sentences with *being* also tend to violate the rule that the subject of a gerund must be possessive. For example, a wrong answer choice might say "The company being insolvent caused investors to panic" rather than "The company's being insolvent…" So you will usually have two clues that the version with *being* is wrong.

It's true that "being" is <u>usually</u> wrong on the GMAT. But if an item with "being" doesn't break either of the rules described above and if you're sure the other choices are wrong, don't be afraid to choose the answer with "being." (And, it should go without saying, don't hesitate to pick an answer that includes the phrase "human being"—that isn't even the same "being." GMAT writers may be using that phrase to throw off test takers who have memorized the "never pick *being*" rule.)

For more practice

OG, 12th edition, Questions: 39, 76
OG, 13th edition, Questions: 24, 31, 51, 60, 66, 76,
99, 100, 110, 117, 122, 124

Exercise 34: Find any mistakes in the phrasing or usage of idioms.

1. Being a well-known author, Neil Gaiman is often asked for autographs.

2. The district manager reported that hopefully, there would be a significant improvement in sales for the next quarter.

3. Simplified Chinese characters have fewer strokes as contrasted with traditional Chinese characters.

6.3 HANDLE WITH CARE: PHRASES THAT ARE NOT ALWAYS WRONG BUT REQUIRE CAREFUL THOUGHT

1. in that vs. because

The phrase "in that" does not mean exactly the same thing as "because." "In that" is used when the writer is about to explain <u>in what way</u> something is true. "Because" is used to explain <u>why</u> something is true.

These examples show the contrast:

> The famous athlete is a hypocrite in that he frequently criticized public figures who were unfaithful to their wives, while he himself was unfaithful to his wife.

Here the writer isn't explaining <u>why</u> the athlete is a hypocrite—the cause—but explaining <u>in what sense</u> the athlete is a hypocrite.

> The famous athlete is a hypocrite because he was raised to be one.

Here the writer is giving the cause—how the athlete got to be this way.

> The geographic designation of the new national monument Grand Canyon-Parashant is somewhat unusual in that much of the northeastern and northern boundary follows the drainage divide of the Virgin River, an ecological rather than a political boundary.

The writer is explaining <u>in what way</u> this is unusual.

> President Clinton was able to declare Grand Canyon-Parashant a national monument without the aid of lawmakers because the law gives the president that authority.

The writer is explaining <u>why</u> the president was able to do this.

2. due to or because of vs. because or since

For either "due to" or "because of" to have a chance of being correct, it should be followed by a noun, not a clause. An expression like "due to the fact that sales have declined" is guaranteed to be too wordy for the GMAT; look for something short and sweet like "because sales have declined" instead. "Due to" and "because of" have been known to turn up in the non-underlined portions of real GMAT SCs, so we know the GMAT writers don't consider them poison.

However, we can see in the official materials that when "due to" or "because of" appear as part of the underlined portion of an SC, the official GMAT writers usually use it in the incorrect answer choices that are wordy and awkward. In general, don't choose an answer with "due to" or "because of" unless you're certain that it's not too wordy and that the other four choices are wrong.

Note that the GMAT also allows the word *since* to be used to mean *because*—it has appeared with this meaning in official practice materials on the GMAC site.

3. double vs. twice

The usage of "double" and "twice" on the GMAT causes a great deal of confusion. (Some of the explanations in the Official Guides don't help much, either.) We have gone through every example available from official sources, from the last 5 editions of the Official Guide and the Verbal Review supplements to the released GMATs, and determined that these are the rules that the official material follows:

In these sources, "double" when used correctly is always used as a verb, as in these examples:

> Prices <u>have doubled</u> over the last six months.

> With modern fertilizers, the crop yield <u>has more than doubled</u>.

> Scientists recently found five new species of moth, <u>doubling</u> the number of moth species known to inhabit the region.

Note that while there is a widespread rumor on online GMAT discussion boards that "more than doubled" is not accepted on the GMAT, this rumor is mistaken; "more than doubled" does in fact appear in the credited answer choice in official materials. See, for example, Official Guide 10th Edition Question 72. An expression such as "increased by more than double" is always wrong because it's too wordy. While commentary in the Official Guide(s) mentions that "double" <u>could</u> be used as an adjective, in every official example in which "double" was correct, it was used as a verb.

In contexts in which a verb would not be appropriate, the adverb "twice" is preferred, as in these examples:

> The company spends twice as much on advertising as on product safety.

Fourteen car burglaries were reported this year, twice as many as were reported last year.

A recent survey found that 80% of residents favor the tax proposal, twice the number reported by the previous survey.

In short: If "double" is used as a verb, as in "prices have doubled" or "recent findings double the number of fossils available for study", it may well be the correct answer. If "double" is not used as a verb, "twice" (especially an expression such as "twice as many" or "twice as much") is usually the preferred choice. The expressions "twice the number" and "twice the figure" are definitely accepted. The very similar expressions "double the number" or "double the figure" have never appeared as either rejected or credited choices in official materials, but based on the Official Guide comment that "double" can be an adjective, we can predict that they would probably be accepted. On the other hand, an expression such as "double the apples" sounds awkward and unclear; the Official Guide describes this merely as "vague" and does not go so far as to call it outright ungrammatical (see Official Guide 12th Edition, discussion of question #125), but such constructions with "double" never appear in any credited answer choice. When in doubt, unless "double" is used as a verb in one of the answer choices, look for an expression such as "twice as many" or "twice as much."

4. determined through vs. determined by

The verb "determine" can be used with either the preposition "through" or the preposition "by." The meanings are different, however. To say that something is "determined through" something else is to describe the means by which scholars or investigators determine the nature of that thing. To say that something is determined "by" something else is to talk about the cause of whatever the phenomenon is.

For example: Physical characteristics such as height are determined by the interaction of dominant and recessive genes inherited from the parents; this understanding was initially determined through a series of experiments on plants.

5. be able to/be capable of

Be cautious when a GMAT sentence uses the phrase "able to" or "capable of." These phrases are often unnecessarily wordy (look for something shorter such as "can" or "could"), and may be fully incorrect if the sentence is intended to say only that something is possible, not that the subject of the sentence has some sort of ability.

For example: "Computers may be capable of being programmed to pilot airplanes." Does this really make sense? While the computers can be programmed, this isn't a capability that the computers have. It is the human programmers who have the capability of making this happen. Notice that the verb is in the passive form ("capable of being programmed"). This should be a tip-off that the choice of the word "capable" is wrong, because it doesn't make sense to say that something is capable of having someone else do something to it.

Contrast:

INCORRECT: Researchers have discovered that the liver has the capability of being damaged by certain painkillers.

INCORRECT: Researchers have discovered that the liver has the ability to be damaged by certain painkillers.

INCORRECT: Researchers have discovered that the liver is able to be damaged by certain painkillers.

CORRECT: Researchers have discovered that the liver can be damaged by certain painkillers.

6. *act as* vs. *act like*

To act <u>as</u> something is to fill a role or act in some sort of official capacity: "While the Director is in the hospital, Ralph will act as director to keep the project going." To act <u>like</u> something is simply to act in a particular way: "Ralph is acting like a small child."

7. *as a means to* vs. *as a means of*

"As a means to" is used to talk about a goal; "as a means of" is used to describe the way something is done. For example:

Some people write fan fiction as a **means of** artistic expression. (Fan fiction is itself a form of artistic expression, not something that people do as a stepping-stone toward artistic expression.)

The ancient Egyptians used mummification as a **means to** immortality. (Mummification is not, itself, a kind of immortality; it's a technique used to achieve immortality.)

8. "so X as to Y," "so X that Y," "X enough to Y" and "X enough that Y"

There is some confusion as to the GMAT's position on the idiom "so X as to Y." "So X as to Y" was at one time considered correct in official materials (as recently as OG-10). In the Official Guide 11th Edition item 33 (which is the same as 12th Edition item 37), however, "so X as to Y" is described as "not a correct idiom", though there is no further explanation. In item 33 of the 11th Edition, however, the answer choice that included the idiom "so X as to Y" also had an incorrect verb tense, unlike the case in all the older examples in which the idiom was considered correct. In short, we are not sure whether "so X as to Y" has been permanently rejected by the GMAT writers or whether it was just not the right idiom for the context of item 33 of the 11th Edition of the Official Guide, perhaps because of confounding factors involving verb tense. The expression "so X that Y" always appears to be an acceptable idiom.

An alternate idiom with almost the same meaning is "X enough to Y" (note: not "X enough that Y"). There is a subtle difference in meaning between the two, but it is probably not a large enough difference to make one idiom flat-out wrong in a context where the other one is right. "So X as to Y" is used to comment on the surprising quality or intensity of X, whereas "X enough to Y" is merely saying that X had met some minimum threshold required to make something happen. For example:

> The expression on the Mona Lisa's face was so enigmatic as to be the subject of speculation by generations of art critics.

> Stock prices have risen so high as to cause a frenzy of speculation.

> Global temperatures have risen high enough to melt some glaciers.

> Average temperatures inside a volcano are not always hot enough to melt rocks.

The bottom line: "so X as to Y" was at one time listed as a correct idiom in official GMAT materials. Grammarians still believe it is correct. More recent editions of the OG prefer the idiom "so X that Y." "X enough to Y" is also considered correct on the GMAT, but "X enough that Y" is <u>always</u> wrong.

9. *try to VERB* vs. *try VERB-ing*

Both "try to do" and "try doing" are good English, but they have different meanings. "Try to do X" means "attempt to do X"—the person may or may not be able to do it. "Try doing X" means that the person will do X experimentally, perhaps to see if he likes it. There's no question about whether the person <u>can</u> do X, only what the results will be. Note the contrast:

> John tried to ice skate, but he fell down repeatedly.

> John tried ice skating, but decided he preferred skiing.

Exercise 35: Identify any idiom that is incorrectly used and replace it with an appropriate idiom.

1. In an attempt to increase sales, the company tried to lower prices, but even this failed to attract more customers.

2. Determined to improve his department's performance, the manager tried convincing the employees to care more about the quality of their work, but was unable to do so.

3. The heat inside a volcano is often hot enough that it melts rock.

4. Some dieters use herbal supplements and fasting as a means to lose weight.

5. Though most clothes are washed after one day's use, jeans are able to be worn two or three days in a row before they are washed.

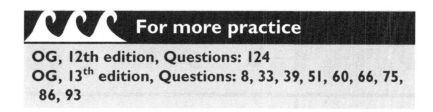

For more practice

OG, 12th edition, Questions: 124
OG, 13th edition, Questions: 8, 33, 39, 51, 60, 66, 75, 86, 93

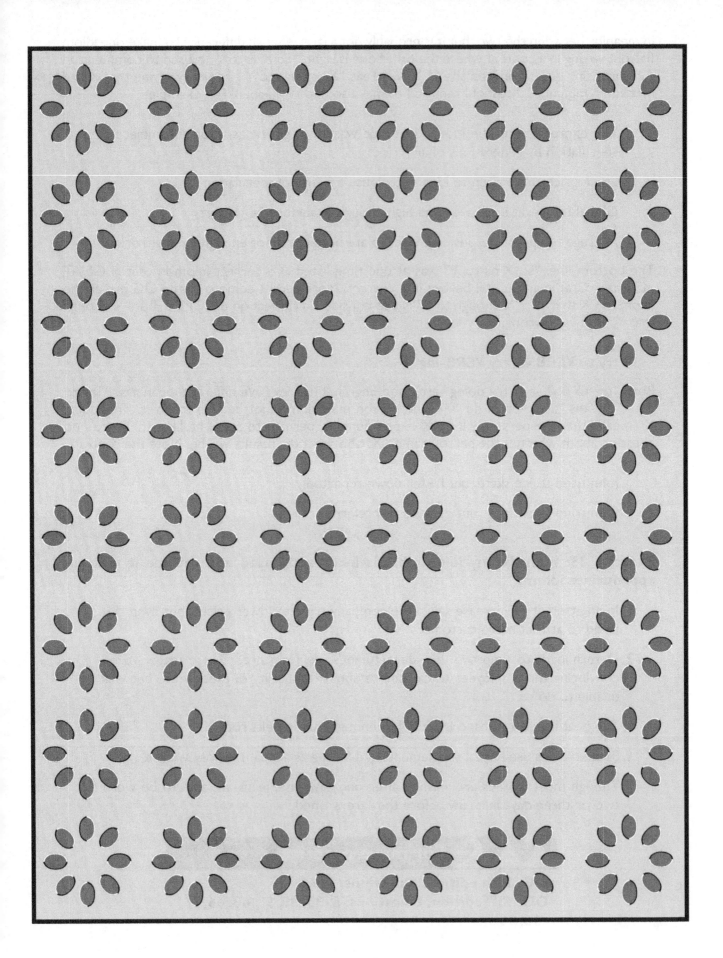

6.4 CAN YOU MEMORIZE EVERY POSSIBLE IDIOM?

Can you memorize every single idiom the GMAT might ever test? In a word, no. You can study the list of idioms that have come up in official GMAT materials in the past and focus on those that seem particularly likely to come up on a real GMAT, but the fact is that there's no limit to the phrases that GMAT writers might choose to focus on.

However, there is a useful technique for dealing with any Sentence Correction question that depends on an idiom. The GMAT commonly tests the usage of various words, particularly verbs, with a focus on the words that accompany them. For example, in English the word "discuss" is used without a preposition, as in "We need to discuss the problem", not "We need to discuss *about* the problem." The GMAT often gives you a verb and tests whether you know what should go along with it. Often, the question will use large, unfamiliar words to make it hard to tell whether the word is used correctly.

The key to solving these is to mentally step back from the question and construct your own phrase using the same verb. Use ordinary, everyday words so that you can more easily hear which phrasing sounds correct. When you feel you know which one is right, go back to the GMAT question and eliminate the choices that use the verb incorrectly.

For example, suppose the GMAT question looks like this (for simplicity's sake, we'll just give two answer choices):

> A controversial study has found that methamphetamine usage may <u>exacerbate the effects of HIV by enhancing a retrovirus's ability for replicating rapidly</u>.

> a. exacerbate the effects of HIV by enhancing a retrovirus's ability for replicating rapidly

> b. exacerbate the effects of HIV by enhancing a retrovirus's ability to replicate rapidly

The question hinges on whether the correct phrasing is "a retrovirus's ability for rapid replication" or "a retrovirus's ability to replicate rapidly." The unusual words can easily be so distracting that they make it hard to hear which one is right; perhaps neither one sounds entirely normal to you. So take a step back from this sentence and make up a test phrase using more common words. Ask yourself which sounds better, "John's ability to play the piano" or "John's ability for playing the piano"? If English is your first language (or if you're a fluent, non-native speaker), you can probably hear immediately that the correct version is the first one. Then you can go back to the GMAT question and determine that (b) is the better choice.

That technique will get you through a lot of sentences that depend on choosing the right preposition or other grammatical form, without your needing to do a lot of memorization (assuming you speak English natively or at least fluently). But the GMAT also tests distinctions that aren't as obvious to all speakers. In some cases, everyday spoken English would allow for two or three different ways of expressing something, but the GMAT considers only one of the versions to be correct.

Regionalisms—the way that something is commonly said in one part of the U.S. but not another—may also be tested: the GMAT sometimes contrasts the standard ("correct") written form of an expression with a non-standard variant that's commonly used in just one part of the country. This means that an idiom trap that seems obvious to someone from the East Coast might seem very tricky to someone from the Midwest, or vice versa. The bottom line: even a highly educated native speaker of English needs to review the list of idioms that the GMAT considers "correct", and memorize any that don't seem obvious. If you encounter a phrase you haven't memorized, try placing it in a more familiar, simpler context and see whether it sounds right.

6.5 DISTINCTIONS YOU DON'T NEED TO WORRY ABOUT

There are a handful of idiom pairs that GMAT test takers sometimes worry about needlessly: both members of the pair are considered correct on the GMAT.

I. compared to/compared with

This pair of phrases appears on many GMAT idiom lists, but GMAT experts who have examined large numbers of official items report that the difference between these two (to the extent that there is a difference) is never the key factor in determining the right answer.

2. in contrast to/in contrast with

According to the explanation of item 16 given in OG-11, either idiom is correct.

3. help VERB/help to VERB

Both patterns appear in examples in the Official Guides and both are listed as correct.

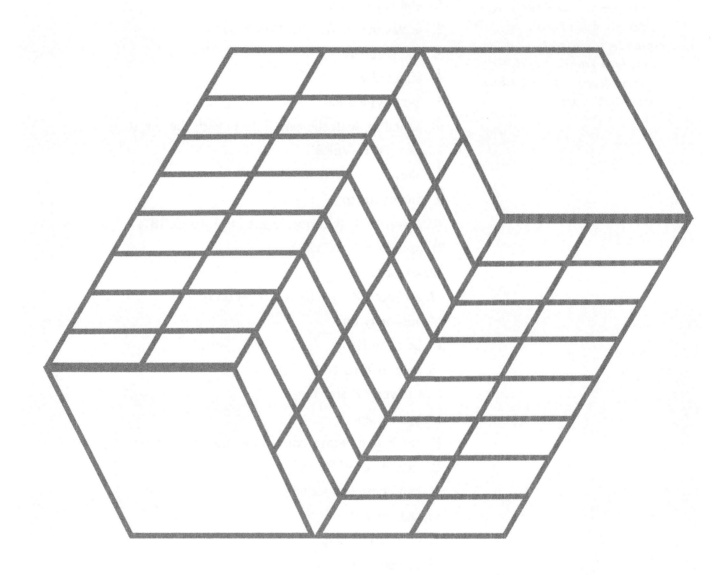

This list includes the idioms discussed above as well as others that are less commonly tested but could possibly come up. Of course, no list can include every phrase that might ever appear on the GMAT, but the majority of the phrases listed below have appeared in official GMAT materials.

1. ability to VERB
2. acclaimed as (not "acclaimed to be")
3. acquiesce in
4. afflicted with
5. aid in VERB-ing
6. aimed at, with the aim of (not "with the aim to")
7. allow X to VERB
8. allow for
9. analogous to
10. argue for X (but not "argue for X to VERB")
11. associate X with Y
12. attest to
13. attribute X to Y (X is attributed to Y)
14. authority on
15. be at fault for
16. believe X to be Y
17. between X and Y
18. both X and Y
19. call X [a meeting, convention, etc.] to consider Y
20. capable of VERB-ing
21. center on (something)
22. change in
23. claim to be able
24. collide with
25. X is composed of Y
26. X comprises Y
27. conceive of X as Y
28. connection between X and Y
29. consider X Y
30. could well VERB (meaning "probably could" or "could easily")

You will have a growing knack for gravitating toward wilder, wetter, more interesting problems. More and more, you will be drawn to the kind of gain that doesn't requite pain. You'll be so alive and awake that you'll cheerfully push yourself out of your comfort zone in the direction of your personal frontier well before you're forced to do so by divine kicks in the ass.

Rob Brezsny[117]

In the depths of winter I finally learned there was in me an invincible summer.

Albert Camus[118]

31. credit X with Y (X is credited with Y)

32. dated at

33. decide on X

34. decide to VERB

35. different from

36. distinction between X and Y

37. distinguish between X and Y (not "distinguish X from Y")

38. double the figure for (as in "200,000 events of this type happened in 2009, double the figure for 2008")

39. doubt that (not "doubt whether")

40. either X or Y

41. enough to (not "enough that")

42. equipped to VERB (not "equipped for VERB-ing")

43. estimate to be

44. evidence of

45. except for (not "excepting for")

46. expect X to VERB (not "expect X that it should VERB")

47. expend on (not "expend for")

48. for instance (not "as an instance")

49. from X to Y (not "from X up to Y")

50. grounds for VERB-ing (not "grounds to VERB")

51. have sympathy for

52. help VERB/help to VERB

53. in contrast to/with

54. in danger of doing

55. instill X in Y

56. invest in (not "invest into")

57. likely to (not "liable to")

58. liken to

59. make X VERB

60. mistake X for Y

61. native of (describing a person born in a place)

62. native to (describing the natural habitat of a species)

63. neither X nor Y

64. not only X but also Y

65. not so much X as Y

66. oblivious to

67. opportunity to VERB (not "opportunity for VERB-ing"—"opportunity for" would be acceptable with a noun, however)
68. opposed to
69. order X to VERB
70. owe restitution to X for Y
71. permit X to VERB
72. persuade X to VERB
73. prefer X to Y
74. prized as/for
75. prohibit X from VERB-ing (not "prohibit X to VERB")
76. pronounce X Y (not "pronounce X to be Y" or "pronounce X as Y")
77. rate for (when "rate" means "price")
78. rate of (when "rate" means how quickly something is happening)
79. regard X as Y
80. require X to VERB (not "require that X VERB")
81. reluctant to VERB
82. rival X for Y
83. see X as Y
84. seek to VERB
85. separate from
86. subject to
87. subscribe to
88. substitute X for Y
89. suspicious of
90. sympathize with
91. targeted at
92. tendency to
93. think of X as Y (not "think of X to be Y")
94. be tolerant of
95. try to
96. twice as many as
97. view X as Y (not "view X to be Y")
98. X is to Y what W is to Z
99. worry about, be worried about (not "worry over" or "be worried over")

Exercise 36: Idiom Review. Fill in the missing word—if any—in the blank. If nothing is needed, draw a slash mark.

1. Asian elephants are different _____ African elephants.

2. Some trainers consider Asian elephants ____ easier to work with.

3. The Maya are credited _____ having invented an extremely complex writing system.

4. Modern Maya have decided to try ____ learn their ancestors' writing system.

5. Mayan writing is estimated _____ more than 2,000 years old.

6. One set of Mayan inscriptions is dated _____ 1300 years old.

7. The Mayan writing system was initially viewed _____ nothing but pictograms.

8. Some anti-cancer drugs are specifically targeted _____ the cancer cells' ability to create new veins.

9. Some people think of cancer _____ incurable, but in fact it can often be successfully treated.

10. Drug companies often must expend millions of dollars ____ the development of a new drug.

11. The self-absorbed actor often seemed oblivious __ other people's feelings.

12. The game warden said he was unwilling to acquiesce _____ the plan to capture the wild zebras.

13. The cable company's business plan depended on the idea that people would be willing to pay exorbitant rates ____ mediocre entertainment.

14. Some people regard the internet ____ mere entertainment, while others consider it ____ a significant business tool.

15. In a national emergency, the vice president may be called on to act _____ the president.

16. The senator caused a huge scandal by getting drunk and acting _____ a fool at a fundraiser.

17. It is difficult to have a lawyer disbarred without significant evidence _____ wrongdoing.

18. Michael Jackson was acclaimed _____ the best dancer since Fred Astaire.

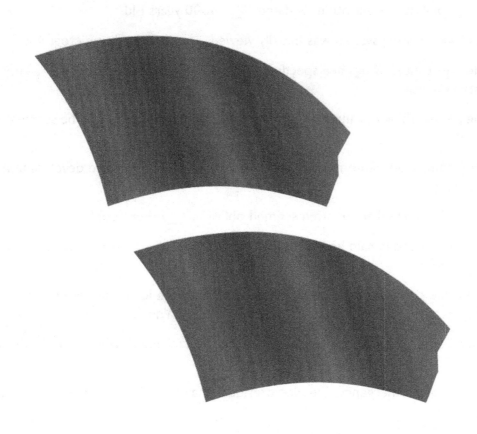

Exercise 37: Decide which of the phrases between brackets is correct.

1. Some linguistics were at first reluctant [to admit/about admitting] that the Mayan writing system was more or less phonetic.

2. The reason the Mayan writing system was unknown for centuries was [because/that] the Spanish conquistadors had done their utmost to suppress it.

3. In the 1980s, scholars claimed [the ability/to be able] to read large segments of ancient Mayan text.

4. The Maya are [attributed with/credited with] the invention of an independent writing system unrelated to any other.

5. There are signs all over the train station prohibiting [passengers from smoking/passengers to smoke].

MODULE 7: CLAUSES AND CLAUSAL CONNECTORS

MODULE 7: CLAUSES AND CLAUSAL CONNECTORS

The one thing that every single sentence must have is a clause. At minimum, a clause is a subject and a verb. Some sentences consist of just one clause:

John ate cake in the kitchen.

It rained all day long.

Without a doubt, vanilla ice cream is better than chocolate.

In each example, there is just one subject and verb, so there is just one clause. More complicated sentences can have more than one clause. In the following examples, we've put each clause in brackets. Notice that each clause has a subject and a verb.

[After the company acquired its chief competitor], [its stock value rose significantly].

[Unless the government intervenes], [analysts believe [that prices will fall]].

[John said [that he was eating cake in the kitchen]].

Some clauses function as modifiers of other clauses. For example:

[If it rains], [the reservoir will overflow].

The clause "if it rains" is a modifier of the clause "the reservoir will overflow." Notice that if the sentence were only "The reservoir will overflow", it would still sound like a complete sentence. If the sentence were reduced to just "If it rains", that would sound incomplete. A clause that is worded so it can function as a modifier of another clause doesn't sound correct by itself—you can hear that something is missing.

In evaluating sentences on the GMAT, you need to notice when a sentence sounds as if there's a piece missing. Then ensure that the version you pick is complete in terms of having all the clauses that are supposed to be there and having them connected to one another with appropriate connecting words. In this section we'll show you the things you need to check for.

7.1 MAKE SURE THAT THERE IS AN INDEPENDENT CLAUSE

Every sentence must have a main clause—that is, a clause that does not function as a modifier of any other clause but that could stand by itself as an independent sentence. In this example, the main clause is underlined:

> When he got back from the store, before he did anything else, <u>John took a shower</u>.

There are three clauses in the sentence. The first two—"when he got back from the store" and "before he did anything else"—function as modifiers. You can determine that if those stood alone as sentences, they would sound incomplete. The main clause is "John took a shower." It could stand alone as a whole sentence and still sound OK.

One or more of the choices on a GMAT SC question may be a complicated sentence that has no main clause. For example:

> Although the meat, upon inspection, was found to have been inadequately refrigerated, <u>but it was not contaminated with dangerous pathogens</u>.

The underlined portion of the sentence [the (a) choice] cannot be correct, as the sentence simply has no main clause—no clause that could stand by itself as an independent sentence. A better version would be:

> Although the meat, upon inspection, was found to have been inadequately refrigerated, it was not contaminated with dangerous pathogens.

It's very common for the GMAT to offer an answer choice that would produce a sentence that has no main clause. Avoid this trap by reading your choice back into the sentence and making sure that the complete sentence has a main clause.

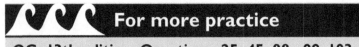

For more practice

OG, 13th edition, Questions: 25, 45, 88, 99, 103, 108

7.2 CLAUSES AND CONNECTING WORDS

A sentence can have multiple clauses (that is, multiple combinations of subjects and verbs). Clauses often require connecting words such as *that*. For example, this sentence is not quite right:

> The CEO announced the company's stock would recover quickly.

The word "that" is missing. It should say "The CEO announced *that* the company's stock would recover quickly."

The GMAT rarely, if ever, tests something as simple as a single clause missing the word "that." However, questions do focus on two clauses that are supposed to be parallel, one of which has "that" while the other does not. For example:

> **INCORRECT:** The alleged perpetrator denied that he had been at the scene and he had had any prior contact with the victim.

> The clause "he had had any prior contact with the victim" should be parallel to "that he had been at the scene," and so it should begin with the word "that":

> **CORRECT:** The alleged perpetrator denied that he had been at the scene and that he had had any prior contact with the victim.

The GMAT also sometimes substitutes a preposition instead of "that", creating sentences similar to these:

> **INCORRECT:** The board was particularly worried <u>about the company's stock had plunged sharply just one week earlier</u>.

> **INCORRECT:** Many of Pasteur's contemporaries were skeptical <u>of invisible living organisms could be the cause of disease</u>.

> Each of the underlined clauses should begin with "that," not "about" or "of."

The connecting word "although" is sometimes the focus of GMAT questions. "Although" (like the related "though" and "even though") means that the idea expressed in one clause <u>appears</u> to be incompatible with another; by using "although," the speaker is saying that actually, both things are true at the same time. For example:

> Although the company president denied the rumors, independent sources confirmed that the buyout was scheduled to take place.

GMAT questions sometimes use "although" incorrectly, particularly to join clauses that don't express ideas that appear incompatible:

> **INCORRECT:** Although the computer weighs only two pounds, it is the lightest on the market.

The connecting words "while" and "whereas" are sometimes tested. "While" is correctly used to describe something that occurs <u>at the same time</u> as something else. "Whereas" is used to

That is why we need to travel. If we don't offer ourselves to the unknown, our senses dull. Our world becomes small and we lose our sense of wonder. Our eyes don't lift ot the horizon; our ears don't hear the sounds around us. The edge is off our experience, and we pass our days in a routine that is both comfortable and limiting. We wake up one day and find that we have lost our dreams in order to protect our days. Don't let yourself become one of these people. The fear of the unknown and the lure of the comfortable will conspire to keep you from taking the chances the traveler has to take. But if you take then, you will never regret your choice.

Kent Nerburn[121]

introduce <u>a contrast or comparison</u>, but not necessarily to make any claim that things happened at the same time. Note the difference:

> While Nero fiddled, Rome burned.

> Whereas Americans in the 1800s needed to consume a large number of calories in order to do heavy farm work all day, modern Americans typically do not need all of the calories they consume.

Note: The clauses that are compared with the use of *whereas* should be parallel in structure, and the things that are compared should be as similar as possible in terms of structure and number. For example:

a. Whereas many corporations in the United States must bear the cost of providing health insurance to their employees, most corporations in other industrial countries can rely on their national governments to provide universal health care.

b. Whereas the typical corporation in the United States must bear the cost of providing health insurance to its employees, in other industrial countries most corporations can rely on the national government to provide universal health care.

Of these two, (a) is more parallel: the two clauses have the phrases in the same order, and both refer to "corporations" (plural). (b) has the phrases within the two clauses in very different orders, and awkwardly compares "a typical corporation" to "most corporations."

For more practice

OG, 12th edition, Questions:
OG, 13th edition, Questions: 17, 23, ,36, 96, 116, 130, 136

7.2.1 WATCH OUT FOR: "IF" VERSUS "WHETHER"

The distinction between "if" and "whether" is tested fairly often on the GMAT. In everyday conversational English, *if* is often used in contexts in which the GMAT would insist on the use of *whether*. To clarify the difference between *if* and *whether*, first recall that a clause (a phrase with a subject and a verb) can be the subject or object of a verb. For example, in "I know <u>that John is a genius</u>", the clause "that John is a genius" is the object of "know." A clause can also be the object of a preposition, as in "We need to talk about <u>what to wear to the party</u>." A clause that serves as the subject or object of a verb or preposition is called a "noun clause"—it is a clause that plays the role of a noun.

Now, the rule that governs "if" versus "whether": "If" should never be used to introduce a noun clause; *whether* should be used instead. For example:

> I don't know <u>whether John is a genius.</u> (Not "I don't know if John is a genius.")

> <u>Whether John is a genius</u> is unclear to me. (Not "If John is a genius is unclear to me.")

> Nobody told me <u>whether I should show up for the meeting</u>. (Not "Nobody told me if I should show up for the meeting.")

The word "if" may <u>sound</u> right to you in some of these examples, but if so, that means that you're judging by the standards of conversational English rather than formal (GMAT) English. On the GMAT, you should select *if* only if the clause is setting up a condition—regardless of whether it appears at the beginning of the entire sentence or at the end:

> If it rains, we'll stay home.

> We'll stay home if it rains.

If you're not sure, a good rule of thumb is this: if <u>both</u> "if" and "whether" sound right to you—pick "whether." This technique works because in spoken English we often use the word "if" where formal written English would require "whether", but we <u>don't</u> mix them up in the opposite way—we never say "whether" where formal written English would require "if." If you think both words sound right, you can be pretty confident that formal written English (and the GMAT) would require "whether."

 GRAB A CLUE: If some answer choices include *if* and others have *whether*, and both sound correct—pick *whether*.

Note: Never pick *whether or not*, because the writers of the GMAT consider the *or not* to be redundant—it's included in the meaning of *whether*.

Exercise 38: In each of the sentences below, choose either *if* or *whether*. Only one is correct in each case.

1. I don't know if/whether he'll be on time.

2. A company spokesperson declined to comment on if/whether the recall would be expanded further.

3. If/whether the effects of global warming can be reversed is far from clear.

4. If/whether the effects of global warming can be reversed, clearly the nations of the world should begin the effort to do so immediately.

5. The suspect refused to clarify if/whether there had been others involved.

6. No one told the company president if/whether the issue had been resolved.

7. If/whether any other food products were involved in the outbreak, the FDA will expand the range of the warnings.

8. Everyone affected by the food poisoning outbreak is likely to recover if/whether medical attention is given promptly.

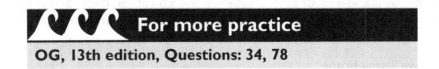

For more practice

OG, 13th edition, Questions: 34, 78

7.3 WATCH THE PUNCTUATION

The GMAT doesn't focus intensively on punctuation, but there are two punctuation mistakes that are sometimes tested: comma splices and misuse of semi-colons.

7.3.1 WATCH OUT FOR COMMA SPLICES

A comma splice is a construction in which two clauses that <u>could</u> each stand alone as a sentence are joined together with nothing more than a comma. Another name for this is a "run-on sentence." Comma splices are always incorrect. Two clauses should be joined with a connecting word such as *and* or *but,* or a semi-colon (see below), or one should be subordinate to the other and introduced with a word such as *although*. These are examples of comma splices:

- The stock's meteoric rise came as a surprise to investors, many had expected more modest gains.

- Elephants may have developed from aquatic mammals, they may have been similar to hippopotami.

- The torrential rains were devastating, the high winds were even worse.

Exercise 39: Determine which of these sentences has a comma splice.

1. Refusing to surrender but knowing he was going to die soon, the chief wrote out his final statement to the tribe.

2. The manager realized that his division would have to improve its performance dramatically, he therefore instigated a complete overhaul of departmental procedures.

3. Only two things in life are certain, death and taxes, but people invest a great deal of money and energy in an effort to avoid both.

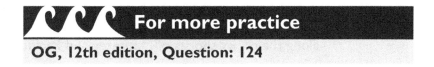
For more practice
OG, 12th edition, Question: 124

7.3.2 BE CAREFUL WITH SEMI-COLONS

A semi-colon (the ; symbol) is just what it looks like: a compromise between a comma and a period. It indicates that two clauses are somehow closely connected in meaning, so that the writer might have used a comma; however, since the two clauses are each full, independent clauses, the writer cannot simply place a comma between them—that would make a comma splice. So the semi-colon does some of the same work as a period: it separates two independent clauses. The elements on each side of the semi-colon <u>must</u> be independent clauses, and cannot be introduced with words such as *and, but,* or *although.* Taken on their own, each clause on either side of a semi-colon should be able to stand on its own as an independent sentence. This sentence, for instance, would be considered wrong on the GMAT:

The discovery of a living coelacanth, a creature long thought to be extinct, came as a shock; although the discovery was a welcome surprise.

There is an important exception to the rule that the material on either side of a semi-colon must consist of complete independent clauses: when the sentence includes a list of parallel phrases, and each phrase contains one or two commas witin it, then semi-colons may be used to separate the phrases so that the grouping of ideas is easier to see. Here is an example:

Tourists visiting the California Bay Area are generally drawn to the scenic beauty of the area, enjoying hiking, camping, and picnicking in the redwood forests of the Santa Cruz Mountains; spending weekends surfing, sunbathing, or playing volleyball at one of the many beaches of Santa Cruz County; or going whale-watching, exploring tidepools, or looking for otters along the rocky shores of Monterey and Pacific Grove.

That sentence has a lot packed into it, and it would be harder to read if the semi-colons were replaced with commas:

Tourists visiting the California Bay Area are generally drawn to the scenic beauty of the area, enjoying hiking, camping, and picnicking in the redwood forests of the Santa Cruz Mountains, spending weekends surfing, sunbathing, or playing volleyball at one of the many beaches of Santa Cruz County, or going whale-watching, exploring tidepools, or looking for otters along the rocky shores of Monterey and Pacific Grove.

In this kind of sentence, semi-colons can be used to separate members of a list (i.e. parallel phrases), and recent material in the Official Guide suggests that the GMAT may test this rule.

Exercise 40: Decide whether each of these sentences has an independent clause on each side of the semi-colon.

1. No political system, however cleverly designed, can solve every problem; for every solution to a problem inevitably creates another problem.

2. Snowflakes are an example of the fact that a seemingly simple molecular structure can give rise to fantastically complex shapes at the larger level; no two of them are exactly alike.

3. Some people find the theory of wormholes in space fantastic; nevertheless, a number of highly respected physicists have endorsed it.

4. Although business analysts endlessly repeat the advice to "Buy low, sell high," making it sound like a simple principle to implement; the fact is that predicting the best time to buy or sell is notoriously difficult.

5. There is no reason to expect gasoline prices to stay low indefinitely; sooner or later, demand for gasoline will once again push the price up.

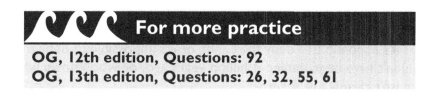

For more practice

OG, 12th edition, Questions: 92
OG, 13th edition, Questions: 26, 32, 55, 61

GMAT questions often ask you to judge which way of expressing an idea is the best way. After you have eliminated answer choices that clearly break grammatical rules, it comes down to your judgment. Some of the choices you may be presented with are one-of-a-kind—the GMAT writers will come up with a new, unique way of scrambling up a sentence. However, some examples of "poor expression" recur with enough frequency that they are worth studying so that you can recognize them.

One such pattern is the choice between a gerund and what is called "shell noun" (by linguists, not GMAT writers—for all we know, the GMAT people may not have a term for it). The contrast involves a pair like this:

a. In light of the recently discovered evidence, there seems to be no way to deny <u>the fact that the Earth was formed over 4 billion years ago.</u>

b. In light of the recently discovered evidence, there seems to be no way to deny <u>the Earth's having formed over 4 billion years ago.</u>

In (a), the noun "fact" serves as a shell noun: a noun that helps to "package" the ideas expressed as "that the Earth was formed over 4 billion years ago." It's clear that what we are finding impossible to deny is this fact.

In (b), the same ideas are expressed much less cleanly: "the Earth's having formed over 4 billion years ago" strings out the concepts in a messy, disorganized way. It sounds almost as if the writer means that it's impossible to deny the Earth, or it's impossible to deny the Earth's having formed, or it couldn't have been denied 4 billion years ago, or who knows what it's trying to say. The sentence isn't cleanly put together.

The contrast between a neat, tidy construction with a shell noun and a sprawling, confusing mess with an -ing is a pattern that comes up fairly often in official GMAT materials. Below are a few more examples which we have constructed. For each pair, version (a) would be the credited choice on the GMAT. Version (a) has a shell noun, the word *that* and a complete clause—a subject and a verb. Notice that the (a) version for each pair sounds neater and cleaner than the (b) version.

a. Though geologists were at first skeptical, the theory that the continents lie on moving plates is now widely accepted.

b. Though geologists were at first skeptical, the continents' lying on moving plates is now widely accepted.

a. Though nowadays, women's participation in politics is taken for granted, the idea that women deserved the right to vote seemed ridiculous at first.

b. Though nowadays, women's participation in politics is taken for granted, women's deserving the right to vote seemed ridiculous at first.

a. The data recovered from the airplane's black box strongly support the idea that an electrical failure caused the crash.

b. The data recovered from the airplane's black box strongly support the idea of an electrical failure causing the crash.

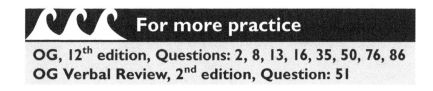

For more practice

OG, 12th edition, Question: 8, 76
OG, 13th edition, Question: 3, 16, 20, 36, 50, 90, 117

Very similar is the contrast between a neat clause introduced with "that", and a sprawling string of phrases, as in this pair:

a. Although recent developments have raised hopes <u>for the economy possibly beginning to recover,</u> most economists are skeptical <u>about the current rate of job creation adequately addressing the problem of unemployment.</u>

b. Although recent developments have raised hopes <u>that the economy is possibly beginning to recover,</u> most economists are skeptical <u>that the current rate of job creation will adequately address the problem of unemployment.</u>

The (b) version would be the credited choice on the GMAT.

There is one additional detail that plays a role in the incorrect version and frequently comes up in similar sentences on the GMAT: the incorrect version misuses the gerunds (-ing forms). It is technically grammatical to have a gerund with its own "subject", as in "the economy's beginning to recover." The "subject" of the gerund must be possessive, though—in other words, "the economy's beginning to recover" is correct, but "the economy beginning to recover" is not. The GMAT usually uses this rule only as another strategy for creating wrong answer choices. That is, the GMAT often has incorrect answer choices in which a regular, non-possessive noun is put together with a gerund, as in the (a) version above. It's very rare that the GMAT will actually include a noun-plus-gerund combination in the credited answer choice—even when it's technically grammatical, it's usually too wordy. Usually the GMAT is looking for a much tighter, cleaner phrasing with the word *that* and a clause (a subject and a verb), as described above. Aside from subtleties of smoothness or wordiness, you should automatically eliminate any answer choice that has a non-possessive noun as the subject of a gerund.

For more practice

OG, 12th edition, Questions: 2, 8, 13, 16, 35, 50, 76, 86
OG Verbal Review, 2nd edition, Question: 51

MODULE 8: SPECIAL ISSUES OF MEANING

MODULE 8: SPECIAL ISSUES OF MEANING

By now, you should be aware that meaning, not just mechanics, comes into play frequently in Sentence Correction questions. For instance, you have to understand what the sentence means to know what the subject of the verb is, or to know whether modifiers are in the best positions, or to know whether a comparison makes sense. In all kinds of sentences on the exam, meaning is an important consideration that helps you sort out what's what. But in this section, we want to talk about cases where meaning doesn't just play a supporting role in helping you identify an error. Here we want to focus on cases where the entire problem revolves around meaning—often subtle aspects of meaning that require you to be on your toes.

When a Sentence Correction question appears to have two or three (or more) correct answer choices, and you can't identify any rule or idiom that would differentiate the credited answer from the distractor(s), there's a fair likelihood that the problem will hinge on a subtle aspect of meaning. There are indications that the GMAT now has an increasing percentage of questions in which two answer choices are grammatically possible, but one expresses the intended meaning more clearly. It's therefore even more important that you be aware of meaning and not simply look at the sentence in terms of grammar rules.

First of all, there is one general principle: Do not change the meaning of the original sentence unless you have a good reason. What constitutes a good reason? First, the credited answer must make sense. If the (A) version seems to be saying something absurd, choose an answer that makes more sense. Second, the credited answer expresses the intended meaning clearly and effectively. If (A) makes some sense but another version makes _more_ sense and seems to be what the writer wanted to say, then choose the version that expresses the meaning more effectively. In all other cases, stick with the meaning of the (A) sentence. Don't choose an answer that changes the meaning unless you have a good reason.

Beyond that general principle, we've identified a few common problems that arise with respect to meaning: wordiness and redundancy, faulty equations, and things that simply don't make sense—or that appear to make sense until you look more closely.

8.1 WORDINESS (AND REDUNDANCY)

Wordiness and redundancy are two slightly different ways that a GMAT sentence may contain unnecessary words. Redundancy means that the same idea is unnecessarily expressed twice. Wordiness means that the sentence uses more words than needed to express the idea; often the extra words actually make the sentence less clear. We'll focus first on wordiness, but some of the principles will apply to redundancy, too.

You should check for wordiness and redundancy only _after_ you've already eliminated answer choices that break hard-and-fast grammatical rules such as subject-verb agreement, use of pronouns, correct formation of comparisons, etc. Some test takers are tempted to eliminate answer choices that "just sound too wordy" immediately, and end up striking out the correct answer choice first. Worse, they then feel they have to choose from what's left, and end up convincing themselves that a "small" grammatical error in their answer choice will be OK just this once. The GMAT doesn't work that way. The GMAT is completely rigid with respect to grammatical rules, whereas wordiness and redundancy are in the eye of the beholder, so there's more wiggle room. What sounds bad to you may actually be the best choice.

The bottom line: Check for wordiness and redundancy, but only after <u>after</u> you've eliminated answer choices that break grammar rules.

The key to avoiding both wordiness and redundancy is simple, however:

Choose the shortest version that expresses the meaning clearly.

The wordy version of a sentence is often unclear or confusing. Focusing on clarity will also help you eliminate choices that are simply vague, regardless of how many words they have.

A rule of thumb: A word is better than a phrase, and a short phrase is better than a long phrase.

But again, you need to make sure that the sentence is clear: a word is better than a phrase, provided that the word expresses the meaning clearly. Let's look at some examples.

A word is better than a phrase:

Wordy: The poet <u>served as an inspiration to</u> many younger writers.

Better: The poet <u>inspired</u> many younger writers.

Wordy: A chemical in the sunscreen may <u>be an irritant to</u> sensitive skin.

Better: A chemical in the sunscreen may <u>irritate</u> sensitive skin.

Wordy: The lawsuit demanded that the company <u>provide compensation to</u> victims of discrimination.

Better: The lawsuit demanded that the company <u>compensate</u> victims of discrimination.

Wordy: The stock was sold for a sum lower than its original cost.

Better: The stock was sold for less than its original cost.

Notice that in each case, the better version isn't just shorter: it's more direct. It states precisely what the writer means without beating around the bush. If you always look for the version that is most clear and direct, you'll be able to recognize wordiness.

A short phrase is better than a long phrase:

Wordy: The new product was designed with the intention of being competitive with established products.

Better: The new product is intended to compete with established products.

Wordy: Management unveiled a new organizational scheme, the aim of which is the maximizing of profits along with reducing overhead.

Better: Management unveiled a new organizational scheme aimed at maximizing profits while reducing overhead.

Wordy: In extreme cases, the patient may die unless there is a doctor who can administer adrenaline quickly.

Better: In extreme cases, the patient may die unless a doctor administers adrenaline quickly.

Make sure the sentence still makes sense. Be careful not to pick a version that is so short that the meaning is unclear. Here are some examples of making things too short.

Clear: The flu presents a serious danger to senior citizens unless they are vaccinated each year.

Too short: The flu presents a serious danger to senior citizens unless vaccinated each year.

The too-short version doesn't make it clear who is getting vaccinated; it sounds as if possibly it's the flu itself getting the shot.

Clear: The artist's best-known work was a painting of a lighthouse on a cliff.

Too short: The artist's best-known work was a cliff lighthouse painting.

The too-short version condenses the prepositional phrases (OF a lighthouse, ON a cliff) into a much smaller phrase that is so compact, it's hard to interpret. Shorter isn't better if the reader would have a hard time understanding the meaning.

8.1.1 REDUNDANCY

Redundancy is a little different from wordiness. A wordy sentence uses too many words to express the meaning; a redundant sentence says the same thing twice. There is a limitless number of ways that the GMAT writers could create a redundant sentence, but a few patterns in particular have come up in official materials and should be noted. The GMAT writers seem to feel strongly enough about these that you can quickly reject answer choices that contain them (you may well see other expressions on the GMAT that you feel are redundant, but in general, you should use your own opinions about redundancy as the last criterion to evaluate answers—eliminate outright grammar errors first).

 GRAB A CLUE: If more than one version of the sentence sounds OK to you, check to see whether one has redundancy.

- **to enable someone to be able to do something**: To enable someone means to make them able; you don't need to say "be able" again.

- **rising increases:** a sentence that talks about "rising cost increases" or says that "increases have been rising" is redundant.

- **previously... in the past:** if the sentence says that someone did something "previously", it's redundant to add "in the past", and vice versa. Same comment applies if the sentence says "**currently...now.**"

- **regain again**: if something has been "regained", then the person has it again, and vice versa; there's no need to say both.

- **is doing and will continue to do**: the statement that someone "will continue" doing something automatically implies that the person has already been doing it, so specifying that the person "is doing" or "has been doing", whatever-it-is, is redundant.

- **increase/rise up to**: if the sentence says that prices are rising or increasing, the idea that they're going "up" is already clear, so "up" is redundant.

- **whether or not:** The writers of the GMAT consider this common expression redundant, on the grounds that "or not" is implied in the meaning of *whether*. This one seems to come up frequently on the GMAT; if you see it in an answer choice, you can immediately eliminate that choice from consideration. The GMAT never includes this expression in a credited answer.

Don't eliminate a phrase that is in fact necessary, just because you're concerned about redundancy. In section 3.3.2, we gave you examples of contexts in which you may need to add a noun to make the sentence clear while avoiding incorrect usage of *which*. In some cases the best version of the sentence will repeat a noun, as in this example:

INCORRECT: Analysts have pointed out a number of instabilities inherent in the current business model, which prudent investors will want to take into consideration.

CORRECT: Analysts have pointed out a number of instabilities inherent in the current business model, instabilities that prudent investors will want to take into consideration.

Even though the word "instabilities" is repeated, it is not redundant; rather it serves to clarify what the modifier ("that prudent investors will want to take into consideration") applies to. Don't assume that every repetition is redundant; think about whether the repetition is necessary.

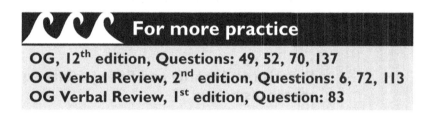

For more practice

OG, 12th edition, Questions: 49, 52, 70, 137
OG Verbal Review, 2nd edition, Questions: 6, 72, 113
OG Verbal Review, 1st edition, Question: 83

8.2 FAULTY EQUATIONS

The GMAT uses this trick often enough that it deserves a name of its own. A Sentence Correction question may state that one thing "is" another—i.e. equate two things—that aren't in fact the same thing at all. For example, "The archaeologists determined that the body buried in the tomb was a 19-year-old woman." That may not sound so bad, but in fact, the body wasn't a 19-year-old woman. It was the <u>body of</u> a 19-year-old woman. The GMAT would credit a different version of the sentence, such as "The archaeologists determined that the body buried in the tomb was <u>that of</u> a 19-year-old woman."

Here's another example: "Scientists declared that the new fossil <u>was a type</u> previously unknown to paleontologists." In fact, the fossil wasn't "a type" at all. The fossil was one instance <u>of</u> a type. The sentence should read "Scientists declared that the new fossil was <u>of a type</u> previously unknown to paleontologists."

Note that in these cases, adding the word "of" or the phrase "that of" makes the sentence longer but not wordy; the addition is needed to make the meaning clear.

Exercise 41: Identify and fix any faulty equations in the sentences below.

1. The photograph on the wall was a man who appeared to be about 20 years old.

2. The Coast Guard announced that the body that washed up in Pacific Grove last week has been identified as Sandra Brown.

3. Peering closely at the faded image, the antiques appraiser could see it was a little girl with a small dog.

4. The pest control expert was chagrined to find that the insects colonizing the 100-year-old maple were a species he had never dealt with before.

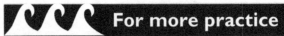 **For more practice**

OG, 12th edition, Question: 69
OG, 13th edition, Question: 131

8.3 THINGS THAT DON'T MAKE SENSE... AFTER ALL

You need to watch out for GMAT Sentence Correction choices that simply don't make sense. One common trick is for the sentence to be phrased in a way that isn't exactly talking about what you think it is—or in other words, what it is talking about doesn't precisely make sense. For example:

> Funding is already in place for the shopping mall's construction, which is expected to open for business next year.

What is it that's going to open for business next year? Logically, the writer must have meant the shopping mall, but as it's worded, it means that the <u>construction</u> will be open for business. Here's another example:

> The plan for the scientific expedition to the North Pole, long delayed due to weather and financial difficulties, will depart next week.

This one is saying that the <u>plan</u> will depart, not the expedition. The sentence isn't entirely clear as to what has been delayed due to weather and financial difficulties, either—is it the plan, the expedition, or the North Pole itself?

Those cases may seem fairly obvious—though on the real GMAT, the sentence will often be longer and more complicated, to make it harder to spot the discrepancy. Some GMAT SCs are much more subtle. They may seem reasonable at first or even second glance, but in fact be saying something strange if you take a really good look at them. For example:

> The county supervisors declared that since the area already had one large shopping mall, a second one should not be built, if only because redundant facilities should be avoided.

The sentence probably seems to make sense, at least at first, but think about this phrase "redundant facilities should be avoided." It's saying literally that if one sees two facilities that serve the same function ("redundant facilities"), one should stay away from them. The sentence is presumably intended to say that <u>construction</u> of redundant facilities should be avoided—not the facilities themselves.

Look at the subtle contrast between these two sentences:

a. Stiffly beaten egg whites—whites that have been beaten until they form solid, stable peaks although they are made of nothing but liquid and air—are used in many recipes.

b. Stiffly beaten egg whites—whites that have been beaten until they form peaks that remain solid and stable although they are made of nothing but liquid and air—are used in many recipes.

Which version is better? The second one clearly spells out what is being contrasted with "although": the peaks <u>remain solid and stable</u> **although** <u>they are made of nothing but liquid and air</u>. The first one is more confusing. It seems to be saying <u>they (the egg whites) form</u>

solid, stable peaks **although** <u>they are made of nothing but liquid and air</u>. In other words, it seems to be saying that the egg whites themselves are made of nothing but liquid and air. Moreover, the sentence reads as if what is surprising is that the egg whites form peaks. The claim that the peaks are stable and solid, the idea which should be the point, is hidden rather than highlighted. The reader can figure out what the sentence is intended to say, but it doesn't say it as clearly as it could.

There is no grand list of all the possible ways that the GMAT writers might construct a sentence that doesn't make sense (or doesn't make as much sense as it could). But you can become more skilled at spotting subtle glitches in meaning by looking at a number of examples and noticing what's wrong with them—and, when you practice actual GMAT questions, noticing what's right with the versions that the GMAT would prefer.

Exercise 42: Underline any part of each sentence below that doesn't make sense, or could be stated more clearly. There will be one in each sentence. Suggest a re-write.

1. The music industry executive said that, because of the economic impact of piracy on recording companies, unauthorized duplicates of songs would be prosecuted to the fullest extent of the law.

2. The Chair of the Senate Foreign Relations Committee testified that the future of the Iraqi state hinged on the success of its effort at establishing democracy, and that a stolen election should be prevented at all costs.

3. The documentary on the history of the Waldorf and Montessori schools showcases two very similar educational systems although they were invented by different people.

The bottom line: even when a sentence appears to be grammatically correct, you need to be sure that it makes sense.

For more practice

OG, 12th edition, Questions: 23, 90
OG, 13th edition, Questions: 100

MODULE 9: DICTION

Module 9: Diction

9.1 BE AWARE OF WORD CHOICE

Some GMAT Sentence Correction questions hinge on the difference between words that sound similar but mean different things. For example, "economic" and "economical" have very different meanings (in American English): "economic" means "having to do with the economy", but "economical" means "affordable" or "inexpensive." (It is surprising how frequently the GMAT seems to test this particular pair.) The verb "decline" (in the sense of dwindle or worsen) is not the same as the noun "declension" (which refers only to a concept in traditional grammar—the system of endings on nouns in a language such as Latin, which uses grammatical endings to signal the role of a noun in a sentence). A sentence that talks about a number declining shouldn't describe it as "declension."

A few other distinctions to be aware of:

Lie vs. lay The verbs "lie" and "lay" often cause confusion for native speakers. The difference is this: "lie" is an intransitive verb—this means that it cannot describe what someone does <u>to something else</u>; it can only describe the position that something or someone is in. For example, "He is lying on the bed." "Lay" is transitive: it is used to describe putting <u>something else</u> into a lying position: "He is laying the books on the table." It is incorrect to use "laying" to describe what someone is doing if they are merely occupying a position, so "He is laying on the bed" is wrong. The past tense of "lie", unfortunately, is "lay" (this is probably why speakers so easily confuse these verbs). The past tense of "lay" is "laid." So it would be correct to say "He laid the books down, and the books lay there for several hours."

Between vs. among The contrast between "between" and "among" is sometimes tested. "Between" is correctly used to talk about two items; "among" is used for multiple items. So "This is between the two of us" is correct. "Among these three companies, Acme is the best" would be correct, not "Between these three companies..."

Much vs. many "Much" is used with nouns that describe something that can't be counted, such as *water, gold, dirt*. "Many" is used with plural count nouns—nouns that have a plural form and can be counted, such as *trees, dogs, ideas*. If a phrase combines words of both types, do not use either "much" or "many" alone to head up the phrase; instead, choose an answer that has both "much" and "many", even if it looks wordier to you than the alternatives. For example:

   a. It takes many hours of work and energy to drill an oil well.

   b. It takes much energy and hours of work to drill an oil well.

   c. It takes many hours of work and much energy to drill an oil well.

   Of these three, (c) is the only correct choice.

Few vs. little The distinction between "much" and "many" also applies to "little" and "few": "little" is used with non-count nouns; "few" is used with count nouns. If the sentence mixes count nouns and non-count nouns, choose the answer that has both "few" and "little"; don't try to make one word cover both. For example:

It can be difficult to make a living in a remote area in which <u>few people and economic activity can be found</u>.

    a. few people and economic activity can be found

    b. there are few people and economic activity

    c. there is little economic activity or people

    d. little economic activity and people can be found

    e. there are few people and little economic activity

    (e) is the correct choice.

Leave vs. let In some parts of the U.S., "leave" is used to mean "allow"; this is considered non-standard in formal written English, and the GMAT has been known to test this point occasionally (see Official Guide 11th Edition Question 64 for an example). Given a choice between "leave", and "allow", or "let", do not choose "leave".

Aggravate vs. irritate "Aggravate" means "to make worse," as in "Poor diet and exercise habits may aggravate a pre-existing heart condition." In everyday English spoken throughout much of the U.S, it is also used to mean "irritate", as in "Her behavior really aggravates me." This is considered non-standard in formal written English. The GMAT usually seems to use "aggravate" in its correct, standard meaning, so you don't need to avoid choosing it in most cases, but if you see it used as a synonym for "irritate" or "annoy", do not choose "aggravate."

Exercise 43: Spot any phrases that seem odd or poorly worded.

1. The differential between field crickets and snowy tree crickets is fairly obvious, as the two species do not have the same coloring.

2. The word "undertaker" is not referential to one who undertakes something, but rather means a person who deals with dead bodies.

3. The security guard was reprimanded for insubordination and laying down on the job.

4. Trade relations between China, Japan and South Korea are complex and heavily influenced by cultural nuances.

5. The newly-elected senator hoped to be placed on committees with substantial power over finances, thus putting him in a better position than most junior legislatures to secure money for his home state.

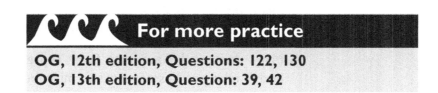 For more practice

OG, 12th edition, Questions: 122, 130
OG, 13th edition, Question: 39, 42

9.2 ESTABLISHED NOUNS VERSUS –ING FORMS

One of the details the GMAT sometimes tests is the distinction between nouns and gerunds (words made by combining a verb with *–ing*). In cases where a verb doesn't have an established noun form, it's often possible to create a noun by adding *–ing*. However, if English <u>already</u> has an established noun, then an invented noun that is "pasted together" with a verb + *-ing* will not serve. If a noun is what is required in the context, choose the established noun over the newly-coined *–ing* form.

In other words, if you are given a choice between *destruction* and *destroying*, or *refusal* and *refusing*, or *coercion* and *coercing*, <u>and if the context clearly requires a noun</u>—choose the established, "official-sounding" noun, not the *–ing*. For example:

a. Many doctors believe that fever represents the body's attempt to destroy invasive microbes.

b. Many doctors believe that fever represents the body's trying to destroy invasive microbes.

Of these two, (a) is the better choice.

For more practice

OG, 13th edition, Questions: 28, 53

MODULE 10: HALLMARKS OF FORMAL WRITTEN ENGLISH

Module 10: Hallmarks of Formal Written English

Throughout this book, we have highlighted grammatical rules that are strictly observed in formal written English, but applied only loosely (or not at all) in everyday speech. There are some additional constructions and/or characteristics of formal written English that have come up in official GMAT materials that you need to be familiar with.

The GMAT may use "exotic" features of formal written English in the non-underlined portion of the sentence merely to create confusion, slow down reading, and/or intimidate the test taker. He or she may naturally react by feeling discouraged when a sentence "doesn't even sound like English." The way to make yourself invulnerable to these manipulations is simple: study the characteristics of formal written English that tend to recur on the GMAT and get used to them. If any of them sound odd to you, read the examples a few times until they sound less odd. Make mental notes on the things that sounded funny to you, but that are actually OK. Notice when these elements come up in practice materials; you don't have to remember the technical names for any of them, but it helps if you develop a reaction like "Oh, there's another one of *those* again" when you see them.

10.1 INVERSION

Inversion—the verb appearing before the subject—was discussed in Section 1.2. It is more common in formal written English than in speech, but it is sometimes used in a spoken context, especially for dramatic emphasis ("Never in my life have I heard such nonsense!"). Sentences with inversion are sometimes correct on the GMAT; at other times, inversion seems to be used merely to create confusion. The only thing you need to know beyond what was said in section 1.2 is that inversion is occasionally used to mean "if", but only in conjunction with these three words: *had, should,* and *were*:

> Had the president been informed, he would have addressed the problem. (Means the same as "If the president had been informed...")

> Were the law of gravity to be repealed, the earth would fly away from the sun. (Means the same as "If the law of gravity were repealed...")

> The secretary informed the ambassador that, should he need anything, the embassy would provide it. (Means the same as "The secretary informed the ambassador that if he needed anything...")

10.2 FOR

The word "for" can be used in older, more formal English to mean "because", as in this quote from John F. Kennedy:

> "In a very real sense, it will not be one man going to the moon; it will be an entire nation. For all of us must work to put him there."

10.3 BUT

The word "but" can be used to mean "only", as in the famous quote from Nathan Hale:

> "I only regret that I have but one life to give for my country."

"But" can also be used to mean "except", as in "The lobbyist has tried everything but outright bribery" or "But for the view, this hotel has nothing to recommend it."

10.4 PERFECT INFINITIVE

The perfect infinitive is the form "to have done", as in "I'm sorry <u>to have woken</u> you up so early." It does not mean exactly the same thing as an ordinary infinitive ("to do"). The perfect infinitive conveys that the action occurred before some other action. In this example, the speaker is sorry <u>now</u> for having woken the person up <u>earlier</u>.

Additional examples:

Archaeologists believe the Mayas to have practiced human sacrifice. (Archaeologists believe that the Mayas practiced human sacrifice in the past.)

Archaeologists believe the Mayas to practice human sacrifice. (Archaeologists believe that the Mayas practice human sacrifice now.)

A thorough investigation of the accident found the driver to have been drunk. (The driver was drunk before the investigation—presumably at the time of the accident.)

A thorough investigation of the accident found the driver to be drunk. (The driver was drunk at the time of the investigation.)

10.5 PASSIVE PARTICIPLE WITH INFINITIVE

In written English, passive participles (such as "known" or "believed") are used with infinitives (as in "he is known to be X" or "it is believed to be the case") far more often than in spoken English. Some of these examples may sound familiar to people who don't read much formal written English, but some may sound more exotic. All of them are correct.

1. The contest winner is believed to be a long-time resident of the neighborhood.

2. The suspect is alleged to have revealed trade secrets to a competitor.

3. The storm was said to have deposited more than three feet of snow in two hours.

4. The artist, long rumored to have ties to an anarchist group, denied any such connections during the interview.

5. The person most widely believed to be a viable candidate for the open congressional seat is a well-known figure in local politics.

6. The defendant was known to have visited the bar on several previous occasions.

7. The nuclear submarine was reported to be lurking just off the coast of Santa Barbara.

Because these constructions are not common in speech, the GMAT tries to trick people by substituting phrasing that may sound more familiar. In particular, the GMAT is likely to substitute "as VERB-ing" in place of "to VERB," as in these (incorrect) examples:

1. The defendant was known as having visited the bar on several previous occasions.

2. The nuclear submarine was reported as lurking just off the coast of Santa Barbara.

It should be noted, however, that there are a few passive participles that do not combine with an infinitive. "Seen", "viewed", "regarded", and "acclaimed" all take "as" (as in "She was seen as a breath of fresh air to the theater, widely viewed as a worthy successor to Garbo, and eventually acclaimed as the greatest actress of her generation"). "Considered" takes neither the infinitive nor "as", but instead directly connects the participle to the predicate, as in "He is considered a gentleman." These participles work the way they do because the basic verbs they are made from work in the same way. For example, "Critics see her as a talented amateur" is correct, whereas "Critics see her to be a talented amateur" is not. These verbs are listed as idioms on the list in section 6.

Especially in the higher-level questions, where details of formal written style become especially important, the GMAT may very well try to add to the confusion by throwing in the distinction between a simple infinitive and a perfect infinitive. This was described in the preceding section, but it's worthwhile to look at it again, this time in examples that combine both grammatical factors. The GMAT has been known to focus on this combination (passive participle plus the distinction between simple infinitive and perfect infinitive) in high-level questions.

a. The politician was known to visit the casino.

b. The politician was known to have visited the casino.

For short sentences like these, both versions are correct, but the meanings are different. (a) means that people knew about the politician visiting the casino at the time that he was visiting; in other words, there was a time when he was known as a casino-visitor. (b) means that people knew that the politician <u>had</u> visited the casino—they knew about it after he did it.

Generally, the GMAT will test the distinction between infinitives by constructing a sentence in which something is now believed to have been a certain way in the past. For example:

The giant tortoise Harriet, one of three tortoises <u>long reputed to be taken from the Galapagos Islands by Charles Darwin on his historic 1835 voyage aboard the HMS Beagle</u>, died in an Australian zoo at the age of 176.

a. long reputed to be taken from the Galapagos Islands by Charles Darwin on his historic 1835 voyage aboard the HMS Beagle

b. long reputed to have been taken from the Galapagos Islands along with Charles Darwin as part of his historic 1835 voyage aboard the HMS Beagle

c. with a long reputation of having been taken from the Galapagos Islands by Charles Darwin on his historic 1835 voyage aboard the HMS Beagle

d. long reputed to have been taken from the Galapagos Islands by Charles Darwin on his historic 1835 voyage aboard the HMS Beagle

e. long reputed taken from the Galapagos Islands by Charles Darwin on his historic 1835 voyage aboard the HMS Beagle

Your answer choice: ____

Explanation: (a) is out because "to be taken" implies that the tortoise is being taken now, or is taken out of the Galapagos Islands regularly. (b) has the right infinitival form, but has odd choices of prepositions—"along with" implying that Charles Darwin was also taken out of the Galapagos Islands. (c) changes the meaning and doesn't flow well. (d) is concise and correct. (e) tries too hard to be concise—"long reputed taken" is unidiomatic and awkward.

Exercise 44: Decide which version of each sentence is correct. (Additional exercises can be found on the website, testprepny.com)

1. The average age in the Senate is quite high; several senators are <u>known to serve</u> in the military during World War II.

    a. known to serve

    b. known to have served

    c. known as having served

2. The crash was so severe that the pilot was considered to be fortunate to survive.

    a. considered to be fortunate to survive

    b. considered fortunate to survive

    c. considered fortunate to have survived

10.6 CLAUSAL SUBJECTS

In written English, a clause can be the subject of a verb, as in this example:

<u>That pigs cannot fly</u> is an observation that has sometimes been subject to dispute.

The subject of the sentence is the clause "that pigs cannot fly." The clause in this kind of construction doesn't have to be introduced by anything more elaborate than the word "that." This usage is not common in spoken English, therefore examples on the GMAT sometimes give people pause. Compare:

Spoken style: The fact that the earth goes around the sun wasn't accepted for a long time.

Written style: That the earth goes around the sun was not accepted as a fact for a long time.

Spoken style: The idea that taxpayers have to pay to have jobs shipped overseas is infuriating to a lot of people.

Written style: That taxpayers must pay to have jobs shipped overseas infuriates many people.

Spoken style: The fact that the former senator had a mistress and an illegitimate child came as a shock to a lot of people.

Written style: That the former senator had a mistress and an illegitimate child came as a shock to many people.

On the GMAT, a clausal subject that begins with the word "that" is not always the credited answer choice. It may be, or the GMAT writers may be trying to take advantage of the confusion that some people feel when they see this kind of structure by constructing answer choices that are essentially gibberish. The way to avoid falling into that trap is to get familiar enough with clausal subjects, as in the examples above, to recognize when they're used correctly and when the sentence dissolves into chaos. If you're someone who already reads a lot, you may have no difficulty with this at all; if you're less familiar with this kind of construction, you should review the examples carefully.

Exercise 45: Indicate whether the following sentences are correct or incorrect. (Additional exercises can be found on the website, testprepny.com)

1. That no one has ever produced a convincing photograph of the Loch Ness monster should not be construed as proof of the monster's non-existence.

2. That reindeer cannot actually fly can hardly be said that it has been proven.

3. That the dark side of the moon is not always dark may not be obvious to those who have only a casual acquaintance with astronomy.

10.7 INFINITIVAL MODIFIERS

In written English, an infinitive can be used as a modifier following a noun. This is far less common in everyday conversational English, so some people may hesitate when they see an example in writing. All of these examples are correct:

Cord blood <u>to be donated</u> must include a minimum of 90,000 cells.

Museum staff have announced that the new wing <u>to be dedicated</u> later this week will offer extended hours for its first month of operation.

Department of Transportation officials denied that the improvement project was a misapplication of funds; the highway <u>to be widened</u> was recently ranked the most congested in the state.

10.8 PARTICIPIAL MODIFIERS

In written English, more commonly than in spoken English, a participial phrase—a phrase based on an *–ed* form or an *–ing* form—may be used as a modifier after a noun. As with the other patterns that are more common in written than in spoken English, if you find these constructions unfamiliar you should study them until they feel more comfortable and sound more normal to you.

Compare the following examples:

Spoken style: The man who got shot by the police was walking in an area that's known for gang warfare.

Written style: The man shot by the police was walking in an area known for gang warfare.

Spoken style: The road that runs from Chicago to LA is famous as the subject of the song "Route 66," which was composed by a popular singer by the name of Bobby Troup.

Written style: The road running from Chicago to LA is famous as the subject of the song "Route 66," composed by popular singer Bobby Troup.

10.9 NOMINATIVE ABSOLUTE CONSTRUCTIONS

Formal written English sometimes makes use of a modifying structure that is very rarely heard in spoken English. A noun phrase can be followed by a passive participle or an *-ing* form to form a phrase that modifies a clause. The underlined phrases in the following sentences are examples:

1. The ship sailed away majestically, its sails billowing in the breeze.

2. The once-successful mogul found himself alone, his reputation destroyed.

3. Its products found to be defective, the company was forced to issue a recall.

4. His theory disproven, the scientist decided to switch to a different field.

The nominative absolute is found in writing, but has never been popular in spoken, conversational English. It may appear exotic to test takers who don't read a lot of formal written English. The GMAT can try to trap people who find it odd-sounding by offering to "fix" the construction by adding a verb; the problem is that unless a semi-colon is used, adding a verb may create a comma splice. All of the following would be incorrect on the GMAT:

1. The ship sailed away majestically, its sails were billowing in the breeze.

2. The once-successful mogul found himself alone, his reputation was destroyed.

3. Its products were found to be defective, the company was forced to issue a recall.

4. His theory was disproven, the scientist decided to switch to a different field.

The GMAT may also offer you a version which tries to "fix" the nominative absolute by adding an unnecessary *being*:

> His hands being crippled by arthritis, the painter held the brush in his mouth.

The sentence would be correct without *being*, so if this were a choice on the GMAT, you should look for the one that reads simply "His hands crippled by arthritis."

The GMAT may also offer you a version that tries to "fix" the nominative absolute by re-writing it as a clause that is unnecessarily wordy and/or full of mistakes. To take the same example, they might give you an incorrect choice like "Because there had been arthritis having crippled his hands." Again, they're looking to trap people who think the nominative absolute sounds weird, and who are therefore vulnerable to picking gibberish rather than the correct answer.

One last way that the GMAT is likely to "fix" the nominative absolute is to add a preposition, typically "with", as in:

> The ship sailed away majestically, with its sails billowing in the breeze.

In most cases, there's nothing wrong with adding the preposition "with" in and of itself. The trap lies in the fact that the GMAT writers may add a mistake to the version that has "with", knowing that many test takers will prefer the "normal-sounding" sentence that uses "with" to the "weird-sounding" nominative absolute. As with other hallmarks of formal written style, the key is to review the examples until the construction feels more familiar, so that you won't automatically reject it on the real GMAT.

The nominative absolute may also appear in the non-underlined part of the sentence—the GMAT writers may add it simply to create confusion and slow the test taker down. They may also use it to give the impression that there's a lack of parallelism or a connecting word missing when in fact there is no error. Let's look at a brief example of how this trap could work:

> The meeting adjourned, <u>the committee members were faced with the task of implementing</u> the decisions they had made and explaining those decisions to the rest of the company.
>
> a. the committee members were faced with the task of
> b. and the committee members faced the task to implement

There is nothing wrong with (a). The initial phrase "The meeting adjourned" is a nominative absolute which could be paraphrased as "Now that the meeting had adjourned." But a test taker who is unfamiliar with the nominative absolute could easily be misled into believing that the phrase is supposed to be part of a list of parallel items: "The meeting adjourned and the committee members were faced..." So (b) is offered as an alternative, but (b) has a mistake: "the task of implementing" is replaced with the incorrect "the task to implement."

Again, if you're likely to be thrown off by these kinds of sentences, the key is to review examples and come to understand that these constructions are normal, correct English. They simply aren't normal for <u>conversational</u> English. Everyday conversation does make use of a few standard phrases that are nominative absolutes, however, and taking a moment to look at them may help you familiarize yourself with the construction:

All things considered, there's no question that he's right.

All other things being equal, this is clearly the best choice.

Weather permitting, we'll have a picnic.

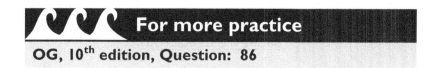

For more practice
OG, 10th edition, Question: 86

10.10 APPOSITIVES

An appositive is a noun phrase that's used to give an alternate description of another noun phrase. It's not essential that you remember the term appositive, but it is essential that you get used to seeing them. If you're a native speaker who reads a lot, you may already be comfortable with them, but you should still be aware of how they're used on the GMAT; test takers who aren't as fluent in formal written English should definitely study their use.

The Prime Minister, <u>a lifelong supporter of animal rights</u>, criticized the bill for doing too little to protect farm animals from abuse.

The construction of the Taj Mahal, <u>a project that took 30 years and thousands of artisans to complete</u>, is considered the finest achievement of designer Ustad Ahmad Lahauri, <u>a Persian Muslim architect of the 17th century</u>.

Appositives were briefly described in section 3.1 above, in the discussion of dangling modifiers, but here we want to talk about how appositives are used more generally by the GMAT writers. Appositives are very common in GMAT SC sentences. They are frequently added merely to increase the length and complexity of sentences, and add to the potential for confusion. They are often placed between the subject and the verb to make it harder to tell whether there is an error in agreement, as in this simplified example:

The United States census, <u>a once-per-decade survey that employs tens of thousands of people</u>, is mandated under the Constitution.

a. a once-per-decade survey that employs tens of thousands of people, is

b. a once-per-decade survey that employs tens of thousands of people, are

It's typical on the GMAT that the real subject (in this case "census"), and the last noun of the appositive are opposites with respect to number. You need to mentally skip over the appositive and match the subject directly to the verb to hear whether it should be "census...is" or "census...are."

You also simply need to be comfortable with reading sentences that are embellished with a lot of extra appositives, and not allow yourself to be distracted or slowed down excessively by all the verbiage. In some cases, the appositives are used just to "bulk up" the sentence and add new and unfamiliar information, encouraging the test taker to slow down and try to take in all the details, when in fact the details are irrelevant to answering the question correctly. Here's an example:

> A 95-million-year-old amber deposit, the first major discovery of its kind from the African continent and one that adds new fungus, insects, spiders, nematodes, and even bacteria to the ecosystem shared by the dinosaurs, <u>may provide fresh insights into the rise and diversification of flowering plants during the Cretaceous.</u>

a. may provide fresh insights into the rise and diversification of flowering plants during

b. may be providing fresh insights into the rising and diversification of flowering plants

c. may have provided fresh insights into the rise of flowering plants that diversified

d. provide fresh insights into the rise of diversified flowering plants

e. may provide fresh insights into the ways that flowering plants could have arose and diversified

The correct answer is (a). The long appositive "the first major discovery of its kind from the African continent and one that adds new fungus, insects, spiders, nematodes, and even bacteria to the ecosystem shared by the dinosaurs" is somewhat interesting, and it can be tempting to read it carefully and try to understand it in detail. If your goal is to score the point on an SC question rather than to learn about a new scientific discovery, it's a big waste of time. Because the appositive itself isn't underlined, and there isn't anything like a pronoun (which might need an antecedent located in the appositive) in the underlined part, you can tell immediately that there isn't much the appositive can do for—or to—you. You only need to glance at it long enough to recognize that it's not the subject, that the subject is "deposit", and "dinosaurs" therefore couldn't possibly have any effect on the correct form of the verb. Run your eyes over it lightly; don't dig in and take the time to think about how interesting it is that scientists found fungus, spiders, nematodes and what-not in a lump of amber.

Appositives are very common in formal written English—and are very, <u>very</u> common on the GMAT!—but they are quite rare in conversational English, except for when the speaker is fumbling for the right description: "This guy I knew, the basketball player I told you about one time, the one who used to work for Coca-Cola, you know, that guy—well, he..." Even when they are used, spoken appositives aren't in the same style as what you'll see on the GMAT. If GMAT-style appositives feel awkward to you, or if you tend to get bogged down in all the trivia that the sentence is throwing at you, review a lot of examples until they feel more comfortable and they don't slow you down so much. Once you get used to seeing them, a lot of GMAT sentences that would have looked long and complicated will start to look relatively simple.

10.11 FORMAL USES OF 'THE' AND 'A'

In formal written English, the articles *a* and *the* are each occasionally used in a way that is not frequently heard in spoken English.

'The' may be used before a quantity phrase to indicate that that phrase is describing the total set of items. Compare:

> The 36 million people who live in California do not spend much of their time worrying about earthquakes. (Implication: there are only 36 million people in California.)

> 36 million people who live in California do not spend much of their time worrying about earthquakes. (Implication: there may be more than 36 million people in California; this sentence is talking about only 36 million of them.) Another example:

> This country was at one time more compact territorially than it is now: the 48 states of the United States were contiguous. (Implication: there were only 48 states at that time.)

> This country was at one time more compact territorially than it is now: 48 states of the United States were contiguous. (Implication: there were more than 48 states, but 48 of the total were contiguous.)

Note that this usage of "the" may be correct even when the quantity expression is more complex than just a number. The following examples may give some readers pause but are, in fact, correct:

1. The more than 300 million people living in the United States represent every race and ethnic group on the planet.

2. The linguist believed that the tonal properties of the more than 35 distinct dialects of Chinese were different.

3. The fewer than 20 chiropractors who offer the controversial treatment say that their patients give it rave reviews.

4. By 1992, the average farm size had increased by 14 acres to 223 acres for the fewer than 40,000 farms remaining.

The word "a" may be used in written English with a proper noun, such as the name of a person or a city, if the writer attaches a modifier, as in these examples:

In a New York filled with new immigrants and unskilled laborers, factories could be run very cheaply.

On a Mars only recently colonized by humans, three people fight for their lives.

The orphans wandered the streets of a bombed-out London after the Blitz.

The film is set in the near future in a crime-ridden United States that has converted Manhattan Island in New York City into a maximum security prison.

For more practice

OG, 13th edition, Questions: 39, 58, 60, 139

ANSWER KEY

Directions for correcting your work:

Follow the questions with exercise numbers rather than page numbers.

MODULE 1: SUBJECTS AND VERBS

Exercise 1: Imagine that each of these noun phrases is a subject and decide whether the verb should be singular (i.e. take an "s") or plural (no "s").

the boys in that room	**plural**
people in Rome	**plural**
half of that book	**singular**
all of the children	**plural**
the girls under the tree	**plural**
the cat and the dog	**plural**
The United States	**singular**
a number of reasons	**plural**
half of those people	**plural**
someone	**singular**
the lion, as well as the tiger	**singular**
neither of the two candidates	**singular**
the reason that they went	**singular**
all of the information in those books	**singular**

Exercise 2: Determine which noun is the simple subject.

1. The exact **reason** that so many people overeat during the holidays is difficult to determine.

2. **Complaints** about inconveniences and delays at the airport have reached unprecedented levels.

3. Due to unforeseen complications, **negotiations** between management and the union are expected to drag on much longer than previously anticipated.

4. The very last **thing** the reclusive multi-millionaire said in the moments before he died was "Rosebud."

5. The **fact** that so many people persist in activities that they know to be bad for their health and/or safety is a puzzle to some psychologists.

Exercise 3: Check for errors in subject-verb agreement.

1. The firefighters' union, after long and tortuous negotiations, have agreed to a compromise.

Subject: union   Verb: have   Agreement: No

2. The principle of "innocent until proven guilty," often invoked in both real-life trials and television legal dramas, is not always properly appreciated by juries.

Subject: principle   Verb: is   Agreement: Yes

3. The famous Victims' Bill of Rights, a topic of much controversy and editorializing, after much delay and protracted negotiations, have finally been adopted.

Subject: Bill   Verb: have   Agreement: No

4. A number of test takers, despite strenuous objections from the school board, has decided to stage the play *Bat Boy: The Musical*.

Subject: test takers   Verb: has   Agreement: No

5. The recent report of increased costs—though still not fully confirmed and in fact dismissed by some analysts—are stirring concerns among some investors.

Subject: report   Verb: are   Agreement: No

Exercise 4: Find and underline the subjects in the following sentences.

1. **Out of the most recent** series of debacles has come a new **appreciation** of the importance of internet security.

2. Only now are any of the **people** involved in the incident ready to talk to the press.

3. From one of America's forgotten small towns comes an unforgettable **story** of love and friendship.

4. Not until relatively recently have **people** realized that the tonsils perform an important function.

5. Only in the past week has the full **extent** of the damage become clear.

Exercise 5: Identify the subject of each underlined verb.

1. The company's rather unconvincing <u>denial</u> of the rumor <u>was</u> both brief and incoherent.

2. The <u>problems</u> not yet identified in the software <u>could delay</u> the release.

3. A <u>technique</u> for making tougher sails for sailboats that sail under harsh conditions <u>was</u> the key to the success of the company.

4. <u>Rumors</u> of a new settlement agreement <u>came</u> as a surprise to the striking workers.

5. The recent <u>discovery</u> of the fossil of a fish with four working, paddle-like legs <u>helps</u> to establish the sequence by which fish developed into amphibians.

6. The <u>significance</u> of the fossils of *ambulocetus*, the so-called 'walking whale," which in many ways resembled modern whales except for the presence of two hind legs, <u>cannot be</u> overstated.

7. Any <u>claim</u> for damages resulting from negligence or misuse <u>must be</u> accompanied by substantial documentation.

8. The <u>ideal</u> of a perfect society in which all of the inhabitants achieve their full potential <u>has</u> never been realized in actual practice.

Exercise 6: Use of the Perfect Tenses.

1. Ever since the Great Depression, which gave FDR the political mandate he needed to enact the sweeping reforms of the New Deal, the majority of Americans thought of Social Security as an indispensable safety net. Wrong; should be "the majority of Americans have thought of Social Security as an indispensable safety net."

2. When the prospectors and speculators known as the 49ers poured into California at the start of the Gold Rush, they had brought with them little beyond their clothes, their prospecting tools and their dreams of instant riches. Wrong; should be "they brought with them little beyond their clothes, their prospecting tools and their dreams of instant riches."

3. At the recently concluded meeting, the board has decided to focus on overseas expansion for the foreseeable future. Wrong; should be "the board decided to focus on overseas expansion for the foreseeable future."

4. Archaeologists have recently discovered that the Maya had had a more complex writing system than is commonly believed to be the case. Wrong; should be "the Maya had a more complex writing system than is commonly believed to be the case."

Exercise 7: Subjunctive.

1. Confident of its strategy despite an unprecedented spike in the rate of customer complaints, the Beatlejuice company has made the bold decision to ignore the growing chorus of critics who demand that the product in question must be recalled.
    C.   that the product in question be recalled

2. The members' organization that had insisted for months that the museum increase hours and reduce admission fees was soundly disappointed by the recent decision by the museum's board to cut back hours and raise fees instead.
    A.   increase hours and reduce admission fees

Exercise 8: Increasing Familiarity with the Present Subjunctive.

1. In front of a glass-enclosed display case outside the American Consulate here, clusters of Chinese gather silently to read material that the Chinese Government has demanded <u>be</u> removed.

2. I'd link to the brawl, but the NBA demanded that youtube.com <u>remove</u> all clips of the incident.

3. Previously Mr. Bancroft has insisted News Corp. <u>pay</u> $66 a share—$6 more than it is offering—to the family in order to win his support for the transaction.

4. "From day one, I thought it was essential that everyone <u>touch</u> the project and <u>get</u> engaged in it."

Exercise 9: Identify any mistakes in the verb forms in these sentences.

Some of these could be corrected in more than one way; the corrections suggested here are based on the most obvious interpretations of the sentences.

1. If I ~~would've had~~ known that you were coming, I'd have baked a cake.

2. Had I but known about the problem, I could have done something. OK

3. The birds in the local area will not return if nothing ~~were~~ is done about the cat problem.

4. If John ~~knew~~ had known about the problem last year, he would have taken care of it.

MODULE 2: PRONOUNS

Exercise 10: Determine whether the pronoun has an appropriate (plural) antecedent.

1. Due to recent shortfalls in sales, the company has announced that they will have to lay off a number of workers. **No: "company" is not a plural antecedent for "they."**

2. Apparently convinced that they would have to act quickly to avert a strike, several top managers called for renewed negotiations. **Yes: "top managers" is a plural antecedent for "they."**

3. Unlike companies in Japan, in the United States they have to pay the costs of workers' healthcare. **No: there is no antecedent for "they."**

4. Announcing that contract negotiations had fallen through, the union declared that they were highly likely to call for a temporary work stoppage. **No: "union" is not a plural antecedent for "they."**

5. In Russia, unlike the United States, they frequently eat lemons with salt. **No: there is no antecedent for "they."**

Exercise 11: Decide which of the two choices should fit into the blank in the sentence.

1. The cheetah (Acinonyx jubatus) is an atypical member of the cat family—unique in terms of speed, _____.

    while lacking climbing abilities, it is placed in its own genus, Acinonyx.

2. Fairies are generally described as tiny humans with wings, having magical powers and _____ which humans are strictly forbidden to enter.

    living in their own land, a place

3. The mandibular third molar (commonly known as the wisdom tooth) is the tooth located distally (away from the midline of the face) from both the mandibular second molars of the mouth, at the extreme posterior of the permanent teeth;

    it usually appears between the ages of 16 and 25.

Exercise 12: Decide whether *it* is used correctly (from the standpoint of formal written English) in each of the following sentences.

1. If the groundhog doesn't see his shadow, it means that winter will soon be over. **Incorrect**

2. It's obvious what the President will have to do. **Correct**

3. When the rains fall for three weeks without let-up, it can lead to dangerous mudslides in the mountains. **Incorrect**

4. The stars appear to twinkle, but it's only because of atmospheric disturbance. **Incorrect**

5. It has now been established that human activity is an important cause of global warming. **Correct**

Exercise 13: Decide whether *it* or *this* is used appropriately in each of the following sentences.

1. Another major bank announced plans for a merger today; this stirred up fresh speculation about future changes in the financial sector. **"This" is incorrect; change to something like "this development."**

2. If you are repeatedly late in paying your credit card bills, it will have a negative impact on your credit rating. **"It" is incorrect; change to something like "this behavior."**

3. Though many people feel a craving for carbohydrates in the winter, this response to cold weather is not universal. **Correct**

4. Though some people were surprised to hear that the new movie had done so well at the box office, it didn't come as any surprise to those who had seen the work in previews. **"It" is incorrect; change to something like "the news."**

5. Columbus was not, in fact, the first white person to journey to North America, but this wasn't proven until the remains of ancient Viking settlements were found by archaeologists. **"This" is incorrect; change to something like "but the fact that other European explorers had come earlier."**

6. It has often been observed that, when all is said and done, there is a great deal more said than done. **Correct**

7. If one studies just a couple of hours each day, it will add up to a considerable time investment after just one month. **"It" is incorrect; change to something like "this effort."**

8. The announcement of massive layoffs came as a surprise to many people, but to some analysts, this development was a long-overdue response to an obvious problem. **Correct**

Exercise 14: Decide whether *it* makes sense in each sentence below. If it doesn't, correct the sentence (you may need to make significant changes).

1. Thanks to modern agricultural techniques, the current crop of alfalfa is much healthier than it was just ten years ago. **No; change to something like "...than the crop was just ten years ago."**

2. A rock from space that crashes on the earth's surface is a meteorite, but if it merely enters the atmosphere but doesn't hit the ground, it is a meteor. **No; change to something like "...but a rock from space that merely enters the atmosphere but doesn't hit the ground is a meteor."**

3. The concept of clean coal sounds like a major step forward in the fight against global warming, but in fact it doesn't exist yet. **No; change to something like "...but in fact clean coal doesn't exist yet."**

4. Federal regulations that were put in place after the Great Depression ensure that the modern banking system is much healthier than it was in the early 20th century. **No; change to something like "...than the banking system was in the early 20th century."**

Exercise 15: Decide whether the word *that* or *those* is used correctly in each of these sentences.

1. The illustrations by Roberts are more evocative than those by Townsend. **Correct**

2. At 2008 fuel prices, battery powered buses are more economical than those of diesel or gasoline powered buses. **Incorrect: "those" doesn't refer to anything.**

3. In an electric vehicle, gasoline is indirectly replaced by whatever is being used to generate domestic electricity, reducing dependence on that of foreign commodities. **Incorrect: "that" doesn't refer to anything.**

4. Last year, the number of applicants to the fellowship program reached 78, double that of the previous year's. **Incorrect: "that" doesn't refer to anything.**

Exercise 16: Decide whether *who* or *whom* is correct in each sentence.

1. No one knows **who**/whom first invented the alphabet.

2. Isabella was thrilled to meet the woman **who**/whom was believed to have painted the portrait.

3. Despite numerous attempts to determine **who**/whom was responsible for the debacle, the investigation never yielded any fruit.

4. **Whoever**/whomever is eventually found to have authorized the decision will have a great deal of explaining to do.

5. The person to who/**whom** the letter is addressed must sign for it.

MODULE 3: MODIFIERS

Exercise 17: Decide which of these sentences have dangling modifiers. For those that are incorrect, write corrected versions (there is more than one way to correct each of the incorrect sentences).

1. Born in Frankfurt, Germany, Frank and her family moved to Amsterdam in 1933, after the Nazis gained power in Germany. **Incorrect; Better: "Born in Frankfurt, Germany, Frank moved with her family to Amsterdam..."**

2. Long unknown to most people, researchers have discovered a new composition by Mozart. **Incorrect; Better: "Researchers have discovered a new composition by Mozart that had been long unknown to most people."**

3. Using a variety of sophisticated techniques, archaeologists have been able to establish the age of the artifacts with reasonable certainty. **Correct**

4. Struck by the remarkable coincidence, the reporter asked whether he could do a feature story on the recently reunited triplets. **Correct**

5. Though outraged by the situation, there was nothing the lawyer could do. **Incorrect: Better: "though outraged by the situation, the lawyer could do nothing."**

Exercise 18: Mark each of these sentences as OK or Wrong with respect to the use of the word *which*. Fix the ones in which *which* is used incorrectly (there will usually be more than one way to fix it).

1. He spent two months' pay on a diamond ring, which cost a fortune. **OK**

2. He spent two months' pay on a diamond ring, which made me angry. **Wrong**

3. There were several factors which contributed to the debacle. **OK**

4. There were several factors nobody had taken into consideration, which shows that the so-called leadership wasn't really paying attention. **Wrong**

5. There are huge cracks forming in that dam, which indicates that the town will soon be in danger if something isn't done. **Wrong**

6. There are several dogs on that plane, which ought to be illegal. **Wrong**

7. There are huge cracks forming in that dam, which wasn't very sturdy to begin with. **OK**

8. There are several dogs on that plane, which is scheduled to take off in an hour. **OK**

9. The congressman is running for reelection, which he promised he wouldn't do. **Wrong**

10. He ran 25 miles, which the doctor had told him would be dangerous. **Wrong**

Exercise 19: Decide whether the underlined word or phrase at the beginning of each relative clause is correct.

1. The plan was an exceedingly complex one, involving multiple stages <u>where</u> no one was quite sure what he was supposed to do next. **Wrong: change "where" to "in which."**

2. There were several doors, only <u>one of which</u> led outside. **Correct**

3. The first minute after the explosion was a time <u>when</u> no one knew what to expect. **Correct**

4. Everyone in the room suddenly began applauding, <u>which</u> startled the cat. **Wrong; one way to fix it would be to change to "...began applauding; the noise startled the cat."**

5. The person to whom the letter was addressed realized that this was a situation <u>where</u> things could change in an instant. **Wrong; change to "in which."**

6. The conference participants—<u>of which one</u> was a Nobel Prize winner—gathered outside the hotel for a group picture. **Wrong; change to "one of whom."**

7. The company directors realized too late that the man <u>that</u> they had brought in was unsuited to the job. **Wrong; change to "whom."**

8. The gallery-goers were astonished by the exhibition, <u>whose</u> creator was a 9-year-old child from the slums of Mumbai. **Correct**

Exercise 20: Decide whether the placement of *only* makes sense (by the standards of Formal Written English) in each sentence; if not, move it to the right spot.

1. Jonathan didn't enjoy watching the movie because he only wanted to sleep. **Wrong; should be "wanted only to sleep."**

313

2. The board of directors announced that it would only need to lay off 300 employees. **Wrong; should be "it would need to lay off only 300 employees."**

3. The novel is incredibly popular in Europe but so far is available only in German. **Correct**

4. If you need anything, you only have to ask. **Wrong; should be "you have only to ask."**

5. The governor's office announced that under the new rules, homeless people would only be allowed to stay in shelters for a maximum of three months. **Wrong; should be "would be allowed to stay in shelters for a maximum of only three months."**

MODULE 4: COMPARISONS

Exercise 21: Decide which of the following comparisons make sense and which need revision.

1. Like Hemingway, Steinbeck's works are often assigned in high school English classes. **Wrong; should be "Like Hemingway's works, Steinbeck's works are often assigned in high school English classes."**

2. Unlike cottage cheese, yogurt contains a significant amount of calcium. **OK**

3. Unlike most other television dramas, the characters in this series change and evolve. **Wrong; should be "Unlike the characters in most other television dramas, the characters in this series change and evolve."**

4. Unlike humans, dogs have a toxic reaction to chocolate. **OK**

5. Like cats, people should be aware that giving aspirin to dogs can be dangerous. **Wrong; should be "People should be aware that, like giving aspirin to cats, giving aspirin to dogs can be dangerous."**

6. Fear of clowns is known as 'coulrophobia'; like most phobias, it is difficult to explain where it comes from. **Wrong; should be "Fear of clowns is known as 'coulrophobia'; as is the case with most phobias, it is difficult to explain where it comes from."**

7.

Exercise 22: Determine whether these comparisons are clear and make sense. If not, fix them. Remember that sentences that <u>sound</u> as if they make sense from the point of view of everyday conversational English may be considered ambiguous (and therefore wrong) on the GMAT.

1. Surprisingly enough, David could eat a lot more than Goliath **could**.

2. Sicle cell anemia is much more common in areas that are plagued by malaria than **in** areas that aren't.

3. Though sucrose contains both fructose and glucose, high fructose corn syrup contains more fructose than **it does** sucrose.

4. This year's model doesn't weigh as much as last year**'s**.

5. Tea bags contain more caffeine than coffee grounds **do**, but brewed coffee contains more caffeine than brewed tea **does**.

Exercise 23: Decide whether the use of as or like is correct in each sentence.

1. Like Monet, Manet is considered an Impressionist. **Correct**

2. Just as St Francis did, St Claire embraced the concept of poverty as a spiritual discipline. **Correct**

3. Like the works of Beethoven and Mozart have been, the works of Bach have been studied by musical theorists for centuries. **Incorrect**

4. Many people feel like their lives are changing too rapidly for them to adjust. **Incorrect**

5. As organic grain, which is subject to specific limitations on the use of fertilizers and pesticides, organic milk must meet rigorous standards of purity. **Incorrect**

6. The day passed as a shadow. **Incorrect**

MODULE 5: PARALLELISM

Exercise 24: Underline all the parallel phrases in these sentences. Identify any mistakes in parallelism and suggest a re-write.

1. Shakespeare excelled at character, plot, dialogue, and ~~did amazing things with~~ language.

2. Goats will eat just about anything: leaves, grass, paper, rags, and tree bark. **No error**

3. There are only two certainties in life: death and ~~you have to pay~~ taxes.

4. John liked visiting Aspen, where he enjoyed hiking, rock climbing, and ~~skied~~ **skiing**.

5. The clever test taker excelled in math, ~~in~~ physics, and gym.

Exercise 25: Decide which of the following sentences have mistakes in parallelism and correct them.

1. John ate pizza and drank wine, although the combination didn't taste very good. **No error**

2. The evil robot ate the pizza, the couch, **and** the table, and drank wine.

3. Sally likes skeet-shooting, scuba-diving, windsurfing, and ~~to lie~~ **lying** on the beach afterwards.

4. The committee decided that the park needed to be re-landscaped and made safer at night. **No error**

5. The dog wants fish, hamburger or to drink out of the toilet. **Wrong; one way to fix it: "The dog wants fish or hamburger or to drink out of the toilet."**

Exercise 26: Identify and correct any mistakes in parallelism in these sentences.

1. King Herod's reign over Judea from 37 to 4 B.C. is ~~not~~ remembered **not** for justice but for its indiscriminate cruelty.

2. **Not only were some very unusual items** listed in the 25-page will ~~were not only some very unusual items~~, but the deceased also left some choice comments about his heirs.

3. Disgruntled vacationers were informed that they could either submit their complaints for arbitration or, if they insisted, ~~they would have to~~ file a class action lawsuit.

4. The discovery of the archaeological site of ancient Troy ~~was both~~ **both constituted** a major accomplishment for the archaeologist and came as a huge shock to those who had always assumed that Troy was a Homeric myth.

5. The new corporate headquarters are ~~either~~ to be constructed **either** in London or in Paris, at a cost of $300 million.

Exercise 27: Decide whether the parallel phrases in these sentences are formed correctly. Fix any mistakes you find.

1. Economic analysts say that the recession ~~has been and~~ will continue to abate.

2. The mortgage crisis was predicted to hit bottom by mid-year, and it did. **OK**

3. Nuclear engineers testified that the plant was running at full capacity and had been for six months. **OK**

4. Union leaders promised to bring the strike to a rapid conclusion, and they have **done so**.

5. Local officials said that the dam was and is cracking due to the excessive pressure. **OK although somewhat wordy; "has been cracking" would be tighter.**

Exercise 28: Make sure that all the lists in the following sentences are closed off properly.

1. The sinking of the Titanic came about as the result of several factors, including excessive speed, poor visibility, unusually large amounts of ice in the water, **and** inadequate maneuverability.

2. Some common superstitions require people to avoid black cats, to be careful in handling mirrors—which bring seven years' bad luck if they break—**and** to go around rather than under a ladder.

3. In the pre-television era, playing cards, telling stories, **and** reading books were common pastimes.

Exercise 29: Each of the following sentences has at least one set of two or more phrases that are parallel to one another. Underline the parallel phrases. If there is more than one series in the same sentence, mark the two series differently (use different colors or double-underline one).

1. The board of directors decided <u>to diversify the company's product line</u>, <u>to hire a new marketing agency,</u> and <u>to plant spies in the competitors' factories</u>.

2. A triathlon is a multi-sport endurance event consisting of <u>swimming</u>, <u>cycling</u>, and <u>running</u> in immediate succession.

3. Joan of Arc reported that <u>Saint Michael</u>, <u>Saint Catherine</u>, and <u>Saint Margaret</u> told her *to dress as a man, to take up arms, to drive out the English,* and *to bring the Dauphin to Reims for his coronation.*

4. Charged with instituting new cost-saving measures, the library committee decided almost immediately <u>to increase overdue fines</u>, an important source of revenue for the library, and <u>to cut back on hours</u>.

5. When the *Californian's* officers first saw the lights of an unknown ship on the horizon, they <u>tried signaling her with their Morse lamp</u>, but <u>never appeared to receive a response</u>.

6. How long the *Titanic* will remain on the ocean's floor is unclear; many scientists, including Robert Ballard, are concerned that <u>visits by tourists in submarines</u> and <u>the recovery of artifacts</u> are hastening the decay of the wreck.

Exercise 30: Choose the correct version of each underlined phrase. (If you wish, you could also change the next line to "Pay particular attention to meaning when making your choice.").

1. The detective identified the murderer after interviewing several witnesses—some of whom were frightened and reluctant to talk—and ~~uncovered~~/**uncovering** several important but previously unknown clues.

2. The startling profit and loss figures released by the board of directors sent stock prices plummeting, panicked investors into selling as fast as possible, and **triggered/** ~~triggering~~ an SEC investigation.

3. Having overpowered its prey, a cat may deliver a lethal neck bite with its long canine teeth, thus either severing the prey's spinal cord with irreversible paralysis or causing fatal bleeding by puncturing the carotid artery or the jugular vein, or **asphyxiate**/~~asphyxiating~~ the prey by crushing its trachea.

4. Some researchers believe that cats who bring prey to their owners are attempting to take care of them much as they would care for a sick or elderly cat, ~~bring/to bring~~/**bringing** food to sustain them until they are well enough to hunt for themselves.

5. Soon after stepping out of the spacecraft onto the surface of the moon, Armstrong made photographic records of the lunar module so engineers would be able to judge its post-landing condition, **making**/~~make~~ a panoramic sweep with the MESA TV camera, and then collected a contingency soil sample using a sample bag on a stick.

Exercise 31: Decide which word in the underlined pair is correct.

1. The young entrepreneur accomplished many of his goals astonishingly early: by the age of twelve he had founded a successful business, set aside enough money for his retirement, met most of the major players in the industry, and ~~wrote~~/**written** a best-selling book.

2. Investigators found signs of widespread fighting, killing, and ~~destroying~~/**destruction** at the battle site.

Exercise 32: Overall review of parallelism. Identify the errors (if any) in parallelism in the sentences below.

1. The source of the fire that killed the Mercury 7 astronauts was never determined, but their deaths were attributed to a wide range of lethal design hazards in the early Apollo command module such as its highly pressurized 100% oxygen atmosphere during the test, many wiring and plumbing flaws, inflammable materials in the cockpit, a hatch which might not open at all in an emergency, and even the flight suits worn by the astronauts ~~may have been a factor~~. **(The list is a list of nouns, but the last item is a clause - remove 'may have been a factor.')**

2. After the capsule splashed down, Grissom began final preparations for egress, opening up the faceplate on his helmet, **disconnected** the oxygen hose from the helmet, unfastening the helmet from his suit, **and released** the chest strap, the lap belt, ~~the~~ shoulder harness, knee straps, and medical sensors. **(Two verbs are in the wrong form—change "disconnected" and "released" to "disconnecting" and "releasing"; there's a missing "and"; and the final list of nouns has inconsistent use of "the"—remove one "the.")**

3. Carnivorous plants employ a variety of traps to capture and digest insects: pitfall traps, flypaper, lobster pots, ~~as well as~~ **and** sticky hairs. **(Incorrect use of "as well as" to close a list; change "as well as" to "and.")**

MODULE 6: IDIOMS

Exercise 33: Choose the version of each sentence that has no errors in the use of idioms.

1. a. The manager decided to try and improve morale, with the aim of increasing productivity.
    b. The manager decided to try to improve morale, with the aim to increase productivity.
    c. **The manager decided to try to improve morale, with the aim of increasing productivity.**

2. a. Rice is to Asia just like wheat is to Europe: the staple grain.
    b. **Rice is to Asia what wheat is to Europe: the staple grain.**

3. a. **Benjamin Franklin is credited with proving that lightning is electricity.**
    b. Benjamin Franklin is credited for proving that lightning is electricity.

4. a. **Asian elephants are different from African elephants in several interesting ways.**
    b. Asian elephants are different than African elephants in several interesting ways.

5. a. Though the fossils were originally estimated at 35 million years old, paleontologists have more recently dated them to be 47 million years old.
    b. Though the fossils were originally estimated to be 35 million years old, paleontologists have more recently dated them at 47 million years old.
    c. Though the fossils were originally estimated to be 35 million years old, paleontologists have more recently dated them to be 47 million years old.
    d. Though the fossils were originally estimated at 35 million years old, paleontologists have more recently dated them at 47 million years old.

Exercise 34: Find any mistakes in the phrasing or usage of idioms.

1. ~~Being~~ a well-known author, Neil Gaiman is often asked for autographs.

2. The district manager reported that ~~hopefully,~~ **he hoped that** there would be a significant improvement in sales for the next quarter.

3. Simplified Chinese characters have fewer strokes ~~as contrasted with~~ **than** traditional Chinese characters.

Exercise 35: Identify any idiom that is incorrectly used and replace it with an appropriate idiom.

1. In an attempt to increase sales, the company tried ~~to lower~~ **lowering** prices, but even this failed to attract more customers.

2. Determined to improve his department's performance, the manager tried ~~convincing~~ **to convince** the employees to care more about the quality of their work, but was unable to do so.

3. The heat inside a volcano is often ~~hot enough~~ *so hot* that it melts rock. *(or "hot enough to melt.")*

4. Some dieters use herbal supplements and fasting as a means to lose weight. **OK**

5. Though most clothes are washed after one day's use, jeans ~~are able to~~ *can be* worn two or three days in a row before they are washed.

Exercise 36: Idiom Review. Fill in the missing word—if any—in the blank. If nothing is needed, draw a slash mark.

1. Asian elephants are different *from* African elephants.

2. Some trainers consider Asian elephants easier to work with.

3. The Maya are credited *with* having invented an extremely complex writing system.

4. Modern Maya have decided to try *to* learn their ancestors' writing system.

5. Mayan writing is estimated *to be* more than 2,000 years old.

6. One set of Mayan inscriptions is dated *at* 1300 years old.

7. The Mayan writing system was initially viewed *as* nothing but pictograms.

8. Some anti-cancer drugs are specifically targeted *at* the cancer cells' ability to create new veins.

9. Some people think of cancer *as* incurable, but in fact it can often be successfully treated.

10. Drug companies often must expend millions of dollars *on* the development of a new drug.

11. The self-absorbed actor often seemed oblivious *to* other people's feelings.

12. The game warden said he was unwilling to acquiesce *in* the plan to capture the wild zebras.

13. The cable company's business plan depended on the idea that people would be willing to pay exorbitant rates *for* mediocre entertainment.

14. Some people regard the internet *as* mere entertainment, while others consider it a significant business tool.

15. In a national emergency, the vice president may be called on to act *as* the president.

16. The senator caused a huge scandal by getting drunk and acting *like* a fool at a fundraiser.

17. It is difficult to have a lawyer disbarred without significant evidence *of* wrongdoing.

18. Michael Jackson was acclaimed *as* the best dancer since Fred Astaire.

Exercise 37: Decide which of the phrases between brackets is correct.

1. Some linguists were at first reluctant [to admit/~~about admitting~~] that the Mayan writing system was more or less phonetic.

2. The reason the Mayan writing system was unknown for centuries was [~~because~~/ that] the Spanish conquistadors had done their utmost to suppress it.

3. In the 1980s, scholars claimed [~~the ability~~/to be able] to read large segments of ancient Mayan text.

4. The Maya are [~~attributed with~~/credited with] the invention of an independent writing system unrelated to any other.

5. There are signs all over the train station prohibiting [passengers from smoking/ ~~passengers to smoke~~].

MODULE 7: CLAUSES AND CLAUSAL CONNECTORS

Exercise 38: In each of the sentences below, choose either *if* or *whether*. Only one is correct in each case.

1. I don't know if/whether he'll be on time. **whether**

2. A company spokesperson declined to comment on if/whether the recall would be expanded further. **whether**

3. If/whether the effects of global warming can be reversed is far from clear. **whether**

4. If/whether the effects of global warming can be reversed, clearly the nations of the world should begin the effort to do so immediately. **if**

5. The suspect refused to clarify if/whether there had been others involved. **whether**

6. No one told the company president if/whether the issue had been resolved. **whether**

7. If/whether any other food products were involved in the outbreak, the FDA will expand the range of the warnings. **if**

8. Everyone affected by the food poisoning outbreak is likely to recover if/whether medical attention is given promptly. **if**

Exercise 39: Determine which of these sentences has a comma splice.

1. Refusing to surrender but knowing he was going to die soon, the chief wrote out his final statement to the tribe. **OK**

2. The manager realized that his division would have to improve its performance dramatically; he therefore instigated a complete overhaul of departmental procedures. **Comma splice; replace with semi-colon.**

3. Only two things in life are certain, death and taxes, but people invest a great deal of money and energy in an effort to avoid both. **OK**

Exercise 40: Decide whether each of these sentences has an independent clause on each side of the semi-colon.

1. No political system, however cleverly designed, can solve every problem; for every solution to a problem inevitably creates another problem. **no**

2. Snowflakes are an example of the fact that a seemingly simple molecular structure can give rise to fantastically complex shapes at the larger level; no two of them found to be exactly alike. **yes**

3. Some people find the theory of wormholes in space fantastic; nevertheless, a number of highly respected physicists have endorsed it. **yes**

4. Although business analysts endlessly repeat the advice to "Buy low, sell high," making it sound like a simple principle to implement; the fact is that predicting the best time to buy or sell is notoriously difficult. **no**

5. There is no reason to expect gasoline prices to stay low indefinitely; sooner or later, demand for gasoline will once again push the price up. **yes**

MODULE 8: SPECIAL ISSUES OF MEANING

Exercise 41: Identify and fix any faulty equations in the sentences below.

1. The photograph on the wall was **of** a man who appeared to be about 20 years old.

2. The Coast Guard announced that the body that washed up in Pacific Grove last week has been identified as **that of** Sandra Brown.

3. Peering closely at the faded image, the antiques appraiser could see it was **a picture of** a little girl with a small dog.

Exercise 42: Underline any part of each sentence below that doesn't make sense, or could be stated a lot more clearly. There will be one in each sentence. Suggest a re-write.

1. The music industry executive said that, because of the economic impact of piracy on recording companies, **people who make** unauthorized duplicates of songs would be prosecuted to the fullest extent of the law.

2. The Chair of the Senate Foreign Relations Committee testified that the future of the Iraqi state hinged on the success of its effort at establishing democracy, and that a stolen **theft of the** election should be prevented at all costs.

3. The documentary on the history of the Waldorf and Montessori schools showcases two very similar educational systems **that were very similar,** although they were invented by different people.

MODULE 9: DICTION

Exercise 43: Spot any phrases that seem odd or poorly worded.

1. The ~~differential~~ **difference** between field crickets and snowy tree crickets is fairly obvious, as the two species do not have the same coloring.

2. The word "undertaker" ~~is not referential~~ **does not refer** to one who undertakes something, but rather means a person who deals with dead bodies.

3. The security guard was reprimanded for insubordination and ~~laying~~ **lying** down on the job.

4. Trade relations ~~between~~ **among** China, Japan, and South Korea are complex and heavily influenced by cultural nuances.

5. The newly-elected senator hoped to be placed on committees with substantial power over finances, thus putting him in a better position than most junior ~~legislatures~~ **legislators** to secure money for his home state.

MODULE 10: HALLMARKS OF FORMAL WRITTEN ENGLISH

Exercise 44: Decide which version of each sentence is correct.

1. That no one has ever produced a convincing photograph of the Loch Ness monster should not be construed as proof of the monster's non-existence. **Correct**

2. That reindeer cannot actually fly can hardly be said that it has been proven. **Incorrect**

3. That the dark side of the moon is not always dark may not be obvious to those who have only a casual acquaintance with astronomy. **Correct**

4. That there are 12 days of Christmas is confusing to many people who are not familiar with the ancient European traditions from which this one came. **Correct**

5. That the moon is the primary factor determining the timing of the rise and fall of the tides, although now understood fully, at one time controversial and considered rank superstition by those who considered the theory to be an outgrowth of astrology. **Incorrect**

Exercise 45: Indicate whether the following sentences are correct or incorrect.

1. That no one has ever produced a convincing photograph of the Loch Ness monster should not be construed as proof of the monster's non-existence. **Correct**

2. That reindeer cannot actually fly can hardly be said that it has been proven. **Incorrect**

3. That the dark side of the moon is not always dark may not be obvious to those

who have only a casual acquaintance with astronomy. **Correct**

Additional Resources

Tools for Organized Study & Study Spreadsheet

You'll want to create a study spread sheet to track scores and mistakes.

On the very top of the sheet:

1. Date, Test or Book pages/Online etc.

2. Quant, Verbal or Integrated Reasoning

On the Left hand side:

3. Number the rows 1-40 (every page will be 1-40, so that's why you need problem set range on top)

Columns should be as follows:

1. A, B, C, D, E—for answering the multiple-choice questions.

2. Correct/Incorrect.

3. Too Slow—If a question takes you longer than 1.5 minutes, or you guessed on it, whether you get it right or not, indicate this. Take time to understand the question or why it took you so long and explore off the clock if there are any short cuts you missed in doing the question.

4. Too Fast—Identify why you went too fast. Did you think you understood, did you guess, were you overly confident, did you not answer what the question was asking?

5. Guess.

6. Type of Question/Topic tested.

7. Notes.

DATE:_____   TEST # _____ Book/Pages/Online

Q#	Q/V/I	A	CORR./ INCORR.	SPEED	Guess	TYPE	NOTES
1							
2							
3							
4							

Basic Grammar Review

Most of the grammatical concepts you need to understand to do GMAT SCs are explained within the main body of the manual. This brief review is intended only to help test takers who are not sure of the meanings of basic grammatical terms such as noun, verb, subject, object, etc.

The main parts of speech are nouns, verbs, adjectives, adverbs, and prepositions.

Nouns describe things—people, places, concrete objects, and abstract ideas. Some frequently used nouns are: *cat, name, place, democracy, truth, water, sand, construction, translation.*

Verbs describe actions or states of being, and can be marked to communicate tense (time). Some frequently used verbs are: *run, eat, live, believe, sleep.*

Adjectives are used with nouns to add description. Some frequently used adjectives are: *happy, intelligent, uncertain, useless, true.*

Adverbs are used with verbs, adjectives, or other adverbs to add description. Most of them end with -ly, but not all do. Some frequently used adverbs are: *happily, quickly, slowly, well (as in "She speaks French well"), truly.*

Prepositions are words that describe relationships, often spatial relationships but often more abstract relationships. Some frequently used prepositions are: *on, to, in, with, about, for, of, from, after, onto, off of, between.*

Grammatical Categories:

The **subject** of a sentence is typically the noun that describes the person or thing who does the action described by the verb. The subjects in these sentences are bolded:

> The **CEO** decided to announce a change.
> The **report** startled the investors.
> **Someone** did a study on the safety of eating apricot pits.

In a **passive** sentence, however, the subject is not actually doing the action, but is instead the person or thing that the action is done to:

> A **change** was announced by the CEO.
> **Investors** were startled by the report.
> **A study** was done on the safety of eating apricot pits.

The **object of a verb** is the noun that follows the verb and describes the person or thing that the action is done to:

> The CEO announced a **change**.
> The report startled **the investors.**
> Someone did a **study** on the safety of eating apricot pits.

Note that the difference between an active sentence and a passive one is that in a passive sentence, the noun that would be the object of the verb in an active sentence becomes the subject instead.

The **object of a preposition** is the noun that comes after the preposition:

> The elephant walked into **the room.**
> The swan flew over **the lake.**

Verbs in English often require various auxiliary ("helping") verbs and endings in order to form the various verb tenses.

Verb Forms:

Verbs in English often require various auxiliary ("helping") verbs and endings in order to form the various verb tenses. The verb tense distinctions that are commonly tested on the GMAT are discussed in Module 1. Here we present a chart of what the verb tenses look like:

> **Simple present:** John sleeps.
>
> **Simple past:** John slept.
>
> **Simple future:** John will sleep.
>
> **Present progressive:** John is sleeping.
>
> **Past progressive:** John was sleeping.
>
> **Future progressive:** John will be sleeping.
>
> **Present perfect:** John has slept.
>
> **Past perfect:** John had slept.
>
> **Future perfect:** John will have slept.
>
> **Present perfect progressive:** John has been sleeping.
>
> **Past perfect progressive:** John had been sleeping.
>
> **Future perfect progressive:** John will have been sleeping.

English also has a class of modal verbs—verbs that don't change forms to mark various tenses, but instead combine with other verbs to express different nuances concerning time, intention, and possibility or probability. The modals in these sentences are bolded:

John **could** go.

The elephant **might** fly.

The earthquake **should** have been predicted.

The economic crisis **may** have already ended.

The commonly used modals are *can, could, will, would, should, may, and might.*

Verbs in English can form words known as **participles**.

The **past participle** is a form like *broken, taken, gone, done, eaten,* etc. For the vast majority of verbs in English, the past participle is formed by adding -ed, so it looks exactly the same as the past tense (the GMAT often exploits the potential for confusion here). The past participle can be used as an adjective (as in "The broken clock"); it is also used to form the passive form of a verb (as in "The clock was broken by the elephant").

The **present participle** is formed by adding *-ing* to the verb, as in *breaking, taking, eating,* etc. The present participle is sometimes called the **gerund**; there is controversy and confusion over the correct usage of these two terms, even among professional grammarians, so in this manual we simply refer to the *-ing* form.

Grammar Rule Chart

Rules	Clues	Correct	Incorrect
Verbs must agree with their subjects.	• The subject is third person. • The verb is present tense. • Choices include *is* and *are* or "s" and no "s."	**Correct:** The recent increase in mortgage failures is a sign of the times. **Correct:** The dog, along with the cat, is going to the vet.	**Incorrect:** The recent increase in mortgage failures are a sign of the times. **Incorrect:** The dog, along with the cat, **are** going to the vet.
Use present perfect for actions extending from the past to the present.	The sentence <u>includes</u> the time expression *since* or a phrase such as *in recent months.*	**Correct:** Since the protests began, attention **has been riveted** on Wall Street.	**Incorrect:** Since the protests began, attention **was riveted** on Wall Street.
Use simple past if the specific time of the event is given.	Choices include both perfect and past verbs.	**Correct:** At last week's meeting, the board **voted** to raise prices.	**Incorrect:** At last week's meeting, the board **has voted** to raise prices.
Use past perfect only if two past events are mentioned.	Choices include past perfect and simple past.	**Correct:** Many researchers believe that the Native Americans originally **migrated** from Asia.	**Incorrect:** Many researchers believe that the Native Americans **had** originally **migrated** from Asia.
Use present subjunctive (the bare verb form) after expressions of necessity/demand.	• Expression such as *demand, require, it is necessary.* • One (wrong) choice includes should.	**Correct:** Academy regulations require that all research **be** both original and unpublished.	**Incorrect:** Academy regulations require that all research **should be** both original and unpublished.
Use past subjunctive were (not was) after if.	• presence of *if.* • choices include *was* and *were.*	**Correct:** If prices go up, profits will fall. **Correct:** If prices went up, profits would fall. **Correct:** If prices had gone up, profits would have fallen.	**Incorrect:** If prices go up, profits would fall. **Incorrect:** If prices went up, profits would have fallen. **Incorrect:** If prices would have gone up, profits would have fallen.
they/them/their must have a plural antecedent.	Sentence includes *they, them* or *their.*	**Correct:** The company announced plans to expand **its** operations.	**Incorrect:** The company announced plans to expand **their** operations.

Rules	Clues	Correct	Incorrect
it must have an antecedent (or be a "dummy subject").	Sentence includes *it*.	**Correct:** The drop in prices came as a surprise, but **it** didn't affect profits. **Correct: It** came as no surprise that the price plummeted.	**Incorrect:** Prices plummeted, but **it** didn't mean that the economy was in trouble.
this must have a noun.	Answer choices include *this*.	**Correct:** Stock prices plummeted; **this development** came as a surprise to economists.	**Incorrect:** Stock prices plummeted; **this** came as a surprise to economists.
that, when used in a comparison, must have an antecedent (a noun that it replaces).	Answer choices include *that* or *that of.*	**Correct:** The land area of England is smaller than **that** of California.	**Incorrect:** Though it is an entire country, England is geographically smaller than **that** of California.
that or those, used in a comparison, must have an antecedent that matches in number.	Answer choices include both *that* and *those*.	**Correct:** The conductivity of gold is greater than **that** of aluminum. **Correct:** The nutrients in wheat are superior to **those** in corn.	**Incorrect:** The conductivity of gold is greater than **those** of aluminum. **Incorrect:** The nutrients in wheat are superior to **that** in corn.
Use who for subjects and *whom* for objects.	Choices include both *who* and *whom*.	**Correct:** T.S. Lawrence was an individual **who** was often misunderstood. **Correct:** The Taj Mahal is a monument built by a grieving husband for the wife **whom** he loved.	**Incorrect:** T.S. Lawrence was an individual **whom** was often misunderstood. **Incorrect:** The Taj Mahal is a monument built by a grieving husband for the wife **who** he loved.
Use *do so* rather than *do it* to stand in for a verb.	Choices include both *do it* and *do so.*	**Correct:** The trainer did not punish the lion because he believed it would be dangerous to **do so.**	**Incorrect:** The trainer did not punish the lion because he believed it would be dangerous to **do it.**
-ing modifiers at the beginning of the sentence must describe the subject.	Sentence begins with an *-ing* phrase.	**Correct:** Reporting on the recent drop in profits, the company cited a number of mitigating factors.	**Incorrect:** Reporting on the recent drop in profits, a number of mitigating factors were cited.

Rules	Clues	Correct	Incorrect
past participle modifiers (*-ed* or *–en*) at the beginning of the sentence must describe the subject.	Sentence begins with a past participle phrase.	**Correct:** Based on impeccable research, the study proves that the scientists were right.	**Incorrect:** Based on impeccable research, the scientists now know that they were right.
A noun phrase at the beginning of the sentence and acting as a modifier must describe the subject.	The sentence begins with a noun phrase that isn't the subject, followed by a comma.	**Correct:** A lifelong fan of baseball, Stephen Jay Gould wrote numerous essays on the subject.	**Incorrect:** A lifelong fan of baseball, Stephen Jay Gould's essays on the subject are famous.
which, when used in a relative clause, must modify the noun phrase it's attached to.	Some answer choices include *which*.	**Correct:** The heiress sold the famous painting, which had been in the family for generations.	**Incorrect:** The heiress sold the famous painting, which infuriated the relatives hoping to inherit it.
where, used in a relative clause, should describe a location.	Some answer choices include *where*.	**Correct:** The company's founder returned to the small town where he had grown up.	**Incorrect:** The bank faced a situation where liabilities exceeded assets.
only must be placed just before the phrase it delimits.	Choices have *only* in different positions.	**Correct:** The company failed **only** because of its marketing strategy.	**Incorrect:** The company **only** failed because of its marketing strategy.
Put phrases in an order that makes the meaning clear.	More than one choice sounds reasonable, but the phrases appear in different orders.	**Correct:** In two dense volumes, the author, using crystal-clear prose, tells the fascinating story of an English village.	**Incorrect:** The author tells the fascinating story of an English village using crystal clear prose in two dense volumes.
Compare "apples to apples," not apples to oranges.	The sentence begins with *like, unlike* or *in contrast to*.	**Correct:** Unlike the United States, Canada has a single-payer healthcare system.	**Incorrect:** Unlike the United States, health care in Canada is a single-payer system.
Use than for unequal comparisons; use as X as for equal comparisons.	The choices vary between *than* and *as*.	**Correct:** England is almost as large as California; the U.K. is larger than California.	**Incorrect:** England is almost as large than California; the U.K. is larger as California.
Make sure comparison phrases are completed.	Choices include complex phrases such as *as more X* or *as X as.*	**Correct:** Platinum is at least as expensive as gold.	**Incorrect:** Platinum is more expensive or as expensive as gold.

Rules	Clues	Correct	Incorrect
Make sure comparisons make logical sense.	Sentence includes *than*; some choices include additional words but others don't.	**Correct:** Acme Paperweights, Inc. consumes more resources than does Anvil Ledgers.	**Incorrect:** Acme Paperweights, Inc. consumes more resources than Anvil Ledgers.
Phrases in a list must be parallel.	Phrases joined by commas or *and/or/but.*	**Correct:** The committee decided that the park needed to be re-landscaped and made safer at night.	**Incorrect:** The committee decided that the park needed to be re-landscaped and better security at night.
Paired expressions must be complete and the phrases following them must be parallel. Paired expressions (memorize them and watch for them): *not only… but also* *not…but* *both…and* *either…or* *neither…nor* *from…to* *between…and* *just as…so*	Part of one of the paired expressions appears in the prompt.	**Correct:** Not only the company's stock price plummeted in response to the recent scandal, but also its reputation, which may never recover.	**Incorrect:** Not only the company's stock price plummeted in response to the recent scandal, but its reputation suffered irreparable damage.
If part of a verb phrase is omitted, the "missing piece" has to appear elsewhere in the sentence.	Partial verb phrases such as *has not and will not* or *has been and will.*	**Correct:** The doctor said that the patient **has not recovered** and likely **will not recover.**	**Incorrect:** The doctor said the patient **has not** and likely **will not recover.**
A past participle can be parallel to an *–ing* form.	Sentence includes an *–ing* word and it's clear that it must be parallel to something.	**Correct:** The hero, **bleeding** from numerous papercuts and **pursued** by rabid wolverines, scampered to safety.	**Incorrect:** The hero, **bled** from numerous papercuts and **pursued** by rabid wolverines, scampered to safety.

IMPORTANT IDIOMS

Correct	Incorrect	Example
Ability to do	Ability for doing	He has a notable ability to dissemble.
Acclaimed as	Acclaimed to be	Ella Fitzgerald is acclaimed as a great singer.
Appear to be	Appear as	The sun appears to be the same size as the moon.
Attribute [effect] to [cause]	Attribute [cause] as the cause of [effect]	Researchers are unsure whether to attribute pancreatic cancer to consumption of high fructose corn syrup.
Claim to be able to	Claim the ability to	Some psychics claim to be able to see the future.
Consider X Y	Consider X to be Y	Many people consider Barack Obama a good speaker.
Credit X with Y	Credit X as Y	The Chinese are credited with the invention of paper money.
Dated to	Dated to be	Hunting tools found in North America have been dated to the 12th century BCE.
Different from	Different than	British English is different from American English in numerous ways.
Distinction between X and Y	Distinction of X from Y	The distinction between the vowels in "ship" and "sheep" is not always easy to hear.
Equipped to do	Equipped for doing	The hospital is equipped to treat 700 patients.
Estimate X to be Y years old	Estimate X at Y years old	Scientists estimate the earth to be four billion years old.
Forbid X to	Forbid X from	Federal law forbids stockbrokers to use inside information.
Known to be	Known as being	The moon is now known to be slightly moist.
Mistake X for Y	Mistake X as Y	Some people mistake the Red-Bellied Black Snake for the Eastern Small-Eyed Snake.
Targeted at	Targeted to	The most recent advertising campaign is targeted at undecided voters.

EXPRESSIONS THAT ARE USUALLY OR ALWAYS WRONG ON THE GMAT

Wrong Expression	Explanation & Remedy
liable to	choose "likely to" instead.
the reason why/the reason is because	redundant—choose something simpler such as "The reason is."
hopefully	incorrect if used to mean "It is *hoped*."
on account of	choose *because* of instead.
as to	wordy and vague—choose *about* instead.
so as to	wordy—to express purpose, "To" is preferred.
as contrasted with	choose "In contrast with," "In contrast to" or "unlike."
being	not always wrong, but make sure that it is needed; if the sentence is grammatically correct without including "being", don't choose it.

GENERAL GMAT TIMELINE

Taking your GMAT should be one of the very first things you do in your application process, though you may have also begun investigating schools you would like to attend. Remember that although the GMAT is only one part of your application package, it should definitely not be something you just need to "get out of the way." In addition to time for careful preparation, you should factor into your timeline the possibility of taking the test twice. Although your first score might end up being as high as you need, you don't want to assume that it will be, thus putting you in the position of scrambling at the last minute to find another test date if you don't perform as well as you'd like. Additionally, your score has a five-year shelf life. If you don't plan on attending school until a few years down the road, you can still take the test and get it out of the way.

You have two fundamental options when setting a GMAT date:

Time is not an issue: You have the luxury of taking the test when it is convenient and when you are ready, and can deal with the application due dates later.

Time is an issue: Give yourself 8 months to a year to implement your optimal application plan. Ideally, you want a timeline that starts in January and includes time to prepare for and take the GMAT, complete your application, and get your references in order.

If you plan on applying to business school this year and entering next year, you'll be working within the "round" system. For many schools, there are 3 rounds; Round 1 starts in the fall, Round 2 starts early in the new year, and Round 3 starts in the spring.

Round 1 is typically around October, Round 2, January, and Round 3, April. If you use these as a reference to extrapolate deadlines you will quickly see how far in advance you need to start working on the GMAT and your application. We suggest you contact some schools you might want apply to to find out their specific Rounds dates.

If you use these dates to extrapolate deadlines, you will quickly see how far in advance you need to start working on the GMAT and your application.

Some people can successfully prepare for the GMAT in 3 weeks. Others need 6 months.

We advise you plan on 2 to 3 months of GMAT study because that will prevent burnout and keep you from placing undo importance on the test. Then, add a buffer of another month or two to accommodate taking the test a second time if you need to. Keep in mind that for most people the GMAT is not a test you can successfully cram for.

Here is a sample timeline. Adapt as necessary.

January-March:

GMAT preparation
GMAT Registration (plan for 2–3 months ahead)
Extra Curricular Activities

March

Organize your goals and start visiting schools

April/May

Take the GMAT
Accomplishments and Leadership experiences

May:

Re-take the GMAT
Visit schools.

June:

Re-take the GMAT

July

Confirm recommenders
Retake GMAT
Create an error-tracking spreadsheet

September

Finished essays and applications
Recommendations should be IN

October

Applications submitted

CONCLUSION

Congratulations! You have completed all the modules to have the best success on the Sentence Correction questions, as well as an optimal mindset on the GMAT. Still, there is more to go over. Within a couple of days before the test, you should do the following:

- Relax a bit. Yes. Really. You've done all the hard work. You need to enter the test fully energized and focused. No diagnostics or marathon study sessions for you, my friend. You can do some light studying, but really allow your brain to integrate so it's fully fresh on test day.

- Make sure your meals, social time, exercise and downtime is 'scheduled.' Eat healthy, sleep deeply, and if any issues come up, go back to Chapter One to figure out how to get into the best mindset. Start with EFT.

- Don't plan on making any 'huge' life decisions at this time, like changing jobs, getting engaged or divorced, or quitting a habit. New exercise routines? Nope. Wait until after the test. Keep things as normal and routine as possible. Just up the ante on being good to yourself.

- Visualize success. We've already gone over this but there is never too much of this good thing. Imagine your ease entering the test center… taking the test… and visualize that stellar score at the end. Doesn't it feel great?!

- If you have the Full Potential Audio Series, break out Bonus Disc 6 to listen to the night before the test/day of the test. Don't have the audio series? No problem. Re-listen to the audio modules we told you about previously. Here is the address again: www.testprepny.com.

- Confirm your plans for AFTER the test. What are you going to do to celebrate *you*? We'd love to hear what it is (we love a good GMAT after party), so drop us a line. That makes it more likely to happen.

- After the test, now what?

This is a great time to reflect on how you performed. Many students take the test twice. We told you that a long time ago. Are you one of them? If so, reflect upon which questions had you stymied, and write them down. Go to different forums such as BeatTheGMAT.com, GMAT Club and Businessweek online forums to see what your colleagues are saying. Having trouble still? Well, find yourself a tutor, mate!

And whether you find yourself registering for the GMAT again, get your ducks in a row. What is the next most important step for your candidacy? Getting your application together, of course. And lucky you; remember all those techniques we started out with in the first section? Well, they are really helpful to use when going through the stressful application process.

We welcome thoughts and feedback on the book—and can likely point you in the best direction, whether it's working with a tutor or admissions consultant—so don't be shy. We'd love to hear from you. Just call! 646-290-7440. You might even hear Eloise the office dog barking in the background.

Bara Sapir and the Test Prep New York Story

My own journey of discovery in this area began when, as a University of Michigan graduate test taker, I was hired to work for a large test prep company to teach the GRE. I was told to familiarize myself with the company's manual and use it as a script; then I was thrown into the teaching arena. Two years later, when I moved to New York, I worked for the same company again. This time the test was the GMAT, a test I had never seen; I taught two classes at the same time they trained me. I was learning the material the day before—or the same day as—my test takers saw it.

I quickly realized that the help my test takers needed—and the help I felt they deserved, considering the amount of money they were spending in an effort to raise their scores—couldn't be provided by simply reading the script provided by the test prep company. I began to improvise, drawing on my background in psychology, creativity, and spiritual studies to help these test takers to transcend the material. I listened to what they were saying about their lives, their goals, and their concerns. I took seriously the difficulties they had in applying the material to actual test-taking conditions. I coached them through mental blocks and insecurities, and helped them to tap into inner resources to succeed. I took small steps and followed my intuition.

My methods were sometimes unorthodox, but the results were astonishing. One test taker improved 750 points on her GRE (the GRE at that time was in 3 sections, with a maximum score of 2400). SAT test takers improved 300+ points. When I moved into the GMAT arena, I saw similar improvements, far above the norm. What made a difference, I believe, was that I was engaging with the test takers as people, partnering with them in finding ways to overcome obstacles and reach for their goals. I didn't realize it at the time, but I was providing what the company I worked for left out of the equation: a living dynamic and a soul to the teaching.

I began to research the field of performance enhancement and the role of mental states in performance, to flesh out and develop my intuitions and the integrated approach I had begun to pioneer. I developed solutions to help the dozens of test takers who came to me after the big test prep company methods or self-study had failed them. I created viable, flexible options for those who didn't want a one-size-fits-all approach. I realized that an effective system of test preparation includes room for creativity and elasticity (as all good teaching requires), together with a more serious treatment of the content material and the integrated use of mindset tools, so test takers could go into the testing situation fully prepared to achieve peak performance. These tools became the foundation of the unique method we apply at Test Prep New York.

These exciting insights are the foundation of the mind-enhancing methodology which first put Test Prep New York on the map. As word of mouth has spread, the company has grown to include a robust staff, second to none. Karen van Hoek, the content developer of this book, is our lead verbal specialist. We have an impressive staff consisting of academics and professionals, many of whom have had significant teaching experience and understand what test takers really need to master to perform their best on these admissions tests. These experts believe in giving clients solid training in both strategy and content—not gimmicks, tricks or short cuts that don't produce consistent results. That Test Prep New York has become a leader in the arena of test prep companies is no surprise: we offer a high quality alternative that is both enriching and transformative. We consistently see our clients produce some of the best score improvements in the industry, and go on to enter their choice MBA programs.

For some, our approach offers viable and consistent methods to save test takers who fall through the cracks of the one-size-fits-all approach offered by the big test prep companies. For others, it's a one-stop-shop to their test-taking process. Each year, we help hundreds of test takers earn their best scores and perform beyond what they thought was possible.

Take John. He worked in the State Department under Condoleezza Rice and was comfortable working in one of the most senior offices of the nation, surrounded by leaders; yet the peculiar pressure of preparing for a test got to him. His colleagues' awareness of the fact that he was studying for the GMAT made him feel uncomfortable, and he felt an immense pressure to perform to impress them. When he went into take the test, he found himself staring at the screen like a deer in headlights. He simply couldn't think, let alone answer a question. We met with him for five hours the weekend before he retook the test. Without reviewing a single GMAT question, we taught him how to get into the best mindset and feel confident while taking the test. He went into the test and scored 230 points higher than on his first diagnostic. And he recently graduated from Harvard Business School with his MBA.

Or take Tim, an uber-smart non-profit executive who had gone through every major test prep program out there—but couldn't budge his score beyond a 670. He knew this score wasn't going to grant him entry to a top school like Tuck (Dartmouth) or Ross (Michigan). While other services gave him generic test-taking tricks, it wasn't enough for him. We customized an action plan for Tim that focused on his quant areas that needed help, and focused on ways to improve his confidence and score. End result? Tim scored in the mid-700s and became a believer and advocate for our brand of education and coaching, and graduated from Ross last year.

While for Tim it was primarily a matter of bolstering his quantitative acumen and helping him get into a productive test-taking zone, and for John it was an attitude adjustment, for each of these candidates, and all our others, we implemented a specific plan for GMAT preparedness including solutions to overcome mental barriers, improve their weakest areas, and get them closer to GMAT success.

Our success includes:

- Use of top-notch materials: Our materials are based on a sober and exhaustive analysis of what the test asks for. We provide an accurate mirror of what you will see on the GMAT, how it translates to what you need to know to answer each question, and how to go through the steps methodically. We don't teach you simple gimmicks or tricks, but we do teach you test-taking strategy that will help you integrate the knowledge and skills.

- An analysis of our clients: Our diagnostic tests, psychological and emotional intakes, consultations, and educational evaluations identify test takers' academic weaknesses, learning styles and psychological barriers to success. Our approach is to address these head on and help test takers with critical thinking, as well as providing nuts and bolts skills that work for the test and for life.

- Learning from the best instructors in the industry: Drawn from the halls of academia, exiles from other test preparation companies, educators, MBA brainiacs who love to teach, lawyers, surgeons, etc.—high-scoring enthusiasts make up our roster of tutoring professionals. They score high, are experts in imparting information, and don't work from a one-size-fits all GMAT (or GRE, LSAT, etc.) script model.

- And finally, embracing and implementing scientifically proven methodologies, practices and traditions to help the test taker get out of his or her own way.

Our program works, consistently, because we combine the most simple ingredients— and we get great results. Which is why people almost always say to us, "I wish I had come to you first."

The time to set out on that path is now.

CONTRIBUTORS

The following TPNY affiliated professionals contributed their expertise to this book. They often work with our clients to provide their expertise to find balance and health in their daily lives as well as when they are preparing for a high-stakes exam.

Acupuncture

Yiska Obadia is a licensed acupuncturist, massage therapist, Journeydance teacher, and holistic health practitioner practicing in NYC. Her work is focused primarily on emotional and mental well being and personal transformation. She is an advocate for increased self-love, personal responsibility and self-care. www.yiskaobadia.com

Aromatherapy

Carmella McDonald holds Certificates in Swedish Massage, Anatomy/Physiology, Shiatsu and Moxabustion, Oriental Diagnosis, Kampo (Japanese Herbs), Masunaga Shiatsu, Reflexology and Macrobiotic Cooking, Vodder Manual Lymphatic Drainage, Low Level Laser Therapy, Graduate Diploma in Ryodoraku Electro-Meridian Laser Therapy and Mineral Therapy, Colour Therapy, Reiki, Angelic Attunements, Feng Shui 9 Flying Stars, Energy/ Environmental Space Clearing and Smudging, Sacred Geometry. She established a clinic at the University of Technology in Sydney, Australia. She holds a Diploma in Aromatherapy with a Chemistry Course in Aromatherapuetic Essential Oils, and is member of the International Federation of Aromatherapists (Australian Branch). In addition to practicing, she was Publicity Officer for the International Federation of Aromatherapists (Australian Branch) handling all media inquiries and interviews, and also assisting on aromatherapy articles for Cleo and Instyle magazines. She is currently practices in New York, and consults www.carmella.info

Homeopathy and Herbal Medicine

Dr. Christopher Trahan, O.M.D, L.Ac. is a Doctor of Oriental Medicine, a licensed Acupuncturist, a Medical Herbalist and a classically trained homeopathic physician. He combines Chinese, Ayurvedic, and western natural healing systems in his practice at the Olympus Center for Holistic and Integrative Medicine. He has over 30 years of clinical experience. He is in Manhattan and maintains an Herbal Pharmacy of over 300 Chinese and Western Herbs. He own Olympus Center in New York City maintains complete western herbal, homeopathic and oriental herbal pharmacies along with three treatment rooms for acupuncture and other therapies. olympuscenter.com

Massage

Frank Hughes is certified in Structural Integration from the Florida School of Massage and has been a nationally certified massage therapist since 1991. In addition, he holds certification in connective tissue massage, neuromuscular therapy, shiatsu, myofascial release, cranial sacral therapy, trager, and spent 6 months in Thailand studying with master teachers Picheste, Chaiyuth, Mama Nitt, Asokanada, and Chongkol. He has worked in a variety of settings ranging from a complementary care center to holistic spas including the GoodLife Spa in St. Marten, and the Yoga Center of Negril. He is also a certified hatha yoga teacher from Sadie Nardinid, gyrokinesis and gyrotonic apprentice from Body Evolution, and has been trained in pilates mat with Kelly Kane and Linda Farrell. Currently, he is enjoying living and working in his Williamsburg, Brooklyn studio, a massage, music and movement space which offers wellness coaching, and where Frank teaches Thai massage for individuals and partners, yoga and pilates-based movement classes as well as practicing his unique style of integrative Thai massage. http://frankhughes.weebly.com

Nutrition

Jodi Krizer Graber is a nutrition and wellness coach specializing in stress management, sugar addiction, and eating disorders and is the founder of Bravo! Wellness. She is a graduate of the Newhouse School of Public Communications at Syracuse University and holds a master's degree from New York University. After 20 years as an arts executive in New York City and having recovered from an eating disorder in her mid-30s, Jodi saw a need for wellness coaching for busy, high-achieving professionals. She received her certification from The Institute For Integrative Nutrition and is a raw foods expert. She speaks frequently on issues relating to nutrition, wellness and self-care. More information can be found at www.bravowellness.com.

Sound Therapy

Katie Down is a multi-instrumentalist, sound health practitioner, and licensed music therapist. She has designed and facilitated workshops in vocal and instrumental improvisation in Croatia, Macedonia, Slovenia, South Africa, and the U.S. Her instruments include flute, guitar, piano, voice, Middle Eastern percussion, glass instruments, didjeridu, ukulele and many more. She conducts sound meditations utilizing therapeutic drone instruments and incorporates therapeutic drone as an effective intervention for trauma, anxiety, and depression through her private practice. As an educator, Katie has been a proponent for arts as a vehicle for social change and has created numerous workshops and curricula for grades K through 12, working with arts organizations as both the education director and as a freelance teaching artist. Katie is also a professional sound designer and composer for theatre and film, working off Broadway and regionally. Her award-winning designs have received critical acclaim and she continues to incorporate her passion for creating sound as a character into her work as a music therapist, providing inroads for creative expression and development. www.katiedown.com.

Yoga and Pilates

Ophra Wolf, owner of Force and Flow Integrated Bodywork (www.forceandflow.com) in Brooklyn, NY, has been investigating the mind-body connection through movement, performance, and bodywork for over fifteen years. She is a highly sought after Yoga and Pilates instructor and has a vibrant bodywork practice grounded in the ancient art of Thai Massage. Her work as a dancer and theater performer give her a rare depth of insight into the art of presence and expression, distinguishing her as an extremely effective instructor. She is known for her unique ability to catalyze transformation in clients of all ages and abilities, and to help individuals align their body, mind, and spirit with their highest potential. forceandflow.com

Tevis Rose Trower is a pioneer in the field of work-life satisfaction. Fueled by the question "Why do we 'hate' work?," in 2001 she founded New York-based Balance Integration Corporation, providing sustainable success and employee engagement tools to optimize human assets within corporations. Heralded in Megatrends 2010 as Corporate Mindfulness Guru for the new millennium, Tevis teaches corporate professionals how to apply time-tested mastery techniques to resolve modern work-life challenges. As a faculty member in Advanced Management Studies at NYU's School for Continuing and Professional Studies and under the auspices of Balance Integration, Tevis has created mastery programs for numerous leading organizations including Google, AOL, Viacom, Yahoo!, Edelman Public Relations, Disney, Cleary-Gottleib, and the Young Presidents Organization (YPO). She presents at Kripalu, Omega, and studios around the globe. Her work has been cited in countless publications including Yoga Journal, Business Week, Forbes, Investors Business Daily, Glamour, and AMNY. She is also a former U.S. Army Reservist and board member of the New York Yoga Teachers' Association. balanceintegration.com/

Gratitude and Acknowledgments

We teach our clients to master a foundation of knowledge, from which all the other questions are dependent. If any piece of that basic knowledge is in skewed, the rest of the card castle will look, rise up, or fail, a bit differently. To this end, I'm grateful for my foundations, my family and friends who have provided such an intriguing, inspiring, and growth-oriented foundation. To my parents, Rosalie and Dr. Lowell Saferstein who provided a life-long canvas of possibility imparting a thirst of knowledge, a quest of curiosity, and a magical childhood in a day when recreation was not an interactive screen but in tide pools, nature hikes, classical quartets, backyard 'digs', and artistic creation. Their endless support and belief in me has benefitted our countless clients to whom I impart the absolute possibility of manifesting one's visions. I honor my grandparents of blessed memory for being my champions in just about every decision I've made, and their unconditional love. Also to my friends, over the years, with whom I've have shared constellations. Whether central now or if we have moved on, this crew of characters have touched me and remain influential in how we learned from one another. My community in/from Ann Arbor has continued to keep an open heart, tune, and home (thank you Gaia, Beth, Josh, Orly, and John Roegner), and my NY friends who have created a web of fun and support that has helped me keep my nose to the grindstone while having a place to connect and tune in that has continued to support growth and community. I thank Jo Ellen Kaiser, Jay Michaelson and Dan Friedman of Zeek. To the inspiring memory of Tom Cole and the Aspen maverick posse he introduced me to, who inspired and propelled me to start TPNY and reach a wider audience (Mark Pincus, Gary Leff, Tim Garneau and others). To Beth Shoenfeldt, Ladies who Launch, Collective-E, RHH-b-school, SCORE, WIBO, the Makor Artist Collective, VSC, and inspiring women's/business organizations who helped shape my path. To Princeton Review on whose giant shoulders we stand. Special thanks to Katie Down, Martha Lipton, Mary Beth, Susannah Macomb, Eileen Eichenstein, Beatrice Aranow, Driftwood and Low Down, whose friendship and/or collaborations, personal and professional, help keep my soul free. Hallelujah to my new Bay Area community and friendships. Yum. I am truly blessed. And to my sweetest rescue pup, Eloise, who cannot really understand a word I say or write, but loves me and cheers me to no end, nonetheless. Alan Brown who has been a test prep hero and friend through and through, helping to develop the TPNY/TPSF brand and business expertise; he has provided me, selflessly, and joyously, with more than the basic sustenance in completing this book along with a deep belief in our work. Of his unconditional friendship I'm grateful. Thanks to the champions of education I've had the privilege to learn from and work and study with along the way, including, as far back as I can remember, through high school (M. Sorkin and Mich), University of Michigan Art School and Graduate School (Dr. Victor Meisel and Joel Isaascon), and the JTS Davidson School of Education, namely, Areyeh Davidson, Neil Gilman, and Janet Walton at Union Theological. Also a special mention to Jo Milgrom whose friendship and mentoring I cherish.

In more pragmatic terms, I am thankful Jo Ellen Kaiser, who I have had the pleasure of working with at Zeek journal, the editor of this manual. She was instrumental in helping us to articulate our intentions and words clearly. Janet Goldstein started us on the path and Andrea Cutler's graphic abilities in incorporating my watercolor into a stunning cover image. Karen van Hoek, a friend and colleague, has been an inspiration and pleasure to work with since TPNY began.

Other artists, contributors, researchers, assistants, and interns and have also been instrumental in getting this book done effectively, namely Christina Tsui, Michael Vitale, Jason Leahey, Victoria Kittelsen, the contributors of this book (listed within) and artists Agungmalang Setya Nughra and Raf Domingos. Many thanks go to Eliezer Estrecho who was a hero in layout design and to Dawn Varga Danka for the final editing, proofreading, and project managing the completion of the book. An admirable task.

Thank you also to the thousands of clients, dozens of tutors, and interns who have worked with TPNY/TPSF, taught me to be better educator, and inspired me. In truth, there is never enough room to be grateful.

—*Bara Sapir*

I'd like to thank the many TPNY students who have worked with me over the years and shared with me their questions, confusion, and reflection on how they approach the GMAT. The hours we've spent examining GMAT traps and looking at how they avoided them, or why they fell into them, have informed every page of this work. Thank you to my friends Leora Druckman and Daniel Peisach, who have provided the nurturing space in which this work was completed. I am grateful to them, and to Neil Clennan and Martha Stokely, for steadfast friendship during difficult times. Extra special thanks to Susan Radovsky for friendship and encouragement through-out the writing of this work; I couldn't have finished it without you.

—*Karen van Hoek*

Bibliography

Amen, Daniel G. MD. *Change Your Brain, Change Your Life*. Three Rivers Press, 1998.

Andreas, S. and Andrews, C. *Heart of the Mind: Engaging Your Inner Power to Change with Neuro-Linguistic Programming*. Real People Press., 1989.

Bandler, Richard. *Time for a Change*. Meta Pubication, 1993.

Bandler, Richard. *Using your Brain for a Change*. Real People Press, 1985.

Beilock, Sian. *Choke: What the Secrets of the Brain Reveal About Getting It Right When You Have To*. Simon & Schuster, 2010.

Church, Dawson. *The Genie in your Genes*. 2nd edition. Energy Psychology Press, 2009.

Cizek, Gregory J. and Burg, Samantha S. *Addressing Test Anxiety in a High-Stakes Environment*. Corwin Press, 2006.

Csikszentmihalyi, Mihaly. *Flow: the Psychology of Optimal Experience*. Harper & Row., 1990.

Dilts, Robert. *Changing Belief Systems with NLP*. Meta Publications, 1990.

Elman, Dave. *Hypnotherapy*. Westood Publishing Company, 1984.

Erikson, Milton and Rossi, E. *Hypnotherapy: An Exploratory Case-Book*. New York: Irvington Publishers, 1979.

Gallwey, W. Timothy. *The Inner Game of Tennis*. Random House, 1974.

Grinder, J. and Bandler, R. *Frogs into Princes: Neuro-Linguistic Programming*. Real People Press, 1979.

Grinder, J. and Bandler, R. *Trance-Formations: Neuro-Linguistic Proramming and the Structure of Hypnosis*. Real People Press, 1981.

Hall, M. and Bodenhamer B. G. *The User's Manual for the Brain, volume 1*. Crown House Publishing, 2001.

Hammond, C. E. *Handbook of Hypnositic Suggestions and Metaphors*. 1st edition. W.W. Norton & Company, 1990.

Jensen, Eric. *Enriching the Brain*. Jossey Bass, 2006.

Johnson, Susan. *Taking the Stress out of Taking Tests.* Barnes and Noble Books, 2000.

Kein, Gerald and Banyan, Carl. *Hypnosis & Hypnotherapy: Basic to Advanced Techniques for the Professional.* Abot Publishing House, 2001.

Lankton, S. *Answer Within: A Clinical Framework of Ericksonian Hypnotherapy.* Crown House PubLishing, 2008.

Lipton, Bruce. *The Biology of Belief: Unleashing the Power of Consciousness, Matter and Miracles.* Hay House, 2008.

Moore-Hafter, Betty. *Tapping your Amazing Potential with EFT—Creative Ideas and Teaching Tools using Emotional Freedom Techniques and Concepts from Hypnotherapy.* Betty Moore-Hafter.

Myss, Caroline. *Anatomy of the Spirit: The Seven Stages of Power an Healing.* 1st edition. Three Rivers Press, 1997.

Newman, Ed. Phd. *No More Test Anxiety.* Learning Skills Publications, 1996.

Pert, Candice. *Molecules of Emotion: The Science Behind Mind-Body Medicine.* 1st edition. Simon & Shuster, 1999.

Restak, Richard, M.D. *The Naked Brain.* Three Rivers Press. 2006.

Schwartz, J. and Begley, S. *The Mind and the Brain: Neuroplasticity and the Power of Mental Force.* Harper Perennial, 2003.

Talbot, Michael. *Beyond the Quantum.* Bantam, 1988.

Temes, R. *The Complete Idiot's Guide to Hypnosis.* Alpha, 1999.

Tiers, Melissa. *Integrative Hypnosis: A Comprehensive Course in Change.* 2010.

Endnotes

1. http://thinkexist.com/quotation/whether_you_think_that_you_can-or_that_you_can-t/7814.html.

2. topquotescollection.com. Not from a published book.

3. Gallwey, W. Timothy. *The Inner Game of Tennis*. Random House, 1974.

4. The Inner Game of Tennis (WE DON'T NEED THIS ONE)

5. Pronoia is the Antidote for Paranoia (WE DON'T NEED THIS ONE)

6. C. George Boeree, "B.F. Skinner," http://webspace.ship.edu/cgboer/skinner.html, (accessed Jul 6, 2011).

7. http://www.apa.org/monitor/dec01/anewtake.aspx.

8. Margaret E. Kemeny. "The Psychobiology of Stress," Current Directions in Psychological Science, Vol. 12, No. 4, Aug 2003, 125.

9. Ibid., 125-126.

10. Beth Azar. "A New Take on Psychoneuroimmunology." American Psychological Association, Vol. 32, No., 11, Dec. 2001, 34.

11. Dawson Church, Ph.D., The Genie in Your Genes, (Santa Rosa, Energy Psychology Press, 2008), 253.

12. Susan Folkman and Judith Tedlie Moscowitz. "Stress, Positive Emotion, and Coping," Current Directions in Psychological Science, Vol. 9, No. 4, Aug., 2000, 115.

13. Barbara L. Fredrickson, "The Broaden-and-Build Theory of Positive Emotions" Philosophical Transactions: Biological Sciences. Bol. 359, No. 1449, Sep. 29, 2004, 1369.

14. Fredrickson, 1370.

15. Ibid., 1370

16. Ibid., 1370.

17. Reprinted with permission of Franklin Covey from First Things First, 1st ed., 1994, Franklin Covey, Steven R. Covey, A. Roger Merrill, and Rebecca R. Merrill, Simon & Schuster Adult Publishing Group, January 1994.

18. "A study published today in the journal Neuroscience, journal of the International Brain Research Organization, confirmed that exercise increases the chemical BDNF—brain-derived neurotrophic factor—in the hippocampus, a curved, elongated ridge in the brain that controls learning and memory." http://www.ohsu.edu/news/2003/092603bdnf.html

19. Shephard RJ. Curricular physical activity and academic performance. Pediatric Exercise Science, 1997;9:113-125

20. http://www.fi.edu/learn/brain/exercise.html#physicalexercise

21. http://www.smartertechnology.com/c/a/Smarter-Strategies/Meditation-Proven-to-Boost-Brain-Efficiency/

22. Andrew Vickers Catherine Zollman. "ABC of Complementary Medicine: Hypnosis and relaxation therapies" BMJ: British Medical Journal. Vol.319, No. 7221 Nov. 20, 1999.

23. Sandra Blakeslee, "This is Your Brain under Hypnosis" http://www.nytimes.com/2005/11/22/science/22hypno.html

24. History Learning Site, Franz Mesmer, http://www.historylearningsite.co.uk/franz_mesmer.htm (accessed Jul 6, 2011)

25. http://www.thelivingmoon.com/43ancients/01documents/History_Mesmerism.html

26. Researchers have long known that people can keep only a handful of items in working memory. (The limit was initially put at 7, plus or minus 2—often cited as the reason phone numbers are 7 digits long—but further research bumped it down to 4.) http://blogs.discovermagazine.com/80beats/2011/06/21/each-half-of-the-brain-has-its-own-memory-storage/ (accessed Jul 6, 2011)

27. THE JOURNAL OF ALTERNATIVE AND COMPLEMENTARY MEDICINE Volume 16, Number 11, 2010, pp. 1145–1152 "Effects of Yoga Versus Walking on Mood, Anxiety and Brain GABA Levels: A Randomized Controlled MRS Study". Chris C. Streeter, MD,1 Theodore H. Whitfield, ScD,2 Liz Owen, BArch,3 Tasha Rein, BA,1 Surya K. Karri, MD, MPH,4 Aleksandra Yakhkind, MS,5 Ruth Perlmutter, MA,6 Andrew Prescot, PhD,7
Perry F. Renshaw, MD, PhD,8 Domenic A. Ciraulo, MD,1 and J. Eric Jensen, PhD9
Abstract

28. J. Krishnamurti (1895-1986) – Indian philosopher (pg. 461 zen book)

29. William Shakespeare, Hamlet. Act 5 Scene 2 (pg. 459 zen book)

30. Richard Saul Wurman (born 1935) – American architect and graphic designer (pg. 458 zen book)

31. Isaac Asimov (1920-1992) – Russian born American science-fiction writer and biochemist (page 457 zen book)

32. Aristotle, Metaphysica 980a, 21 ff. (The Works of Aristotle, Engl. Transl. ed. by William David Ross, 12 vols., Oxford 1908 ff., Vol. VIII).

33. R. G. Collingwood (1889-1943) – British philosopher and historian (zen book 327)

34. Andrew Jackson (1767-1845) – Seventh President of the United States (zen book, page 311)

35. Maya Angelou, I Know Why the Caged Bird Sings (New York: Random House Inc., 1969).

36. Chozan Shissai, Way of the Sword: The Tengu-geijutsu-ton of Chozan Shissai, trans. Reinhard Kammer (Boston: Arkana, 1978).

37. Kathryn Cramer, Ph.D., Hank Wasak, Change the Way You See Everything (China: Running Press, 2006), 10.

38. Alexander Graham Bell, "Bell Telephone Talk," How They Succeeded, (Lothrop Publishing Company, 1901).

39. Confucius. The Analects of Confucius. New York: Random House, Inc., 1989.

40. Miles Davis (1926-1991) – American jazz musician, trumpeter, bandleader and composer

41. Napoleon Hill, Think and Grow Rich (New York: Tribeca Books, 2011).

42. Brain Tracy, Eat That Frog!: 21 Great Ways to Stop Procrastinating and Get More Done in Less Time (San Francisco: Berrett-Koehler Pulishers, Inc., 2007).

43. Theologia Germanica, trans. Susanna Winkworth, (London: London Printing, 1901).

44. As quoted in Sango Mbella, Sophia's Fire (Pittsburgh: G&V Pittsburgh, 2005), 133.

45. Ambrose Bierce, The Devil's Dictionary (New York: Oxford University Press, 1999).

46. Viktor Emil Frankl, M.D., Ph.D., (1905-1997) – An Austrian neurologist and psychiatrist who was also the founder of logotherapy.

47. Henry Ward Beecher, "Henry Ward Beecher to His Son," Our Paper, Volume 10, 1878.

48. Maxwell, Florida Scott, The Measure of my Days (New York: Penguin Books, 1972).

49. Viktor Frankl, The Progress Challenge: Working and Winning in a World of Change (World Gumbo, 2010).

50. Lee Iacocca, Iacocca (New York: Bantam Books, 1984).

51. Henry Ward Beecher (1813-1887) – A Congregationalist clergyman, social reformer and abolitionist

52. Leonard C. Schlup and Donald W. Whisenhunt, It Seems to Me: Selected Letters of Eleanor Roosevelt (Kentucky: University Press of Kentucky, 2001).

53. Thomas Jefferson (1743-1826) – The principal author of the Declaration of Independence and the third President of the United States

54. Herbert Otto Quoted as saying by a reporter.

55. Samuel Johnson (1709-1784) – An English poet, essayist, journalist, literary critic, biographer, editor and lexicographer.

56. George Sylvester Viereck, "What Life Means to Einstein: An Interview by George Sylvester Viereck," The Saturday Evening Post, Vol. 202, 1929.

57. Eckhard Tolle. The Power of Now: A Guide to Spiritual Enlightenment. Vancouver: Nameste Publishing, 1999.

58. Kathryn Cramer, Ph. D, Hank Wasiak, Change the Way You See Everything (China: Running Press, 2006) 82.

59. Sark, Succulent Wild Woman (New York: Fireside, 1997), 23.

60. Mary Crowley Zen book. Page 267

61. As quoted in Dreyfus: His Life and Letters, edited by Pierre Dreyfus (London: Hutchinson, 1937).

62. The Long Discourses of the Buddha, trans. Maurice Walshe (Boston: Wisdom Publications, 1995).

63. Sabrina Ward Harrison, The True and the Questions: A Journal (San Francisco: Chronicle Books, The True and the Questions.Chronicle Books, 2005), 27.

64. Jennifer Edwards (born March 25, 1957) – American actress

65. Sexton, M. Glory Bound (1996). On Black Sheep [CD]. Alberta: Kitchen Table Music.

66. Joseph Campbell with Michael Toms, An Open Life (New York: Harper & Row, 1989).

67. Jeremy Collier (1650-1726) – An English theatre critic, non-juror bishop an theologian.

68. Albert Schweitzer, Out of My Life and Thought: An Autobiography (Baltimore: Johns Hopkins University Press, 1998), 90.

69. Henry David Thoreau 18. Conclusion, Walden

70. George S. Patton, Letter Sent to Son, 1944.

71. Leonardo da Vinci, The Notebooks of Leonardo da Vinci, ed. Irma A. Richter (New York: Oxford University Press, 1982).

72. William Shakespeare, The Life of King Henry the Eighth (Charleston: BiblioBazaar, LLC, 2007).

73. Lily Tomlin quoted in People Magazine December 26, 1977

74. Arthur C. Clarke, Profiles of the Future (New York: Henry Holt & Co., 1984).

75. Thomas Edison (1847-1931), American inventor and businessman.

76. Cramer and Wasiak, 25.

77. Plato. *Plato: Republic*. Trans. GMA Grabe. Indianapolis: Hackett Publishing Company, Inc., 1992.

78. Robert Frost, The Poetry of Robert Frost (New York: Random House, 2001), 64.

79. William James, Talks to Teachers on Psychology and to Students on… (Harvard College Lamont Library, 1900)

80. Marianne Williamson, A Return to Love (New York: HarperPerennial, 1992).

81. Jean Paul Getty (1892-1976) – An American industrialist and the founder of the Getty Oil Company

82. Jean de La Bruyère (1645-1696) – A French essayist and moralist

83. Napoleon Hill, Think and Grow Rich (San Diego: Aventine Press, 2004).

84. Gustavus F. Swift, "Gustavus F. Swift's Mottoes," The Inland Printer. Vol. 32, 1903-1904.

85. Brezsny, 18.

86. The Mathnawi of Jalaluddin Rumi, trans. Reynold A. Nicholson (England: Gibb Memorial Trust, 1990).

87. As quoted by Glenn T. Seaborg, "Need We Fear Our Nuclear Future?" Bulletin of the Atomic Scientists (Jan. 1968).

88. Brezsny, 277.

89. Nachmanovitch, 22.

90. Joseph Campbell with Bill Moyers, The Power of Myth (New York: Anchor Books, 1991), 41.

91. Miguel de Cervantes, Don Quixote, trans. Edith Grossman (New York: HarperCollins Publishers Inc., 2003).

92. Brezsny, 23.

93. Agnes Demille and Martha Graham, Dance to the Piper (Boston: Little, Brown & Company, 1951).

94. Eric Whitman Sigg, The American T.S. Eliot: A Study of the Early Writings (New York: Cambridge University Press, 1989), 73.

95. Logan Pearsall Smith, Afterthoughts: Life and Human Nature (London: Statesman and Nation Pub. Co., 1930).

96. Neale Donald Walsch (born September 10, 1943) – Author of the series Conversations with God.

97. Johann Wolfgang von Goethe (1749 - 1832) – A German writer, pictorial artist, biologist, and theoretical physicist

98. Ralph Waldo Emerson, Literary Ethics (Charleston: Nabu Press, 2010).

99. Albert Camus, The Myth of Sisyphus, trans. Justin O'Brien (New York: Vintage, 1955).

100. Seneca, Epistulae Morales ad Lucilium (Moral Letters to Lucilius) (Cambrige: Harvard University Press, 1925).

101. George Walton Lucas, Jr. (born May 14, 1944) – An American film producer, screen-writer, and director, and the founder and chairman of Lucasfilm Ltd. He is best known as the creator of the space opera franchise Star Wars and the archaeologist-adventurer character Indiana Jones.

102. Rob Brezsny, Pronoia is the Antidote for Paranoia (Berkeley: North Atlantic Books, 2009).

103. The Upanishads, trans. Swami Prabhavanada, Frederick Manchester (New York: Signet Classic Publishing, 2002).

104. George Sheehan, Personal Best (Emmaus: Rodale Press, 1989).

105. Danny Kaye (born David Daniel Kaminsky; 1913-1987) – A celebrated American actor, singer, dancer, and comedian.

106. Alex Ayres, The Wit and Wisdom of Mark Twain (New York: Harper & Row, Publishers, 1987).

107. Joan Chandos Baez (born January 9, 1941) – An American folk singer, songwriter and activist

108. Joseph Campbell with Bill Moyers, The Power of Myth (New York: Anchor Books, 1991).

109. Marcus Aurelius, Meditations, trans. Meric Casaubon (New York: Cosimo Books, 2005).

110. The Blue Cliff Record, trans. Thomas Cleary, J.C. Cleary (Boston: Shambhala Publications, Inc., 1977).

111. Tom Cole. Friend to author. (1964 - 2006)

112. Foster C. McClellan, Thoughts for a Friend (Auckland: Unity Books, 1980).

113. Lennon, J. (1984). Grow Old With Me. On Milk and Honey [CD]. UK: Polydor Records.

114. SARK, A Creative Companion: How to Free Your Creative Spirit (Berkeley: Celestial Arts, 2004), 55.

115. Brezsny, 62.

116. David Ogilvy (1911–1999) – A British advertising executive.

117. Brezsny, 84.

118. Albert Camus, Lyrical and Critical Essays (New York: Alfre A. Knopf Inc., 1967).

119. Joseph Campbell with Bill Moyers, The Power of Myth (New York: Anchor Books, 1991).

120. Nike Advertising Campaign

121. Kent Nerburn, Letters to My Son (Novato: New World Library, 1999).

122. Martin Luther King, Jr. (1929-1968) – An American clergyman, activist and prominent leader in the Civil Rights Movement.

123. Marcel Proust, Les Plaisirs et les Jours (New York: French and European Publications, 1979).

124. Soren Kierkegaard, Soren Kierkegaard's Journals and Papers (Bloomington: Indiana University Press, 1976).

125. As quoted in Harrison, 48.

126. Walt Whitman, Leaves of Grass (Los Angeles: Indo-European Publishing, 2010).

127. Edwin Friedman (1932-1996) – An ordained Jewish Rabbi and family therapist who founded the Bethesda Jewish Congregation

128. Helen Keller, The Simplest Way to be Happy, 1933.

129. Michel W. Potts, "Arun Gandhi Shares the Mahatma's Message," India – West. Vol. XXVII, No. 13., 2002.

130. Francis Bacon, Francis Bacon: The Major Works (New York: Oxford University Press, 1996).

131. Mary Frances Berry, Josh Gottheimer and Theodore C. Sorensen, Power in Words: The Stories behind Barack Obama's Speeches (Boston: Beacon Press, 2010).

132. Brezsny, 299.

133. Gautama Buddha, Dhammapada, trans. T. Byrom (Boston: Shambhala Publications, 1993).

134. May Sarton, Journal of a Solitude (New York: W.W. Norton and Company, 1973).

135. Francis Bacon, Francis Bacon: The Major Works (New York: Oxford University Press, 1996).

136. Robert Collier, The Law of the Higher Potential (Kingsport: Kingsport Press, Inc., 1947).

137. Harrison, 108.

138. Muriel Strode, A Soul's Faring (Charleston: BiblioBazaar, 2010).

139. Harrison, 108.

140. Brezsny, 249.

141. Brezsny, 31.

142. Mary Catherine Bateson, Willing to Learn: Passages of Personal Discovery (Hanover: Steerforth, 2010.)

143. Abraham Lincoln

144. William Butler Yeats, Responsibilities (Cornell University Library, 2009).

145. Wickes, Frances. The Inner World of Childhood (New York: Appleton-Century, 1966).

146. Louisa May Alcott, Good Wives (New York: Penguin Books Ltd., 2010).

147. Henry David Thoreau, Letter to Harrison Blake (16 November 1857).

148. Stephen Nachmanovitch, Free Play: Improvisation in Life and Art (New York: Penguin Putman, Inc., 1990), 24.

149. Albert Camus, Lyrical and Critical Essays (New York: Alfre A. Knopf Inc., 1967).

150. Cramer and Wasiak, 41.

151. Epictetus, The Discourses (NuVision Publications, LLC, 2006).

Take your studying to the

next level

Test Prep New York's online AWA GMAT writing course can develop your analytical skills and get into a healthy mindset for the GMAT's Analytical Writing Assessment.

Write
~~Right~~ your way to success with Test Prep New York.

- Master reading comprehension
- Learn grammar and syntax
- Develop organization and argument - shaping tools
- Engage in essay-writing exercises

AWA students also learn the latest relaxation and visualization techniques to ignite their creative capacity and help achieve their top score.

Enroll in the AWA writing course today and take your writing abilities to the next level.

GO TO THE
GMAT
PREPARED!

Test Prep New York's Full Potential™ Noteboard will familiarize you with the GMAT material while motivating you to perform your best.

It is identical to the test material with five spiral bound, double-sided laminated work sheets and a marker. Our board also includes inspirational quotes and affirmation exercises to inspire and relax you.

Take the first step towards mastering the GMAT and order your Full Potential™ Noteboard today.

Made in the USA
Monee, IL
11 June 2024

59671010R00208